The Walking Detective

An account of a walk from Cornwall to Caithness

The Walking Detective

An account of a walk from Cornwall to Caithness

Paul Heslop

Froswick Press

Also by Paul Heslop

The Job – 30 Years a Cop (2000)

British Library Cataloguing-in-publication data
A catalogue record for this book is available from the British Library.

Copyright © 2001 by Paul Heslop

Published by Froswick Press, P.O. Box 7, Keswick, Cumbria. CA12 5GD

ISBN 0-9538066-1-8

Printed by TJ International Limited, Padstow, Cornwall, England

Foreword

by

Hunter Davies

I always admire anyone who self publishes. All it takes is money, so you might reply, but it needs more than that. You need content for a start, a good story to tell, skill and energy, belief and perseverance to get it all down, to write out what has been nagging away inside you for years. And usually, with self publishers, they come from a background where not a lot of writing it all down, or self expression has been required. Self publishing is a process of learning – about publishing, about yourself.

You also need to have something of the entrepreneur to go into a new, technical area. Printers will baffle you with their expertise and confuse you with the options. Then there's the problem of having got your masterpiece printed, how do you get shot of it? How does distribution work? Apart from your family and best friend, who else is going to be interested?

Paul Heslop overcame all these problems with his first book, 'The Job – 30 Years a Cop', but then he did have a good tale to tell about his thirty years as a policeman. He did an initial print run of 500 and had to reprint, selling over 1,000 copies. Well done, Paul.

Encouraged by this success, this is his second offering about a mad idea – sorry, unusual idea – to walk from Cornwall to Caithness, mainly on footpaths, with no exact route planned. I welcome his ambition and wish him luck.

Hunter Davies, journalist and author, is a regular contributor to a number of national publications, and has written over 30 books, including: 'The Beatles' (biography), 'A Walk along the Wall', 'The Good Guide to the Lakes' and 'Wainwright' (a biography).

Cover design: Ray Liberty

Interior artwork: Charles Petrie

<u>Warning</u>

This is not a guide book. Anyone using it as one will almost certainly get lost, a situation from which the author absolves himself of all responsibility.

Dedicated to my legs and feet

... they deserve it

CONTENTS

Author's Note

'Isn't that what Ian Botham did?' people ask, when I tell them of my venture. Meaning, of course, I'd walked from Land's End to John o'Groats (or vice-versa) – as many have.

Well, no, it isn't actually. By design, I didn't cover the ground as quickly as possible, by the shortest route, by road. I didn't have 'back-up', with accommodation arranged in advance, and others carrying my kit and spare footwear. Mine was a solo expedition, not on a par with trans-continental epic journeys, admittedly, but my route led, by choice, away from the beaten track whenever possible, and was not undertaken with anyone's help.

I didn't walk 'Land's End to John o'Groats' anyway. Instead, a walk from the southernmost to northernmost part of mainland Britain seemed more appropriate. It seemed to make sense to walk between two extremes, exploring much of Britain's countryside, rather than taking the shortest route.

As a working detective, I was unable to take over two months' leave in one go, and consequently was obliged to complete the journey in four sections. Far from making things easy, if anything it added to the difficulties, due to enforced returns to places where each section had ended, and having to 'get into the groove' all over again. The 'upside' of this enforced arrangement was that in between each expedition I enjoyed planning the next, perusing maps and looking forward to the next stage, as well as being able to enjoy Britain's countryside in different seasons of the year. Britain's merits are manifold; to enjoy them in springtime and autumn (as I did) proved an unexpected bonus. I wouldn't have had it any other way.

Landewednack Church   Cp 2001

I'll walk where my own nature would be leading;
It vexes me to choose another guide.
Where the grey flocks in ferny glens are feeding,
Where the wild wind blows on the mountain side.

Emily Bronte

The train was packed, a sort of long cattle truck out of Paddington. I sat in silence, resigned to a long journey in a crowded carriage where passengers fought their way to the buffet car, and frustrated parents took on their recalcitrant wains in an undeclared war of attrition.

An old lady boarded at Reading. She spared me not a glance at first, but when the train almost emptied at Plymouth she smiled. Her message was clear: thank goodness *they've* gone. Later, probably to break the silence, she spoke.

She was talking about Cornwall.

I was born in Cornwall and I will die there,' she said, with more than a hint of pride. Patriotism, even. I understood. I'm just as proud of my Northumbrian roots, I said, my working class upbringing in a close-knit coal mining community.

The train rattled on.

I told her I was going to Lizard. Her silence seemed an invitation to explain.

Lizard Point is the most southerly outpost of mainland Britain, and I intended to walk to the most northerly, Dunnet Head, near John o'Groats. I would spend tonight in the most southerly house in Britain. A fitting place to start, she agreed.

What route would I take? Along the coast to Plymouth, then north. Where would I stay? Guest houses, youth hostels, my tent, anywhere! Why was I doing this? There were many reasons. I enjoy the freedom of walking; I wanted to explore; I wanted to escape the stresses of a detective inspector's role; I wanted the challenge.

She seemed interested, unlike friends and colleagues who seemed to think the entire notion quite mad and that an unattached, divorced male would be better off on the Costa Brava. Somehow, telling her seemed to make it all worthwhile.

It was May. Outside the train, the fields of Cornwall shimmered in the warm, spring sunshine.

1

The South Cornwall Coast

Cornwall. England's farthest outpost. Land of tin and china clay, smugglers' coves and quaint harbours, tourism and Poldark. As the sea heaved against the unyielding rocks of Lizard Point, a balmy breeze carried the fragrance of a million flowers – primroses, bluebells, a host of others sadly unknown to my untrained eye – all basking in the glow of the warm, spring sunshine beneath an azure sky. I glanced back to see if my host might be watching my departing form. Surely she would be there to witness my departure. Alas, she was not. I left in silence: no fanfare of trumpets, no cheering crowds. I was alone, the way it would be all the way to the end of my journey. The way I wanted it to be.

The coast path runs right past the bottom the garden of the most southerly house. I met a woman once, who'd walked the coast path. She'd set off, she said, joyful at the prospect of having the sea for company day after day, only to discover, after less than a week, she was 'sick of the sight of the bloody sea' (her words). But I was walking the length of the country, not 'doing' the coast path, so I could take whatever route I pleased. Like that woman, I was filled with joy – or would have been, except I had a problem. It was the sack. It weighed the proverbial ton. Anyone would have doubted I could carry it fifty yards, let alone the length of the country. As well as the tent, sleeping bag, cooking stove and the paraphernalia needed to survive in the wild there was enough food for a month's excursion into darkest Africa, and enough clothing to kit out the Eighth Army. Just picking it up and somehow getting it onto my back was a major operation. Did I really intend to carry this lot to a point on the Scottish coast near John o'Groats, traversing en route nice, easy terrain such as the Pennine Way and Scottish Highlands? It was bad enough carting it across London to Paddington station, never mind the length of the country.

My decision to carry such a load was influenced by a fellow I'd met once in the Lake District. He was doing Alfred Wainwright's Coast-to-Coast walk and carried the equivalent of a three storey block of flats on his shoulders. 'You get used to it after a while,' he explained, adding that 'it becomes part of you' for good measure. I saw his point. As I'd not planned a precise route, and thus not booked accommodation in advance, there might be a need to camp out, even in civilised places like Cornwall. But I was here, it was on my back and there it would have to stay. I could hardly slip it into an envelope and post it home.

I teetered to my first objective, Lizard lighthouse, where, in the 17 century, Sir John Killigrew levied a charge on ships' owners who were grateful to pay for the privilege of his guiding light rather than risk their vessels ending up on the jagged rocks of Cornwall's coast. Local people complained, saying it would rob them of 'God's grace' – the booty seized from shipwrecks. Killigrew's scheme failed because of difficulty in collecting dues. Served him right, greedy toad. Today's lighthouse generates up to 4,000,000 candle-power, its flashing beam visible 25 miles out to sea. A foghorn sounds when visibility falls to two miles. I'd heard it through the night, its unmistakable deep moans reminiscent of ships' foghorns on the Tyne when I was a boy. You'd hear them on foggy – or smoggy – nights. Now the Tyne is empty, except for a floating nightclub.

I visited the lighthouse once. Looking around, inside, I accidentally cracked my head against a beam. Thinking I might have damaged the superstructure of Killigrew's masterpiece, I wondered if perchance I had knocked the light out of alignment, so that where before crews of giant oil tankers would have steered a safe course, now the flashing light was visible only to an onion seller in Cherbourg. I never heard of any mishaps at sea afterwards, so it must have been okay. I'm not so sure if my head was ever the same again.

"The Mariners" Church Cove　　　℗ 2001

I staggered on to Church Cove, a whole mile into my journey. Here is Landewednack church, dedicated to St Winwallo, the most southerly on mainland Britain, and where the last ever sermon in Cornish was preached, about 1670. Frederick Simpson, a former rector, is credited with these lines:

> Pause, stranger, as you pass beneath
> Where Norman art and Gothic skill
> Have wrought a miracle in stone
> That time has made more lovely still
> Here, in this shrine, above this sea,
> There breathes the faith that made you free.

3

The church tower served as a lookout post for smuggling which, in medieval times, consisted of illegal exportation of wool and tin, then later, to help to pay for the wars against the French, duties were levied on the import of tobacco, tea, brandy and rum. As far as the local magistrates were concerned, smuggling was a perfectly legitimate business, which was hardly surprising since they were at it as much as anyone. Possibly more than anyone. Smuggling still goes on, only now it's drugs, a modern evil perpetrated by people who will never earn the romantic image of their predecessors. I hope not, anyway. What's a bit of contraband compared to a sack of heroin?

Three hard miles led to Cadgwith, where workers in Britain's once-flourishing fishing industry, and their families, lived in thatched cottages by the sea. Today, Cadgwith is the haunt of artists and tourists. I walked down to the water's edge where the silver sea and increasingly hot sun belied the fact that I was in Cornwall, England, and not Bermuda or Hawaii. I was tempted to lie down, or even go for a swim, and to hell with carting my load any further. I resisted, but when I shouldered the sack again it seemed heavier than ever.

I decided to cut inland. Now, where I can confidently navigate on moor and fell and mountain, it's not always quite so straightforward in England's agricultural lowlands, where rights of way are liable to disappear without trace among brambles and stinging-nettles. I found myself climbing gates and even straddling barbed wire fences, a particularly hazardous manoeuvre for someone carrying six tons and wearing shorts. When I reached Coverack, I spied a small cafe by the sea, dumped the sack gleefully and ordered tea and a Cornish pasty, and sat outside near two young women wearing little except friendly smiles. They peered over their long, tall glasses at the lone male in the sweat-stained shirt and shorts and hiking boots and scratched legs. Their smiles were probably out of sympathy due to my deteriorating condition or, quite possibly – or even more likely – because they regarded me as some sort of nutter. We sat beneath the blazing sun, I with my thoughts about them, they with their thoughts about my thoughts. There was no-one else. We had Coverack to ourselves. As for the pasty, it contained meat and potatoes – as it should – and had a thick 'knob' at one end. The purpose of the knob, a native told me once, was to enable tin miners to hold it in grimy hands – *not* for eating. I ate the knobs before I learnt the truth. No wonder it was a struggle.

Cornwall's coast was the scene of many a shipwreck, and now I spied the treacherous, fang-like rocks known as the Manacles, the scourge of shipping. One tragedy, in 1898, was the loss of the *Mohegan*. She was bound for New York from Gravesend (not a service you can use today), carrying sixty passengers and ninety-seven crew, and a cargo of beer and spirits and church ornaments. On a calm sea and in good weather she struck the Manacles. It may have been carelessness on the part of the crew, but ships in those days did not have the benefit of modern navigational aids. The tragedy was reported in the *Royal Cornwall Gazette*: "As the sea poured into the ship, her lights were quickly extinguished, causing panic as passengers found themselves in total darkness, and women hugged their children close to their sides". According to the testimony of one survivor, George Maule, the crew behaved calmly and without fuss, in true British tradition. Less than fifty people survived the tragedy. As bodies were washed ashore they were taken to St Keverne and buried in the churchyard, where today a large Celtic cross marks their common grave.

Further along the path I found myself in a huge quarry. Everything was white, including me by the time I walked out the far end. It looked like part of Cornwall had been struck by a nuclear missile. If my appearance had aroused the curiosity of holidaymakers before, I was a major attraction now. At Godrevy Cove, the path disappeared, this time amid a forest of brambles and nettles. Watched by near-naked sun-worshippers, I was obliged to negotiate slippery rocks right by the edge of the sea, and ended up at the bottom of a steep, grassy hillside. I'd have to climb this bit, but apart from the weight of my sack threatening a spectacular backward plunge onto the rocks below, there were no problems, except for the ubiquitous nettles and, higher up, the spiky assault of gorse. At the top, dishevelled and covered in white chalk, I looked like a latter-day Ben Gunn. Anyone could have been forgiven for thinking I'd been marooned for years on a remote island, and had only now, at this moment, succeeded in escaping.

At Porthallow (pronounced *Pra-la*) my progress was terminated abruptly by a wasp which, for reasons best known to itself, decided to attack my forearm. Man's instinctive reaction is to try and swat the offending creature with a quick swipe of the hand, a manoeuvre usually guaranteeing a miss by about two feet. But I caught the blighter fair and square, knocking it to the ground where I crushed it to an immediate and violent death. I looked down at my arm where a

volcanic-shaped mound was already forming, with the wasp's sting sticking out. One hears from time to time of someone dying after being stung. I could just hear them in the canteen at work:
'Y'know the DI's walking to Scotland or somewhere?'
'Aye. Has he got lost?'
'No, worse. He's dead. Got stung by a wasp.'
Laughter all round. A wasp. That's what kills 'em. If I'd been trekking across the Sahara and a scorpion had got me they'd have grieved for the loss of a brave man. But a wasp in Cornwall? I was contemplating my immediate future, if I had one, when a young woman appeared. She was early twenties, complete with Cornish accent and cheery smile. For a moment I thought she was going to chide me for murdering the wasp. But she had witnessed this unprovoked attack on my person and wanted to help. 'You poor man,' she declared. 'I'll be okay,' I purred bravely.

She lived nearby, she said, and despite knowing nothing about me invited me to her abode 'for a cup of coffee and a rest'. Her mother was at home, she added, possibly to make it clear that her motive was one of help to the stranger and no other. In a few minutes we were at the door of a thatched cottage, set in a garden of roses. For some reason I thought of Enid Blyton. Yet, stepping inside, I found myself in darkness, a cold, chill atmosphere replacing the glorious spring morn I had left a moment before. Is it like this when you die? Do you pass from sunshine through death's dark veil in just one moment? Had a wasp murdered a detective inspector? Then, when my eyes had accustomed themselves to the gloom, I saw her mother, lying unobtrusively on a sofa in a darkened corner of the room. She offered polite conversation while her daughter went and put the kettle on. We chatted about the weather, walking and wasps until her daughter arrived with the coffee.

'You might take ill after being stung,' she said, 'why don't you stay the night?'

My thoughts, long since departed from Enid Blyton, had moved to Bates Hotel, and the likelihood of the imminent appearance of Anthony Perkins. Self-preservation took priority

'No thanks', I said, explaining it was far too early in the day, that I had to go.

I should not have relished the prospect of staying in that cottage. Sad am I to say so after the hospitality shown by good, kindly people, but there it is. Yet the reason in declining their invitation was genuine.

It was still only mid-afternoon and I wanted to press on. Later, I wondered if I would have done so had the girl and her mother been two voluptuous women whose cottage was a welcoming boudoir.

It was still over three miles to the Helford River, a natural barrier to further progress along the coast. It turned out to be one of those days when it just kept on getting hotter. There was no respite for the man who carried his home on his back and whose clothes were now soaked in sweat and whose skin was burning. To add to my woes – I was enjoying it really – painful blisters were forming and my knees were creaking under the strain of walking the hard, ungiving surface of the lanes. But the injury caused by the wasp didn't appear to getting any worse, and I hadn't died.

Just after six I staggered through Manaccan, once visited by Captain William Bligh. The same Captain Bligh who was mistaken for a French spy and arrested and cast adrift when the crew mutinied on his ship, *Bounty*, in 1789. The same Captain Bligh who, as Governor of New South Wales, was imprisoned when he tried to suppress the traffic in rum. Wasn't a popular bloke, Captain Bligh. He sounds like one of those sneaks at school who were always in for a smack from somebody. We had one, a spotty youth who was hated because he had crooked teeth and wore size fourteen shoes. He was always being picked on, much to the delight of those who hated him, including the teachers. He said big feet meant a big penis. We thought it was his way of getting back at us until we saw him in the shower and had to admit he had a point.

Nearing Helford, I knew I'd have to find somewhere to camp. It was either that or collapse by the roadside. On cue, I spied a man and woman in the field of long grass, atop the hillside overlooking the estuary. This seemed as good as anywhere to call a halt. I called out to them in a loud voice.

'OK to put a tent up in that corner?'

They looked at me, then at one another, then at me, then at one another again. I tried to look tired. It wasn't difficult. I was about to say 'I can't cross the river tonight and I'm knackered' when the gent spluttered into life.

'It'll be okay,' he called out in a thick, Cornish tongue.

'Thanks,' I called back, without further ado tramping through the grass and putting the tent up before they could change their minds. Glancing up, I saw they were still looking in my direction, and the Cornishman spoke again, this time with more than a hint of doubt.

7

'I *think* it'll be okay, anyways.'

They walked off then, leaving me to wonder if, after all, someone might order me off their land. Who were they anyway? And why were they in the long grass in the first place?

The heavy pack had taken its toll; my knees throbbed, and one of the blisters was a monster. Still, the volcano on my forearm was no bigger and I was relieved on that score. I relaxed in the warm sunshine of a wonderful evening, and opened a can or two of that heavy food, if only to make the pack lighter. Could I really carry such a load for hundreds of miles? More to the point, did I want to?

From my elevated position above the estuary, I could see the white sails of yachts dotted about the deep, blue waters of the wide Helford River, giving a Mediterranean feel to the now cool evening. Tomorrow, I hoped the passenger ferry would take me across the estuary. I say hoped because the only indication of a ferry was on my Ordnance Survey map. Whether it ran at all remained to be seen. For all I knew it might have been sunk during the war.

*

I woke to the prospect of another glorious day: sun, sea and green pastures. The white sails on the Helford River had given way to bare masts, like matchsticks bobbing about on a surface as smooth as glass in the calm of an English dawn. Fields of deep green reminded me of my first book, *In Green Pastures*, with pictures of hedgehogs, rabbits and dormice. I took it to school where the teacher held it up to the class, to the sound of 'Aahh' every time a page was turned. From the girls, that is. The boys just sneered.

There are more bones in your feet than the rest of your body put together and this morning I believed it. They deserved a rest, but on went the boots. It took an age to pack the sack – there seemed more to cram in. As I heaved it on to my shoulders, I wondered if today I might get used to it, that it would become a part of me, like the man said. I wasn't optimistic.

Helford was deserted. Maybe there wasn't a ferry after all, or if there was maybe it didn't run on Monday mornings. Yes, that was it. Of all the days of the week I had to pick a Monday. Then I spotted a notice on a stone wall: COVE BOATS. Nearby, a sign warned of the danger of rabies. So, shipping from abroad docked here, never mind the ferry. Just below the sign was a large disc, with a door hinged in the centre, the idea being when someone swings the door across, the disc becomes yellow, so the ferryman on the other side of the river (if he's looking) knows there's someone waiting to cross. I swung the door over and scanned the opposite shore. For a few minutes nothing happened. But then a small boat was heading my way. The ferryman made almost a one-mile trip solely for my benefit, thus saving me a walk of twenty. Helford has a hero. In 1773, when the war against France broke out, Sir Edward Pellew took forty Cornish fishermen and 200 Cornish miners and set off for Portsmouth and put out to sea on a frigate, the *Nymph*. Cornish miners were hardly used to sea-faring battles, but Sir Edward and his crew captured a French frigate. In 1797, another frigate under his command took on a French battleship, *Droits de l'Homme*, and drove it ashore. Two years later, he prevented a mutiny on a ship at Bantry Bay, dashing alone into a crowd of mutineers and seizing the ringleader. In 1802 he became an M.P., and later Commander-in-Chief in the East Indies, where he destroyed the Dutch fleet. In 1816 he bombarded Algiers over the refusal to abolish Christian slavery. He was promoted to Viscount, Commander-in-Chief at Plymouth, then Vice-Admiral, United Kingdom. What a guy! One wonders why Erroll Flynn or somebody didn't play him in a movie.

The coast path followed the north shoreline of the river around Polgwidden Cove, where green meadows lay beneath vast carpets of bluebells. I tramped it under the ungiving weight of the sack. Where my spirits should have soared, where my heart should have brimmed full of joy, it was instead a morning marred by gruelling toil. I pressed on to Maenporth, where a score of people lay sunbathing on the sand, their presence evidently not sufficient cause for any entrepreneur to open an establishment for the sale of Coca-Cola or ice cream. I dropped the sack with relief and sat by the beach. It seemed the entire world was standing still – or lying prostrate – except for a young, buxom lass, perambulating back and forth on the sand, her bikini about six sizes too small. Her attempt to secure the undivided attention of all males present, including me, was a total success. Males alone or with male friends eyed her every move, whilst those with wives or girlfriends were more secretive in their observations. Their women looked on with disgust. Or, more likely, envy.

Watching the shenanigans of sun-lovers was all very well, but it was barely noon and here I was, worn out, dispirited – and going nowhere. The sack was too heavy to carry, and if I'd been honest I would have acknowledged this when I was carting it onto and off trains two days before. This was supposed to be an enjoyable venture, a challenge to be met fair and square, not an ordeal that could only end in failure – as it must. I couldn't go on, not with this load. At Gyllingvase beach, on the outskirts of Falmouth, I gave up the ghost and went into a café for fish and chips.

Later, resigned to defeat, I sat by the beach, and watched the world go by. A world where old folk took it easy, young girls soaked up the sun, young men soaked up the young girls, and small children built castles on the sand. No-one noticed the man in the sweat-soaked clothes, whose boots lay where they had been tossed on the ground nearby. I didn't care. I was content just to sit there, with no more grinding work to do on this lovely day. All afternoon I rested, enjoying the pleasure you feel the moment you stop banging your head against a wall; and all afternoon my conscience niggled away with increasing persistence. Give up? Who, me? Not on your nellie. I knew what I had to do. Get rid of the tent and the sleeping bag and the tins of Heinz 57 varieties, that's what. 'He who would travel happily would travel light', said Antoine de Saint-Exupery, the French novelist – who never even walked the coast path as far as I'm aware. But he was right. All would be well if I could walk free of a heavy load. Carrying a light pack is best. If, on any part of my journey, I failed to secure accommodation, so what? I was in Britain. It was springtime. I wouldn't freeze to death. I wouldn't be attacked by wolves or grizzly bears. Tonight, I'd stay at Falmouth youth hostel, and there abandon the weighty contents of the sack. I hadn't got used to it and it hadn't felt part of me after all.

*

'Open cheery heights, fresh south-western ocean breezes; a brisk, laughing sea swept by industrious sails, and the nets of a most stalwart, wholesome, frank and interesting population'.

Thus wrote Thomas Carlyle, of Falmouth. He may have been standing at the gates of Pendennis Castle on a morning such as the one that greeted me as I emerged from the youth hostel (housed in the castle's barracks), for the entire town was bathed in the sunshine of yet another glorious day. Cheery heights indeed!

The castle was built by Henry VIII to guard the mile wide estuary known as Carrick Roads against French invasion. Its cannon were capable of firing onto any vessels, providing they were not more than

800 yards distant. Beyond that was out of range, so another castle was built at St Mawes, opposite, to provide total defensive cover. Later, during the Civil Wars – Cornwall was Royalist – the garrison held out against Cromwell for five months and survived by eating horses and dogs, and was cheered when, starving and unable to continue, they surrendered and marched out, flags flying. As for the French, they never turned up.

I was the New Man. The numbing weight, the leaden burden, the punishing and unacceptable load I had borne from Lizard was gone, the heavy contents of my sack now entrusted to the care of the warden at Falmouth youth hostel. It was the way it should have been all along. But the efforts of the previous two days had left a price to pay: blisters were firmly established beneath and even in between my toes, and my feet were very tired. It would take them days to recover.

Falmouth was a-bustle: shop assistants sweeping pavements, women peering inquisitively into shop windows, their bored husbands wishing they were on a golf course somewhere. I saw no-one carrying a rucksack. I liked Falmouth. It's always easy to like somewhere when it's bathed in sunshine, not so much when it's raining. But I would have taken to Falmouth either way. I would have taken to anywhere, so high were my spirits, so gay was my mood at being able to walk unhindered. I made my way to the pier, where a timetable informed me there was an hour to kill before I could board the ferry to St Mawes. This suited me. After the relentless charge over the past two days I thought it would do me good to linger. After all, I didn't want to walk the length of the country without seeing anything.

In the 17th century, Falmouth's strategic position made it an obvious choice as a packet port for mail boats. In those early years the packet ships were privately owned, but later were replaced by naval ships, built for speed to flee enemy pursuers. At the time, Britain was at war with the French, Spanish, Dutch, even the Americans, and there was constant danger from pirates. And, along with everyone else, the packets were involved in smuggling. In fact, Falmouth, for all its glorious past and present day prosperity, probably owes its existence to the Killigrews, who made their fortune by smuggling and piracy. Sir John Killigrew embarked on raiding missions personally, and he was Vice Admiral of Cornwall. In the town, a tall granite obelisk stands as a memorial to the 'gallant officers and men of H.M. Post Office Packet Service sailing from Falmouth'. A more solid edifice I never saw. It will stand forever, a fitting tribute to be sure.

Crossing the Fal estuary, the views on this wonderful May morning were stunning. Pendennis Castle took pride of place, closely followed by the white-walled houses of St Mawes, with its castle. Southward, a yacht or two graced an otherwise empty sea. The appearance of a galleon under full sail would not have surprised me in the slightest. Perhaps such an occasion inspired A. Cunningham to write:

> A wet sheet and a flowing sea,
> A wind that follows fast,
> And fills the white and rustling sail
> And bends the gallant mast.
> And bends the gallant mast, my boys,
> While like the eagle free,
> Away the good ship flies, and leaves
> Old England on the lee.

A handful of passengers were making the crossing, among them a young couple who, notwithstanding the presence of strangers, were locked in firm embrace: kissing, tongues halfway down each other's throats, hands groping and fumbling with clothing. You know the sort of thing. Did it myself once (don't ask me what year). It was a bit embarrassing for anyone not taking part, i.e. *moi*. Once or twice they managed to disengage to take a photograph, as though they felt obliged to at least make a token gesture about being in such a lovely place. Not surprisingly, I wasn't considered a suitable object for such a diversion, even though, thanks to my appearance, they might have considered me an old sea dog. Suddenly, the female of the species surprised me by handing me her camera and, lapsing into her lover's arms, she and her new husband smiled for the picture which, I hope, today occupies a special place in their home.

St Mawes loomed up ahead. A hundred years ago, this was a busy port and safe anchorage. Once, the town vied for trade with Falmouth, but in the end succumbed in importance to its near-neighbour. Evidently, it's named after St Mauditus who, around the 5th century AD, along with many other Celtic holy men, infiltrated these parts from Brittany, Ireland and Wales, spreading the Gospel. St Mauditus's Holy Well can still be seen today. There's a solid, stone arch and wooden door, with St Mauditus engraved on it. Evidently there was a time when anyone suffering from worms could call here to be cured, but if you happen to need help in this regard I'd check first. St

Mauditus, it is said, set himself up as a schoolmaster, and preached on the beach. One day when a seal barked and made the pupils angry, he clipped it across the ear. A man of the cloth, too. Tut-tut.

St Mawes Castle, unlike Pendennis, was not laid siege during the Civil War. It would have been, but its defences faced the sea, from which direction attack from the French had always been expected. So, when the Parliamentarians arrived at the gates on the landward side, the garrison had no choice but to surrender without a shot being fired.

I climbed the hill out of St Mawes and took the road for St Just. Or, properly, St Just-in-Roseland. Not that it has anything to do with roses; the name derives from the Cornish, *ros*, meaning a spur of land, or peninsula. It's thought that Bronze Age warriors were the first people to occupy this place, around 4,000 years ago, having crossed the Channel in wooden boats from France. They would have discovered forests and swampland then, but they made their settlements on the hilltops, overlooking the sea.

Walking the road, my thoughts strayed to Cornwall's once-prosperous industry, tin mining. Tradition has it that tin was discovered by St Piran, who came to Cornwall from Ireland around AD 500. The story goes that he picked up a piece of black rock which he used to build his fireplace, and when he was cooking his dinner the rock melted into a white liquid which solidified into metal when cooled. He had discovered tin, so became patron saint to the miners.

At first, the tinners worked the surface, where rich ore was washed up from lodes deposited in river valleys, a process known as streaming. But when streaming could no longer meet the demand, the tin had to be mined. No matter how hard the miners toiled, their fate came down to luck: if they found the ore, they were well paid; if not they faced debt and starvation.

Around the 12th century, the Stannary system was established to develop and control the tin industry for the benefit of the Crown. Or, after 1337, the Duchy, where the son and heir to the throne held jurisdiction. In return for providing funds to the Duchy, the tinners were exempt from serving in the armed forces, they could leave their feudal lords and stake a claim without the permission of the owner of a piece of land, they could divert rivers, do whatever they liked to mine tin without fear of reprisal or redress. They even had their own judicial system, and when they broke the law they were tried by the Stannaries' own Courts and could be imprisoned in the Stannaries' own gaols. It was a hard life for the miners and their families, whilst the Duchy couldn't lose. By the 1870's, the tin was mined abroad at less cost and the tinners went to Wales to mine coal. Nowadays, the ruined engine houses and chimneys and empty mineshafts are all that remain of an ancient industry.

I was walking on tarmacadam, as many rights of way across farmland seemed to be obstructed by crops. To tell the truth, there is little pleasure in walking on roads. Roads without footpaths, anyway. Few drivers consider that just around the next bend there might be someone on foot. Still, the one consolation in road-walking is that the ground is covered quickly, 3 m.p.h., perhaps a little more. And I enjoyed walking the Roseland peninsula, where the road traverses the higher ground and the views are extensive. My aim was to rejoin the coast path at Gerrans Bay, and I kept on apace, marching for the coast.

'I have blundered into the Garden of Eden', wrote H. V. Morton of the church at St Just-in-Roseland. The church stands close to St Just Pool, with rising ground abounding in trees and exotic shrubs, and old graves scattered at random. Truly, this is the most exotic and beautiful churchyard I have seen, and that's saying something. St Just, it seems, was probably a hermit, real identity Iestin, son of Gerranius, a Cornish king. Legend has it that a tin merchant came here and that he brought Christ with him. Jesus, it is said, talked to religious leaders by St Just Pool. I wonder if, like me, he might have thought the only feature detracting from the beauty of this place is the pool at low tide, where the slimy bed of the bay is hardly in keeping with the glorious landscape. One miracle would have made it perfect.

Talking of miracles, nature has blessed Cornwall with many beautiful features. Top of the list must be her beaches and cliffs, occupying most of the 300 mile coastline of England's south-westernmost county. Inland, too, Cornwall is pleasant and largely unspoilt, although there are the scars of industry, much of it the result of tin mining. There is a comparison to be drawn between Cornwall and Durham: tin was mined in Cornwall, coal in Durham. Both produced the inevitable 'spoil heaps'. It may be that, *inland*, Cornwall has not the natural idyllic beauty of, say, Devon or Dorset, but when it comes to those beaches and cliffs, her wild and unspoiled places where mankind has marred the scenery just a little, if at all, then Cornwall is unrivalled.

I reached the coast again at Pendower Beach, where golden sands stretch away to the distant sea. I kept close to the cliffs, for the soft sand near the water's edge is very tiring to walk upon, and in any case, it is the domain of the topless beauty and bronzed Adonis, not quite the territory of a man carrying a rucksack and wearing boots. There is an awesome feeling about walking beneath high cliffs. So close to the hard, unyielding rock, towering above, one feels so insignificant. I made steady progress, there being no need to hurry, not on this one mile of paradise where I picked my way through a thousand rocky outcrops, islands in a sea of yellow sand, seeing not a soul. Until, that is, I came across Sophie. She was wearing a pair of briefs and a friendly smile, and reading a paperback. Looking up, she smiled and called out a cheery 'Hi there.' I turned, expecting to see a bronzed hulk, with bulging muscles and bulging swimming trunks. But there was no-one, just the sun-worshippers in the distance. Sophie was talking to *me*.

'What on earth are you doing?' she asked, shielding her eyes from the sun.

'Walking,' I replied, truthfully.

She still had her smile, only now it appeared it might be out of sympathy, either due to my appearance or possibly my mental health.

'Would you like a sandwich?' she ventured.

I hesitated, not because I wasn't sure but because I was wondering if what was happening was true. I mean, she was practically *naked*. She was holding the sandwiches in her hand, offering them to me. 'I'll never eat them,' she said.

'Go on then,' I said, accepting her kind offer (just this once). We must have been quite a sight, she wearing virtually nothing and me carrying virtually everything. I enjoyed her company, not really wanting to get onto my feet again until my conscience insisted I'd never get anywhere if I didn't. I left Sophie as I found her, wearing a lovely smile. And she was smiling too.

At the far end of the beach I took the country lanes again, to Portloe, an enchanting village with a little harbour. It was once an important pilchards port, with drift and seine boats working in co-ordination, whilst lookouts on the cliff-tops watched out for the purple hue which betrayed the pilchards' presence. Later, the fishermen turned to mackerel, but this market, too, declined. Nowadays, fish are transported live to Billingsgate, or exported, so Portloe remains a true fishing village in a county largely taken over by tourism.

Climbing out of Portloe was hot work, with many ups and downs in the unrelenting heat. The coast path here rates ten out of ten in anyone's book, yet it was all but deserted. People, it seems, just park

15

their cars at one of the little harbours, then venture a short distance along the coast, returning when they have satisfied their desire to 'go for a walk'. Ah, what they are missing, for the *real* walk takes them well away from their cars.

Today, the sea – here known as Veryan Bay – was as flat as a lake, with thousands of gulls circling and crying around little offshore islands. I had it all to myself, as though I had reserved it at great cost, as one would an exclusive holiday retreat. In merciless sunshine I reached Portholland, where I sank to the ground, by the beach. It was deserted except for a young couple playing 'tag'. There was plenty of room. I watched them, idly, just a few yards from an elderly chap who was seated on a small stool. I must have looked weary, for he did no more than offer it to me in an obvious gesture of sympathy. Kindness to a stranger is creditable, but what concerned me was his perception at what he must have regarded as my imminent demise. I fled!

I duly arrived at Porthluney Cove, more golden sands, today a proverbial sun-trap. Strangely, there were few people about, just a few of the inevitable sun-worshippers. I was used to the sight of naked breasts by now, having traversed so many golden sands in such scorching weather. Eyes forward (honest) I continued to yet another cliff-top ascent, this time to Greeb Point where, unexpectedly, I came across some Highland cattle, whose fearsome horns belie their timid nature. They were a long way from home. Further on, I got into a mess in the fields near Boswinger, finally locating a country lane leading to Boswinger youth hostel, which was deserted, save for a fellow who was walking the coast path 'in its entirety' in the opposite direction to me. We spoke little to one another. It might have been different if there'd been a pub to go to, but there wasn't, so we couldn't. Sadly, he lost all credibility when he declared he'd caught a bus at Par. How can he say he's walked the coast path when he caught a bus?

*

It came as a shock to look out of the window to find the sun no longer shining. Instead, a grey sea-fret hung dank and cold about Cornwall's coast. I scoffed a quick breakfast of baked beans. Never saw the guy who was on the coast path. He probably left early to catch the bus.

Gorran Haven is a picturesque village on the coast. At least that's what I read about it. As it was shrouded in mist I never actually saw it.

I saw no people either: not in open country, not in Gorran Haven, not on the path. But thoughts of a cup of tea at Mevagissey cheered me. People who take on the elements and get out on foot are more deserving of a cuppa than, say, motorists who cruise up to nice little bolt-holes, having spent hours on end in the warmth of their cars. Take the Lake District. At Wasdale Head there's an inn where you can get a meal and a good pint to wash it down. I went into the inn on a wet and windy day once, hungry and thirsty after a morning on the fells. Thought I'd treat myself. The place was infested with tourists of the motoring kind, all wearing expensive Gore-tex cags and silly hats and tucking in to pub grub whilst I, bedraggled and forlorn-looking, was obliged to wait like an unwanted beggar.

Today, on the cliff-tops, the mist was unmoving and there were no views. You couldn't tell where sky and sea met. Then the path led down the hill into Mevagissey, with its narrow streets and cob and slate cottages by the harbour. I heard someone remark once that tourists spoil Mevagissey. Tourists 'spoil' lots of places, yet it's the tourists who complain. The trouble is, everyone wants to have these places to themselves, and fail to see that others want the same thing and have as much right as them to be there. There were few people about – tourists or otherwise – when I entered a little café in the village for the cup of tea I'd promised myself, but a small crowd was present to witness events when I emerged. The timing was perfection. As I shouldered the sack, a passing seagull – or possibly an albatross – decided to unload. I became conscious of two things: the sound of the *splat* as part of its breakfast, or possibly a three-course dinner from the night before, hit the ground, and a sudden feeling of warmth across my neck where some of it hit me.

Smiles of sympathy graced the faces of those who had witnessed this bombardment. All I can say is I never knew seagulls were such good marksmen. But there's more to report of this unfortunate incident. One trick I'd learned about backpacking was when washing socks and things in rivers or youth hostels, it's a good idea to hang them on your rucksack to dry out as you walk along. I had put this idea into practice at Boswinger (even though conditions were damp). Now my freshly-laundered socks were covered in a yellow, snot-like gunge. So much for the great plan.

There's a story that a monkey was washed ashore and hanged as a spy at Mevagissey. I have heard a similar tale about Hartlepool. Could the same thing have happened twice, or has someone's imagination run riot? The only other historical gem about Mevagissey is that it was here, in 1812, that Andrew Pears perfected the process of refining soap. Maybe he had an experience with a seagull too.

It was time for the cliff-tops again, and the belated reappearance of the sun, and two more miles brought me to Pentewan, where a sign fastened to a tree said 'Have a nice day'. I rested in the square by an old-fashioned water pump, and decided that Pentewan is a most agreeable place. It might not have been so years before, when a narrow-gauge railway brought china clay from St Austell to the little harbour here. China clay, or kaolin, is formed by gases in the interior of the earth. It's all washed out by high water pressure, then left to settle in huge tanks to dry. The resulting waste forms the 'Cornish Alps', huge slag-heaps visible for miles. The clay is used to make paper, rubber, paint, plastics and insecticides – it's a versatile product, although it's a bit messy. Its export from Pentewan ended when the harbour became choked by waste, brought downriver from the china clay pits.

Further on came Charlestown, with its little harbour, named after Charles Rashleigh who, in 1791, constructed it for the export of the aforesaid china clay. When I arrived in Charlestown, a ship was moored in the narrow harbour and china clay was pouring into its hold, white dust landing on houses, on the ground, on anyone passing at the time. It was also landing on the car belonging to a woman resident, which is why she has to wash it every day. She urged me to the museum, just up the road. I told her I hadn't time. I didn't add that if I stood talking to her much longer I'd be as white as everything else in view, and not for the first time on only the fourth day of my journey. So, I took my leave, pleased at having discovered Charlestown, and once again meeting someone courteous and helpful. I was definitely taking to the natives of Cornwall.

The coast path led around St Austell Bay, keeping to the cliff-tops, which here are relatively level, the going easy. That guy who caught the bus missed this bit, and his was the loss. Further on, at Par, I found myself walking around an enormous china clay works, the inevitable white dust everywhere. I emerged where road and railway and hiker compete for space. It was hard to believe that in just a few short minutes I had forsaken Cornwall's beaches and cliffs for a major industrial site. After Cadgwith, Pendower Beach and Mevagissey, Par was a reminder of the real world. I kept moving, eager to escape.

Just before Fowey, I came upon the Tristan Stone. It's thirteen centuries old and looks it. Cars and lorries swept past as I took a close look. You'd think somebody would stop to see something so old – the stone, that is – but the day-to-day business of the twentieth century is clearly more important.
These words are inscribed:

DRVSTANVS IACIT CVNOMORI FILVIS

Which, translated, means:

Drustanus lies here, son of Coromorus

The legend concerns King Mark, who ruled Cornwall during the 6th century, and Tristan, his son. Tristan had a relationship with Iseult, but she married Mark, though she kept seeing Tristan afterwards. Naturally, Mark wasn't too pleased, so Tristan fled to Brittany, where he married another woman, also called Iseult. Iseult of the White Hands, actually.

Tristan sent a messenger to try and persuade Iseult to join him in Brittany. The messenger's instructions were that if he succeeded in persuading her to sail to Brittany with him, the sails of their ship would be white; if he failed they would be black. Tristan waited, with an eye on the horizon. When the ship appeared, he asked Iseult of the White Hands what colour the sails were. Black, she lied, and Tristan collapsed, dead. Why the stone is in Cornwall when he died abroad is unclear, but eligible males might consider giving anyone called Iseult a wide berth.

At last I came to Fowey (pronounced *Foy*). I made my way directly to the harbour, in reality a wide inlet of the sea, a vast sheltered sheet of water, for centuries a haven for ancient sailing ships, including man o'wars of British naval forces, and today's yachts, speedboats, and ocean-going ships. At any given point over the last two thousand years or so I could have stood here and looked at ships. In 1346, 47 ships sailed from here and took part in the siege of Calais, and in 1457, after a French attack at Fowey, they hung defensive chains across the harbour. Just by the harbour there's a pub, *The King of Prussia*. It's named after John Carter, a famous smuggler, who gave himself the name when playing soldiers, presumably when he was still at school. Carter smuggled contraband into a cove in Mount's Bay, which became known as Prussia Cove. It was an ideal spot, sheltered by overhanging cliffs and (it is said) a number of caves which were connected to Carter's house by underground passages. To protect his nice little earner, he installed a battery of cannon, ostensibly to defend against French privateers, but in reality to fire on anyone who might intrude on his business, including English revenue vessels.

I swear the patrons of *The King of Prussia* were the very crew of Blackbeard, so rather than risk having my throat cut I repaired to the more sedate surroundings of the aptly-named *Safe Harbour*, where I ordered a pint of Cornish bitter. I was served by a barmaid with dreadful teeth who asked kindly after my welfare. What she lacked in physical beauty she more than made up for in her warm, friendly personality, which was just what I needed after such a hard day, especially with sixties music drifting quietly across the room. Then a bloke of sixty and what I took to be his wife came in to the pub, and I couldn't help overhearing what they said to one another. It soon became apparent that this guy was a serious contender for Cornwall's No. 1 Male Chauvinist Pig.

'Pint o' bitter an' a gin an' tonic for 'er,' ordered the Cornish nasty, jerking his thumb over his shoulder. He took the drinks to their table, beer spilling over the rim of his glass. They sat in silence, he with his glass held firm in an enormous fist, she sipping her drink timidly. When he belched loudly his wife showed no reaction at all. What kind of life did she lead with this buffoon? A quiet one, probably, where silence ensures peace.

'Ready then?' he asked finally, getting up whether she was or wasn't. She wasn't, but it didn't matter. He led her out the door. It was as well. Another minute and I might have considered my own pint of Cornish bitter, lovely though it was, might have been better emptied over his head.

*

When I dragged myself out of bed for the morning fry-up in the *Safe Harbour*, I could find no sign of life anywhere in the building. I prowled corridors, rattled door handles in the hope of finding someone to cook my breakfast. Just as it seemed the *Safe Harbour* had turned into a *Marie Celeste*, a woman appeared, carrying a plateful of bacon and eggs, which I ate in a room where the smoke of the previous evening's cigarettes – and lots of evenings before – still permeated the atmosphere. Let it be put on record that breakfast in the *Safe Harbour* was excellent.

Continuing along this glorious coastline, it's ten miles to Looe. I planned to stop at Polperro and (with ample time) treat myself to fish and chips. But first I had to get across the harbour. I found myself on the little ferry to Polruan, in company with around 30 others, locals by the look of them. It's a grand crossing, the white buildings of Fowey falling behind, and the view upriver, where wooded slopes come right down to the water's edge, with dozens of boats, large and small, dotted about the harbour. The writer, Daphne du Maurier, made this her home. If it was inspiration she was after she could hardly have chosen better.

Once, wooden ships were built at Polruan. Whether they still are I am uncertain, although there was a boat repair yard still functioning. Polruan is quiet, whilst Fowey is boisterous; Polruan is quaint whilst Fowey is loud. I liked Polruan's narrow streets, where little cottages overlook the harbour. I liked Fowey *and* Polruan: it's easy to like everywhere along this coast. Except that china clay monstrosity at Par, but you have to accept some scarring. Man has to produce. I climbed the hill, rejoining the coast path, taking a last look back. From here, the small craft bobbing about on the tide looked like toys in a giant's bathtub, a splendid scene in the greyness of the early morning, the sort of place you hate to leave behind.

But I had to leave it behind, and was encouraged to do so by a cold, bracing wind. As ever the path was all but deserted. It led to West Combe, a deep ravine that you have to descend into and climb out of again, then a mile further to another ravine, which you have to descend into and climb out of again – just as I had been doing most of the way from Lizard. Pretty flowers, their little faces peeping defiantly among gently waving grasses, were my constant companions, along with the vast, heaving sea.

I have to confess to knowing little of the flora of Cornwall and England's wild, open spaces. No-one taught me, and I never took the trouble to find out. I can identify a dandelion, a daisy, a buttercup. If I'm stung by a nettle I know a dock-leaf will neutralise the sting (an old wife told me). But, whilst their identities were a mystery to me, I enjoyed the constant sight of Cornwall's flowers, and bluebells, which lay in great carpets over the fields and meadows. There's such variation in the landscape, too, with fields of deep-green, reaching to the edge of high, rugged cliffs, rocky headlands, pounded ceaselessly by the sea, long stretches of golden sands, unspoilt and sometimes inaccessible save for perilous scrambles down steep hillsides, secret coves, and smugglers' retreats. Among this tangle of nature's great work are tiny fishing communities, little harbours and holiday hideaways. Nature will smile with approval at man's work here. I pressed on, atop the cliffs above the wide sweep of Lantivet bay, the sea a deep blue, life-like creature that emanated great power. It heaved and swelled, the blue bursting into white on the rocks below. There were unseen bays, with inaccessible, white beaches. I decided to try and get down to one, but my venture lasted just a few minutes before I turned back, the ground being far too steep and dangerous. I didn't want my venture to end trapped on the coast of Cornwall, ending up like Robinson Crusoe. Not without Man Friday for company, anyway. Or even Ruby Tuesday. A mile from Polperro my progress was checked by a lone woman, heading in my direction where the path was narrow, and led through thick gorse. Naturally, I stepped aside to let her pass. She said she was sorry if I'd scratched my legs on that nasty gorse. I said I was glad I hadn't fallen into the sea. Anyway, she didn't pass me by, not then. Instead, she wanted to chat to the bloke with the rucksack. Like me she was wearing shorts, like me she was smiling, unlike me she was gorgeous. I decided to spare her a few minutes of my time.

'Are you walking the coast path?' she asked.

'Sort of,' I replied. She obviously wanted an explanation.

'I'm walking to Dunnet Head.'

Of course, she'd never heard of it.

'It's near John o'Groats,' I explained.

We talked. About this, about that. We were an instant hit, the Rodgers and Hammerstein of the Coast Path Show. An hour later, we were still there. There was even a chance I might have to forego the fish and chips. The chemistry was right, if you know what I mean. If I hadn't known what *horny* meant before, I did now. Such a pity about the gorse. I've hated the sight of it ever since. Reluctantly, we parted, she to continue her walk along the cliffs, me to eat fish and chips before I starved to death.

Approaching Polperro, there's a grand view of the snug little harbour, where cottages cling to the steep-sided cliffs. Polperro is the haunt of artists and the inevitable tourists. They can't bring their cars with them, though. Instead, they must leave them outside the village and either walk down to the harbour or, more romantically, catch a

22

pony and trap service. It's a rule they should enforce elsewhere. Or, better still, everywhere. I ate my fish and chips outdoors, where it was so cold I was obliged to wolf it down before I froze to death. When, moving on, the path climbed to the cliff-tops again, it seemed higher here than anywhere on my journey so far. There's a fine, granite war memorial, high above the sea. The names of the men immortalised on its fine column could not be better placed.

In 1817, a violent storm ravaged Polperro, and Looe, further along the coast. The *West Briton* reported: "The ruin is dreadful. Of 45 fishing boats, 30 have been dashed to pieces, most incapable of repair. Sixty families have been deprived of bread. The pier has been nearly destroyed and several dwellings washed away. Three new boats and all the timber and tools in the shipwright's yard were carried away. The loss to the proprietor is £800".

Further along the coast, Talland church seems to be chiselled into the hillside, the crosses and gravestones in the cemetery all on different levels. Inside, there's an inscription: *Bengys yu nap a-gar Dew dres pup tra us y'n bys*, which, for anyone who doesn't know Cornish, means: "Blessed is the person who loves God before everything else". In the 18th century, the vicar of Talland had a reputation as an exorcist, and locals were afraid to approach the church at night in case they met evil spirits. Come on, he was smuggling like everyone else, and probably encouraged the spooky tales of the devil to keep people away.

On the map hereabouts are the words *Measured Nautical Mile*, presumably marking the place where a nautical mile was first officially calculated. A nautical mile (2,025 yards) is longer than an ordinary mile (1,760 yards) and is based on the Roman mile of 1,000 paces. So, some Roman soldier, possibly on fatigues, was told to walk 1,000 paces across this southern outpost of Britain – hence the official nautical mile. But where does 1,760 come from? Why not 2,000 yards to an *ordinary* mile? I've often moaned about the invasion of metrication into British measures, but maybe kilometres are more straightforward after all. Anyway, three more ordinary miles led to Looe. Evidently, the name derives from the Cornish (or Celtic?) *lagh*, meaning a stretch of water or a lake. A bit like the Scottish *loch*.

I found myself crossing the famous old bridge across the Looe River. The foundation stone was laid by John Francis Buller on 13 June, 1854. He'd given £500 towards the cost, so he was entitled to the honour. Not even the Victorians could have envisaged the amount traffic the bridge would have to take nowadays. People complained about the 'new' bridge at the time, for they liked the old one. Like today, folk just don't like change.

Naturally, Looe was at the forefront of smuggling. In August, 1816, when a small French ship was spotted drifting at sea, it was brought to Looe harbour and her cargo of fruit was sold. Then the customs officers found twelve toy horses which, when they were taken apart, were found to contain 51 pairs of silk stockings and nine silk shawls. Those naughty French!

Charles Sandoe Gilbert (1760-1831), historian, published a Historical Survey of Cornwall in 1817. Wrote Gilbert of Looe: "The situation of these towns (East and West Looe) which line the eastern and western banks of the river Looe, is beautifully picturesque, being encompassed by an amphitheatre of rapidly rising hills, the sides of which are adorned with clusters of flourishing gardens intermixed with little rustic buildings, in some places fringed with ivy and in others shaded by stately foliage..."

If Gilbert were around today, he would write exactly the same, for nothing of Looe has changed – except for tourism, of course. But as many tourists as there are – and there are many – Looe remains unspoiled. It's just a pity they can't keep the traffic out.

On 21st July, 1588, the Spanish Armada was sighted off Looe: "When the curtain of the night was lifted it was upon a glorious scene for England – the great Armada, lazily advancing, and seawards, right in the wind of it were forming the two divisions of the English fleet. Out of Plymouth was sailing another squadron which as it passed boldly across the Spaniards' front, fired on the leading ships, and then, going about, formed the bulk of the fleet to windward".

If you were educated at any time before, say, the 1970's, you'll know what happened after that. Later, maybe you won't.

My first objective in Looe was Boots the Chemists (there's always a Boots, isn't there?) for a fresh supply of sticking plasters for the blisters. I was resigned to blisters. Strange, how human beings get used to things: set off for a walk one morning from home with feet covered in blisters and the day is spent in agony; walk a long distance route and the pain is acceptable, all part of the experience. Later, I located a guesthouse, with a bedroom overlooking the harbour. My hosts were late fifties, and had lived in the Midlands, where he had worked as a civil servant. But long before he was due to retire, they had decided to do something else with their lives, which they considered routine and boring. They would move anywhere, as long as it was on the coast. Llandudno or Lowestoft for all they cared. When a guesthouse became available at Looe they bought it. Simple as that. They love Looe, love Cornwall. 'We've moved to heaven,' they said. I couldn't have argued. The view from their home across Looe harbour is stunning, where houses, competing for space, adorn the steep-sided slopes, backed by the deep green of the hillside beyond. For me, it's the lack of regimentation that pleases the eye.

Later, washed and cleansed, I headed for the nearest pub where I chatted up the barmaid. Okay, she wasn't interested in some bloke walking. Then my host and his wife bowled in, so I had company for a change. By ten you couldn't move. Then two guys came in, and forced their way to the bar. 'They're old bill,' I told my host and his missus.

They looked across the crowded room, identified the two guys.

'How can you tell?' I was asked.

'Policemen and criminals can always tell,' I said.

They didn't ask which category I fitted into, but they doubted my word anyway. At the bar one of them ordered the drinks. 'You old bill?' I asked casually. He nodded.

'Avon and Somerset.'

Takes one to know one, as they say.

*

'Ever thought about doing the Appalachian Trail?' The American guest was enjoying his full English breakfast. 'Twenty-two hundred miles with camp sites everywhere. You'd love it.' I had told him I'd walked to Looe from Fowey, and this was his response. You know, Texas is bigger than England, the Appalachian Trail is grander than the coast path, etc. 'Say,' he purred, 'could you suggest a day's walk for us?' He meant him and his missus. I had a look at what I regarded as their state of fitness. 'Take a walk to Polperro,' I suggested, and left them perusing their map. Four miles wouldn't harm.

The sea was silver today, with millions of tiny ripples. I was running out of adjectives to describe the joys of the Cornish coast. It was always the same: high cliffs, sandy beaches, lovely churches. Here and there, something different to break the monotony. But a glorious monotony.

Again, the path led to the cliff-tops. Again, I had it to myself. As I progressed around the sweeping curve of the bay, I kept looking back to Looe Island, which seemed reluctant to disappear. It reminded me of an old film I once saw about prehistoric monsters. Some people were shipwrecked on an island where they kept hearing loud roars. Finally, a towering monster – it was a lizard magnified ten thousand times – made the palm trees bend with its mighty roar. Blood dripped from its mouth as it devoured members of the crew. Naturally, the hero and heroine just managed to escape. It was all ham acting, except by the lizard which won an Oscar.

Millendreath Beach was so cold it was deserted. I pressed on, singing at the top of my voice. Didn't notice the young couple in a nearby garden. They looked up – probably thought it was Elvis reincarnate – only to see this bloke wearing a silly hat and shorts and carrying a rucksack. Trying not to feel silly – it wasn't easy – I called out to them in my best cheery voice.

'Don't mind me!' I added a smile for good measure.

Blank looks were their response. Maybe they didn't like Elvis. I left them to their miserable lives and continued to Downderry, where the coast path continues straight on and upward onto Battern Cliffs. It was a long, arduous climb, which took me by surprise. At the top it was so cold I was obliged to put on my cag. I was just about to pee into a hedge (as you do) when two elderly women appeared and almost caught me out with their silent approach. So, it was 'good mornings' all round and pleasant remarks about the weather and the scenery, a nice change. They said they wished they could accompany me on my walk. I said the same. They were the only people I encountered on the path all day.

I duly came to Portwrinkle. I had seen the name on the map, and it fascinated me. Portwrinkle! There are long stretches of sandy beaches here, an hotel, a coastguard station and a few houses. I sat awhile on a bench, with no-one about on what had turned into a cold, blustery day. Portwrinkle would be the last community on the coast path before heading inland onto the cliff-tops for the last time. Here, the map indicated a Ministry of Defence 'Danger Area', where you have to leave the coast and cut inland. I suppose if you didn't you'd step on a mine. Those wishing to avoid losing a limb rejoin the path a few miles further on, where, if they are 'doing' the coastal route they must walk miles and miles around Rame Head. But I was bound for Antony and Torpoint and Plymouth. I lingered here, looked out to sea and reflected on my journey so far: Lizard Point and the punishing start with my heavy backpack to Cadgwith and Coverack, the Helford River and

Falmouth; then glorious Pendower Beach, Veryan Bay, Charlestown, Fowey and Polruan, Lantivet Bay and Polperro. The weather and the scenery had been grand. My feet ached and there were the blisters, but they'd be okay. Reluctantly, I turned my back on Cornwall's coast. I would not see the sea again on my journey – apart from a brief sojourn to Plymouth Hoe – until I reached the west coast of Scotland.

At Antony I went into the *Ring o' Bells* for a sandwich and a pint glass of pineapple and lemonade, then wandered across to St James's church, where the gravestones in the cemetery are grouped so close together the occupants might keep one another warm. There are several Celtic crosses, over which the view east is extensive, to Plymouth and the high moors beyond. Inside the porch was a 17th century nun's prayer, an extract from which reads:

"Lord, keep me from the fatal habit of thinking I must say something on every subject and on every occasion. Release me from craving to straighten out everybody's affairs. Teach me the glorious lesson that occasionally I may be mistaken. Give me the ability to see talent in unexpected people".

Her message certainly lasted; you can see it on postcards now.

At Torpoint, I found myself passing by the main gateway of H.M.S. Raleigh, the naval land-base. I was tempted to take a photo of the guard, but as I reached for my camera I noticed a couple of blokes in naval uniforms looking my way and thought better of it. Imagine the headlines: 'Detective Inspector Arrested for Spying'. Then again, it would have added an extra touch of spice to this book, written in my prison cell. Anyway, Torpoint faces Plymouth across the stretch of the River Tamar known as the Hamoaze. The ferry service started in the 1730's and the town grew with the wars against the American colonies, France and Spain. During the Second World War, women were employed on the ferry for the first time. Previously, male conductors collected the tolls on board, but the women collected them *on the shore*, where they wouldn't be exposed to danger and drunks. It was considered that ferries were no place to employ a woman. Today, women serve on destroyers.

I enjoyed that crossing. The sight of warships moored at Devonport, the wide, blue estuary and the bracing air sweeping in from the sea. I looked at the locals, who routinely make the crossing. The only sights that seemed to be of interest to them were their own fingernails, or their morning newspapers. Used to it, y'see. To them there was nothing out of the ordinary. Only people who aren't used to things take any interest. I guess it's just human nature. A fellow from Sheffield once told me he thought it was interesting to watch ships in the Tyne, loading or unloading their cargoes. I couldn't see what he meant, until he explained he lived in a city without a major river and hadn't seen anything like that before. The same principle applied, except that now, if that fellow stood by the Tyne, he wouldn't see ships any more.

On Devon soil – or, rather, Devon pavements – fresh air gave way to exhaust fumes as cars and lorries drove off the ferry and headed for destinations unknown, a reminder that in a city the combustion engine rules. It was about a mile to the youth hostel, in a suburb called Stoke, an old part of Plymouth. A part the Germans never flattened, and they flattened plenty. The hostel, says the guide, was 'inspired by Greek architecture'; which belies a stark, rather cold building. But perhaps I am unkind. Later, I caught a bus to while away the evening at Plymouth Hoe (catching public transport here was OK, as I wasn't actually continuing the journey) – Plymouth Hoe, where Sir Francis Drake finished his game of bowls before dashing off to sort out that Armada; where ships sailed with convicts, sentenced to transportation; where the Pilgrim Fathers set sail aboard *Mayflower* for the New World. Plymouth Hoe, where I stood with mixed emotions: of pride at the little ships of England's navy sending would-be invaders a-scatter; of shame for my country, who's privileged gentry sent peasants to the other side of the world for stealing a rabbit to feed starving infants; of admiration for the little band who sailed for the New World. And pity for a certain Mr Day who, in the 18th century, tried out the new-fangled sailing craft he'd invented – a submarine. From *The Gentleman's Magazine, 1774*: "Mr Day entered his submarine, let water into her and shut the valve. The ship went down in 22 fathoms at 2 o'clock on Tuesday afternoon. Unfortunately, it never rose again". It's still there, I suppose, with Mr Day still inside.

A more recent institution provided my supper. The Kentucky Fried Chicken was as far as my aching feet would take me. Later, lager louts appeared, shouting, kicking empty beer cans and litter bins. Plymouth, like everywhere these days, was devoid of the boys – and girls – in blue, so I repaired to the sanctuary of the youth hostel. Tomorrow, at last, I would head northward on my journey.

2

Dartmoor and the Quantocks

"In Dem ees a er an' ers a ee,
all 'cept th'aud tom cat an' even ees a 'er!"

Old Devonshire saying

("In Devon, he is a her and she is a he,
all except the old tom cat and even he is a her!")

I'd noticed him the night before as he drifted silently through the corridors of Plymouth youth hostel: fifty-odd, unshaven, unkempt, his clothes in tatters, shoes down-at-heel. Yet he was calm, articulate, and he made his bed with precise care. He was broke, that's all. He complained about the overnight fees of youth hostels and poor bus services, and having to walk miles every day. I felt sorry for him, then I realised that's exactly what I'd been doing. As he fumbled with the old leather belt holding up his trousers, anyone could have been forgiven for thinking he was making his way to the nearest soup kitchen.

Dartmoor. Barren, desolate, a vast area of bog, *inhospitable to walkers*. That's what the guidebooks say; that's where I was going. The moor is the remains of a volcanic, mountainous system formed 300 million years ago. Over the years, the topsoil has been eroded by the elements, leaving tall, granite pillars, the so-called *tors*. It's the highest and wettest large area of ground in the south of England, reaching around 2,000 feet in places, and covering some 200 square miles. 3,500 years ago, prehistoric man built stone huts, either in clusters, or scattered. Many survive today (the huts, not prehistoric man), but I'm not suggesting you could go up and knock at the door of any. I hoped to find accommodation at Princetown, more or less the centre of the moor. If I couldn't I'd have to sleep rough, or perhaps take lodgings in the prison. Imagine the inmates welcoming a detective inspector. Full English breakfast in the morning, guv? Pigs would fly.

Feelings of 'getting somewhere' now prevailed. I felt good, even though this morning meant negotiating the busy roads of a major city, and looking out for the little green man at crossings. Civilisation, y'see. We do it every day, except when you've had the sea for company for nearly a week it seems strange. I marched past Home Park, home of Plymouth Argyle FC. In the *Evening Herald,* on 22 March, 1946, Sir Clifford Tozer, chairman, paid tribute to the 'wonderful support' the club had received – fifteen home matches that season with an average attendance of 18,000; total gate receipts of £16,298. Compare that with today's crowds of a Second or Third Division club, and the inflated salaries of today's players. Argyle were trying to sign new talent, but transfer fees were 'prohibitive' – one club had asked £10,000 for just one player. Mr Tozer was optimistic that the club would achieve great things. When they might do so wasn't put on record.

Slowly Plymouth fell behind, older streets giving way to new roads and concrete footbridges. Some of the locals spared me more than a passing glance. They aren't used to seeing people carrying rucksacks hereabouts; for most 'Britain' walkers it's Land End to John o'Groats. Thankfully, at Widewell I left the road, entering woodland, where I spotted a large sign nailed to a tree. PATH CLOSED, it said, although it looked open to me. *When* was it closed? That's what I wanted to know. Yesterday? Last year? 1946? The route, by Bickleigh Vale and the river, looked good on the map. Maybe I should have gone on. Instead, I returned to the road, cursing whoever was responsible for the sign. I suppose providing more information, like the date, was beyond them.

At Clearbrook, wild, Dartmoor ponies grazed contentedly outside someone's front gate. They peered at me through long, hairy fringes, perhaps anticipating a tit-bit. I had nothing but a friendly word. I've never had anything to do with horses, save an old nag known as 'Ginger's Pony' which pulled a cart around our village when we were kids. Ginger made a few bob delivering coal. The miners received free deliveries, so could afford to sell off one or two, and we lads would hop on to Ginger's cart for the ride. And to count how many times on the journey the horse would break wind. I can't recall old Ginger ever saying a word to us. Maybe he was counting too.

I crossed the Plym and followed the road to Hoo Meavy, where stone cottages are worthy of anyone's camera. This is one of the great merits of walking the countryside. Years before, I took my young family for country walks in Northumberland where we discovered lovely hamlets barely half an hour's drive from Newcastle. The names are with me still: Dye House, Smelting Syke, Lord's Lot. Here were fine houses, secret retreats, unseen and unknown to the motorist who passes them by on his or her 'drive in the country'. Here, too, were rivers and woodlands, quiet byways and lonely farmsteads, no end of surprises for the explorer – on foot. Too many folk are missing out. They should get out of their cars and take to the rights of way (we are fortunate to have them), and listen to the rushing waters of the river, the murmuring of little streams, and see for themselves the birds and animals, and breath in fresh air, and stop awhile to explore that churchyard and take in the view.

Lecture over, it's time to recount that a bridleway led off through Burrator Wood, where bright sunshine beamed through the trees, broad shafts of light crying out for an artist's brush. It ended all too soon at the bottom of the towering wall of Burrator dam. I was obliged to climb the steep hillside to a byroad, where a pretty girl sold ice cream. She gave me a smile and a kind word. The ice cream I had to pay for.

The scene was almost Lakeland, with Sheeps Tor rising from woodland on the opposite shore of the reservoir, Plymouth's main water supply. Four centuries ago, the city had to rely on water flowing in from an artificial channel, or *leat*, which drew water from the headwaters of the Meavy. It was Sir Francis Drake's idea, proving he wasn't just good for fighting the Spanish. But when Plymouth grew, so did its demand for water, so they built the dam and flooded the Gorge, a task that kept four hundred men employed for five years.

P 2001

Leather Tor Bridge

I came upon half a dozen fifteen-year olds carrying rucksacks and maps, all with one thing in common: they were lost. We walked side by side and chatted, but what they were doing did not permit me to assist them in navigation, so when I left them at the end of the reservoir they were still lost. I did point out (on their map) the location of a rendezvous point they had to locate, but their means of reaching it I left for them to calculate.

At Norsworthy Bridge a good track climbed through pinewoods, where a stream crashes down the hillside. It leads to Leather Tor Bridge, a pretty spot. Just beyond the bridge a dilapidated sign leaning at a crazy angle says DANGER FOREST FIRES – TAKE CARE NOT TO START ONE. I always think warnings about starting forest fires are silly: most people are law abiding and wouldn't anyway, whilst potential arsonists who weren't actually thinking about starting a fire have been reminded of the opportunity to do so. Further along the track, Raddick Lane, a rough, stony cutting, leads over the open moor to Crazy Well Pool. Once a tin mine, it's filled with water now. It's as well I had my wits about me, for it remains unseen on approach, until *voila!* – you're standing on the edge looking down into the murky waters below. You wouldn't want to be crossing Dartmoor on a dark night, not with holes like that around. Beyond Crazy Well an ancient and forlorn granite cross marks the path, which runs in a groove over the open moor.

A mile further I turned north across pathless terrain, using the compass to ensure correct navigation. There are no landmarks, no clues. You could walk round in ever decreasing circles till you disappear into your own swamp. This was *freedom*, very much a different sort to the confines of the coast path, grand though that too had been. Open moors, wild places. This is the country I love. Dartmoor is a place with the reputation for lost souls, but I was in heaven. Was it only this morning I was walking through a city?

According to my calculations I was quite near Princetown, yet there was no sign of it. I climbed to the top of one of the famous Tors where I encountered a middle-aged couple doing some kind of thing where messages are left and they have to find them. There was probably a Dartmoor 'letterbox' hereabouts, where walkers leave a postcard with their name and address, so that other walkers who find them later can post them on. Don't ask me why they do it, they just do. It all started around 1850, and it is estimated there are some 300-400 such 'letterboxes' scattered across the moor. Above, a helicopter hovered, and I wondered if the crew was searching for the youngsters I'd seen earlier, those lost souls who even now might be cursing me for giving what they thought was the incorrect position of their rendezvous point? Then the penny dropped: it might be searching for *me!*

The super is on the phone to the chief constable.

'Sorry to trouble you, sir. Just, er, one of our inspectors is missing.'

Fortunately, Chiefy's in a good mood.

'What happened, did he venture outside the station?'

Then he realises a missing inspector might arouse the attention of the media.

'What do you mean, missing?'

'Well, more lost, like.'

'Whereabouts?'

The super swallows. 'Dartmoor.'

The chief is aghast. 'Can't you get the local boys to do your enquiries down there?'

The super dries up, bottle gone, visions of a posting to Traffic, destined to drive around the M25 until retirement. The chief, made of sterner stuff, keeps calm.

'Which inspector is it anyway?'

'The detective inspector.'

The chief breathes a sigh of relief.

'Phew! That's a relief. I was worried about all those parking problems...'

'Oh no, sir, that's all in hand.'

'What about those new pens with the fancy police logos?'

'We've a superintendent working on that one right now, sir.'

'Right. Well, see if your oppo in Devon can send a helicopter out or something.'

And there it was, circling, searching..."

Suddenly I caught a glimpse of Princetown, identified by the grey, foreboding walls of Dartmoor prison. The remoteness of the moor always led me to believe that this was the reason for the prison: if you managed to escape you had the perils of the moor to negotiate before freedom was secured. But Princetown came first, the prison after. It was all down to Thomas Tyrwhitt who, in 1786, was auditor to the Duchy of Cornwall. When he saw Dartmoor, he decided he wanted to 'improve' it, and poured in much of his money and energy to create a 2,300-acre estate known as Tor Royal. Later, several cottages were built, and an inn, the *Plume of Feathers*, on the main road in what became known as Prince's Town. He intended Dartmoor to yield good agricultural produce, but his scheme failed, hardly surprising on land over 1,000 feet high with a thin layer of topsoil and open to high winds and the extremes of the weather.

In 1805, with French prisoners of war overcrowding old hulks floating in the Hamoaze, Tyrwhitt made it known there was a very good site for a prison in Princetown, as it became. In 1812, America went to war with Britain, so American prisoners were incarcerated in the prison too. One of them was Charles Andrews, who kept a journal. Wrote Andrews: "The prison is surrounded on all sides by the gloomy features of a black moor, uncultivated and uninhabited. The place is deprived of everything that is pleasant or agreeable, and productive of nothing but human woe and misery... a depot of living death".
Imagine that in one of today's tourist guides.

When peace was signed between Britain and the US, there was delay in the Americans' release, and they mutinied (they must have wanted to leave Dartmoor for some reason). The officer in charge of the garrison – the prison was manned by soldiers in those days – was Captain Shortland, victim of a practical joke when the Americans lowered a jacket and breeches over the wall, and shots were fired in the belief that a prisoner was escaping. He must have seen the mutiny as an ideal way of getting his own back, so he ordered his soldiers to fire a broadside from three yards. Seven Americans were killed, a further sixty injured.

I stood awhile at the prison gates, where an inscription in Latin, *Parcere Subjectis*, means 'spare the vanquished'. Then I crossed the road to the parish church of St Michaels and All Angels, built by French and American prisoners. In past years, any prisoner who died was buried within the prison walls, but now they are laid in the churchyard, their graves marked by small, granite posts with their initials and the date of their death inscribed. Most are so worn you can't read them. From the church you can see rows of terraced houses, with the inevitable moor beyond. Princetown is hardly a town at all, more a cold, grey windswept village. No doubt in the summer months it gets busy, with holidaymakers taking advantage of its facilities. Today it was quiet, with a blustery wind blowing uninterrupted across the moor. If they close the prison again it might turn into a ghost town, where scavenging crows – or maybe vultures – circle above anyone mad enough to be hiking through. To my mind, Tyrwhitt failed to 'improve' Dartmoor with his creation of Princetown. Better the moor had been left in its natural state.

A kindly woman who normally accommodates prison officers took in old bill for a change. Later, I wandered about, passing a small shop with clothing in the window, advertising 'gentlemen's shits' at only

£8.99, and visited the Plume of Feathers, where, reputedly, a sudden, icy 'presence' has been known to drive ladies from the loo, their knickers around their knees. That's what I read, honest. Being a seasoned detective, I kept observations, succeeding only in verifying the icy 'presence'. No ladies appeared. Maybe they've got used to it.

*

My lady host once lived in Bath, but prefers Princetown. Proof that it takes all kinds to make a world. 'Princetown's friendly,' she explained, 'a close community.' Leaving the village, I took a last look back at England's Colditz. A close community, like she said.

I had no idea of my destination today. I would complete the traverse of Dartmoor, and thereafter take to the country lanes beyond. This uncertainty added flavour to my journey, for is it not real adventure to be unaware of one's destiny?

In half an hour I'd reached Two Bridges, a former staging post for those crossing the moor. One bridge was built in 1792, the other in 1931: hence the name – or so you'd think. But it was Two Bridges *before,* so maybe it isn't so straightforward. It might come from *Torbrygge,* an old name meaning 'at the bridge'. A mile further I glanced at my wrist to check the time. I had lost my watch. This was a minor disaster. Suppose someone asked me the time? (If you want to know the time, ask a policeman). There was nothing for it but to retrace steps and look for it. I called at an isolated cottage to seek permission to leave my sack and recover it on my return. I hoped the occupants weren't still in their beds at what was a fairly early hour. They weren't. Or their dog wasn't, for my knock was greeted by a menacing growl, followed by fierce barking. Fortunately, his master called him back before opening the door to the stranger. Relief, though, was tempered, when I saw that the master looked as mean as the dog. But I am unkind, for my request to leave my sack was granted without hesitation. 'Leave it in the porch,' he said, 'no-one will touch it.' I quite believed him.

Later, watch recovered (lying in the grass), I made a silent approach to the cottage. Brutus was raising decibels before my fingers even reached the handle of the porch door, but this time he wasn't able to put in a personal appearance, for his master had shut him in.

Postbridge, like Two Bridges, was formerly a staging post. For those seeking Coca Cola and Yorkie Bars it still is. In the 1920's it was the scene of a series of motoring accidents, when several drivers who had driven off the road claimed the hand of a ghost had reached through the window and grabbed the steering wheel. What would insurance companies make of that today? "I was driving in the vicinity of Postbridge at midnight in the middle of winter with my window down when this hand reached in and grabbed the wheel..." Goodbye, no claims bonus.

Another couple of miles brought me to the Warren House inn. The inn takes its name from Headland Warren, where man-made mounds were constructed for the breeding of rabbits, introduced to Britain in the 12th century as a special delicacy. It was thanks to the damage rabbits did to crops that myxomatosis was introduced in 1954, causing agonising death to innocent creatures. Having introduced the rabbits, man no longer wanted them. I remember seeing one once, its eye sockets empty, body stiffened after an agonising death. It's a sight I never forgot.

The inn also served as a hostel for tin miners. An old sign once hung outside:

> John Roberts lives here,
> Sells brandy and beer
> Your spirits to cheer;
> And should you want meat
> To make up the treat
> There be rabbit to eat.

I made do with a glass of lemonade.

Bennett's Cross stands by the roadside, half a mile beyond the Warren House. It's mis-shaped form was once a landmark for those crossing the moor; before that, it was a monument to God. For me it was the place to join the Two Moors Way, a long distance route that links southern Dartmoor to Exmoor. Here, the Way runs along a ditch across the moor, where I encountered just one person, a fellow heading south. He never spoke, just walked by as though I wasn't there. As I was the only other human being in about twenty square miles he could hardly have missed me. Maybe he doesn't like crowds. Then I had what seemed to be Dartmoor to myself again, alone in this featureless world of coarse grasses, bracken and heather. That Tyrwhitt chap was surely a great optimist to think he could ever do anything with it. In fact, the only thing man succeeded with was building a monstrous prison, and introducing rabbits, and he did his best to get rid of them.

Ahead lay the green fields of North Devon. There would be many a mile of tarmacadam now, but this is not to say the walking was dreary. Far from it. Dartmoor has 9,000 miles of roads, mostly farm lanes, bordered by neatly-trimmed high hedgerows. There was no-one about: no pedestrians, no cyclists, no cars. Without a map, and the helpful signposts, you'd be just as likely to get lost on the lanes as on the moor.

What I found pleasing were the views, where the hedges permitted any, across deep valleys, where the lanes lead down to meandering rivers. The only sound was the singing of the skylarks, the screeching of crows, and the crunch-crunch of boots on loose gravel. I ignored rights of way; there was not the time to navigate the complexities of a thousand fields with a thousand stiles, and farmyards with hostile dogs. I wanted to cover ground quickly. And anyway, the lanes are rights of way too. Not that I was totally confined to them; after Chagford Bridge, I took to the banks of the Teign where for two glorious miles I savoured the joys of an English Sunday afternoon in spring. Here were green pastures, with trees overhanging the silent waters of the river. Why go abroad? I look at photographs of some exotic island, where barren rock forms a backdrop to gently-waving palms on a golden beach. It's the barren rock I always see. There's no barren rock by the Teign.

I walked with deliberate slowness; when something's as good as this there is little point in hurrying. There were people now, and I said a few 'good afternoons', the way you do. I passed by places with lovely names, like Rushford Mill Farm and Dogmarsh Bridge, then finally climbed uphill to Castle Drogo, the last castle built in England. It was designed by Sir Edwin Lutyens for its owner, Julius Drew, a sort of 19th century Richard Branson who sold tea direct to the British public, thus cutting out the middleman. He made a fortune, and retired at the ripe old age of 33. To occupy his time, he employed a genealogist to trace his family tree, discovering that a distant relative was none other than the Norman, Lord Drogo (or *Dru*). So, with loads-a-money to spend, he built the castle. It was something he wanted, that's all. We throw money at things we don't need today, like grotesque statutes and the infamous Dome, but the national lottery pays for it, so that's OK.

The afternoon was wearing on, and I was wearing out. Thoughts of accommodation came to mind. A look at the map was not encouraging: there were no villages to speak of, no obvious watering holes to aim for. In Cornwall and Princetown there had been lots of 'bed and breakfasts', but I'd not seen one since Dartmoor. There was nowhere for a man of the road. I passed through Drewsteignton, not doing justice to a place with such a lovely name. Hereabouts signposts indicate the name of crossroads. It's a good idea. Lets you know where you are if you're lost. Or stops you getting lost. Or proves you are lost when you thought you weren't. I wasn't lost, but I was tired and I needed a bed. Never mind guesthouses, I would knock on some door, *any* door. No sooner had I made this decision than I was staring at a sign pointing down a narrow lane: BED AND BREAKFAST. The lane led to Eastchurch Farm, in the parish of Hittisleigh. They took me in, plied me with home-made beer, provided an excellent meal and showed me to a huge bedroom with a huge double bed. What more could I ask?

There was a German family staying over, too, their first visit to Britain, they said. Like the many Germans I have encountered (mainly in Scotland – they love it) I found them polite and civil. They quizzed me on the merits of my country, and I was happy to help out (without once mentioning the war). Also, they wanted to know what clotted cream was. Happily, I was able to tell them that Devonians of old had no such thing as a butter churn, so they just stirred the cream until it became clotted. 'It's quite safe,' I assured them.

Before crashing out, I checked my feet. Some of my toenails were turning black, and I wondered how much further I'd get before they fell off. I was past caring. I was immune to pain, and another day in glorious countryside was in prospect tomorrow.

*

St Andrew's church, Hittisleigh, is built of granite, and stands 650 feet above sea level. The base of the font is Norman, and records show that in 1285 the vicar was one Alexander Pont, who had 75 parishioners. How do I know this? Because I took the trouble to find out. It fascinates me to think that when I visit a church I am standing in the footsteps of people, long gone. I like to wander around churchyards, or sit inside where it is cool, to take a moment to reflect, and appreciate what we have, a part of our heritage. I visited many churches on my journey; not all of them, of course, or I should never have reached Dunnet Head. But some, at random, because I fancied doing so at the time. In an age of violence and insecurity, it makes me proud to walk into a church and find peace.

The sun turned out to keep me company, beaming down on fields of waving corn, green meadows, distant valleys. Glorious Devon, as the travel guides say. Cornwall's coast was a joy, Devon's countryside a perfect partnership. I was running out of adjectives. Repetition doesn't make for good reading. I should have been on the Pennines or somewhere, where words like bog and ooze could be used for a change, but that would come in good time. Again, I had no idea of today's ultimate destination. For the record, I passed through Yeoford, then reached Sandford where a solitary woman passer-by called out to me across the street, asking if she might direct me to wherever I wished to go. Unsolicited, unasked, without hesitation. Just plain kindness. I thanked her, told her I knew where I was bound and waved the map to prove it. Then I sat outside the church awhile, spurning the opportunity to take a drink in the Lamb Inn – a decision I'd regret.

Moving on, I became hot and thirsty, the latter an increasing problem as the supply in my canteen dwindled. I had noticed a place called Wolfaridsworthy on the map and it lay conveniently ahead. Just a matter of following the lanes until I got there, when I would call at the inn for a cold drink. As I progressed, that drink became my only thought. I marched in rhythm to the name: Wool-far-ids-worth-y, Wool-far-ids-worth-y. I said it out loud as I went: Wool-far-ids-worth-y. (In fact, the locals say *Woolsery*). Four miles to go: Wool-far-ids-worth-y. Two miles. Wool-far-ids-worth-y. One mile. Wool-far-ids-worth-y. If there is an inn, I never saw it. In fact, I never slowed down or even changed gear at Woolfaridsworthy.

I needed to stop and drink something. It's never been my way, incidentally, to knock at people's doors to ask for water. Not part of the game, as it were. I looked at the map. Further on was Puddington. Would there be a pub? Nope. I checked the map again. Next was Pennymoor, where, in clear letters, the word *inn* appeared, an oasis in the desert of lanes and hedges. Now, instead of a marching word, I thought of *Quench*. The thought of a long, cold drink: *Quench*. I roared on, maximum speed. *Quench-Quench-Quench*. At Pennymoor I marched in triumph to the inn. It was closed.

The map again. Five miles away was Rackenford, with the magic word, *inn*. To reach it became my sole aim in life, my one remaining ambition. Surely there I would find the refreshment I sought, and a bed come to that. Now, as the marching resumed, I felt my skin burning under the merciless sun. The best I could do was to try and use any shade the high hedges might provide. How people walk across deserts I do not know; I was walking in the sun on an English day in springtime and I was jiggered. I saw a John Wayne film once, where he lost his horse in the middle of Nebraska or somewhere. He staggered bravely on under the burning sun, even threw his gun away. John Wayne without a gun is hard to imagine. Somebody rescued him. I needed rescue now.

I found myself crossing Witheridge Moor, something of a surprise after the pastoral landscape surrounding it. It's the haunt of witches. Evidently some of the locals wear witches' hoods, and go in search of the real thing. It did seem a bit spooky. If I hadn't been so single-minded in my quest to reach Rackenford I might have glanced up to see a witch or two myself.

At Rackenford, as you might guess, the Stag was closed. But I calculated it would open soon. It was just a question of whether they would accommodate a lone, sweat-stained, weary bloke who had arrived on foot (as opposed to cool, contented tourists who arrive in cars). I hung about, cold now as the sun disappeared. A cotton shirt soaked with sweat feels like a wet rag when you stop walking and the temperature drops. A woman rolled up in a car, declared she owned the pub and was able to accommodate me for the night (as a guest, that is). She led me to a cosy room. I was whacked and must have looked it, for no sooner had I divested myself of sack and boots and lain on the bed than she reappeared with a pint glass of lager which, she said, was on the house. For the rest of my life, that woman will rank alongside Florence Nightingale and Grace Darling. As for the lager, it never touched the sides.

Later, cleansed and refreshed, I was received in the bar by my host, and her daughter, and even introduced to some of the locals as a sort of celebrity. I ate a steak dinner to Dire Straits, and basked in the glow of a living fire in the inglenook fireplace. There was a warm, friendly atmosphere in the Stag, but dinner eaten and a couple of more pints swallowed, I'd had it. So I said goodnight to the locals and took to my bed, reflecting on the fact that tomorrow's walk would be even longer than today's as I headed for Somerset and the Quantocks, then drifted into sleep, secure in the knowledge that I was going from strength to strength, and that fitness, not weariness, was my reward.

*

It wasn't until the following morning I discovered the Stag is haunted. The story goes that a highwayman called Tom King and the ubiquitous Dick Turpin argued over the innkeeper's daughter, so King betrayed Turpin to the authorities. Centuries later, King's horse was heard galloping through the Stag by the landlord and his wife and daughter, who were seated by the fire. They never actually *saw* King and his horse. I regretted turning in so early the night before, thus missing the opportunity to hear or see it for myself.

Today, I was heading for the youth hostel at Crowcombe Heathfield, in Somerset, 25 miles away. I had not realised just how hard the day would be – Devon is anything but flat! Valerie and Lindsay – mine hosts – saw me off personally. They did me proud. First, though, a visit to All Saints church, or rather the cemetery, where I noticed some of the headstones carried the optimistic message, 'Until we meet again'. Whilst I respect the views and beliefs of others, I have to admit difficulty in believing that, once dead, there can be any after-life, call it what you will. Still, it's a matter for each and everyone, I suppose.

The sun was at it again as I took to the lanes, bound for the Quantocks. At Oakford, I climbed the hill to St Peter's church. The only sound was the screeching of crows, as though they objected to my intrusion. *Deja vu* Hitchcock's *Birds*. The views were wonderful, across rolling landscapes with distant deep valleys. I could have stood here hundreds of years ago, it would have been the same. Different crows, that's all. Today, a leaflet asks you to think of the hundreds of people who have passed under the yew tree outside the porch over the centuries. I always do, as I said earlier.

Here, for the first time on my journey, it *rained*; not much, just a few spots. Certainly not as much as that which inspired Keats to write:

> "Devonshire is a splashy, rainy, misty, snowy, foggy, haily, floody, muddy, slipshod county. The flowers here wait for rain twice a day as mussels do for the tide".

He never walked Devon in May. He couldn't have.

Another mile led to Oakfordbridge, where woodland clothes the steep hillside on the opposite bank of the Exe. A signpost points to Black Cat, presumably the name of a place and not someone's pet. Beyond, a lane leads for an eternity up a long, steep hill, where overhanging branches form a long tunnel, today a bright green canopy, in autumn it will be golden-brown. It's all very beautiful. At the top I glanced into a field where grazing cows reminded me that I'd read somewhere that black Devonian cattle copulate early. Early in their bovine lives or early in the year wasn't clear. This lot didn't do anything anyway. At a pub in Bampton the landlord said it wouldn't be long before the place would be infested with tourists who forsake the M5 for the scenic route to Tiverton, cluttering the place with parked cars, and the inevitable coach parties. It was easy to imagine his pub bulging at the seams, with lots of readies going over the bar. All he took from me was the price of a cheese roll and a glass of lemonade.

The church on top of the hill is St Michaels and All Angels. They were going to pull it down in 1862, when it was in a bad state of repair. Thankfully, it was restored. The cover on the 15th century font was carved by Eleanor Bennett, who died in 1987, aged 104. Her husband died in 1942. Forty-five years is a long time to be without your loved one. Nearby a huge, empty car park is obviously the place where the tourists park their jalopies, like the man said. I called at the gents, where an ad carefully written on the wall in biro invited anyone 'under 25 and horny' to call the phone number given. As I failed to meet at least one of the qualifying requirements I gave it a miss.

Bampton's misfortune is that it lies on the busy road. There's a sort of one-way system that encourages motorists to put their foot down in what they perceive as a golden opportunity to proceed without the usual traffic jam. Crossing the road can be a bit like walking across the circuit at Monaco in the middle of a grand prix. But Bampton is a pleasing place nonetheless, with old, grey stone cottages and its church, and views over rolling countryside. It would have been better before the internal combustion engine, but then, wouldn't everywhere?

Further on, a path led through woodland to the River Batherm – and Somerset. It was an eerie walk, through those lonely woods. I was reminded of an old film about werewolves. A young woman was walking through woods just like these when she felt a 'presence', and thought she heard footsteps. Yet when she stopped and looked about there was no sound and nothing to see. I stopped and looked about. No sound and nothing to see. It's true you get a cold chill down your spine. I was pleased to cross the river and emerge from the woods safe and uneaten. For me, Somerset brings to mind cider and the unique, rolling dialect of the natives. I used to spurn cider, had never tasted it until someone got a few pints in once. I never spurned it again. As for the lingo, there's a wonderful poem by Arthur Clark:

Oim a Zummerzet lad with Zummerzet ways,
And oi loikes zitten out on Zummerzet days,
Wi zum Zummerzet zider and Zummerzet cheese,
And Zummerzet unney from Zummerzet bees...

Zummerzet – sorry, Somerset – was Somerset*shire* until 1122, not that anyone remembers that far back. It was much the same as Devon: quiet country lanes, rolling countryside. I steamed on in the heat, getting into a mess near some farm buildings, where I was obliged to scramble over a barbed wire fence, with one eye on Mrs Farmer who was taking in the free-range washing. I felt like a criminal, expecting her to see me at any moment, with a 'where do you think you are going?' look in her eye. She didn't, and I chided myself for being careless. Then I headed along yet more lanes, through woodlands and across rivers. It was a route-march now, a single-minded effort to reach Crowcombe Heathfield. I was hot, thirsty, footsore and knackered when, at last, I turned up at the portals of the youth hostel.

There's been a youth hostel here since 1940. Evidently it can be 'quiet' from time to time, which means it tends to fall under threat of closure. I find this sad, for youth hostels, surely, exist to provide for the few, as well as the many. As a member, I expect to find them in quiet backwaters, which is, to my mind, the whole point of having them. I hope Crowcombe stays open, along with all the others that might not be seen to 'pay their way'. Let them be subsidised by those that earn the big bucks – and by membership funds, of course.

I was resigned to a night in, for the hostel stands miles from anywhere. To put it another way, there's no pub. That was fine by me, but my heart sank on sight of thirty-odd schoolchildren, for past experience of such parties are of boisterous, ill-disciplined, noisy and totally out of control charges of schoolteachers who don't seem to give a damn. I had an awful experience once where such a crowd drove me, literally, to seek shelter elsewhere. I accept kids will be kids

– I was one once – but I cannot accept anarchy. Have fun, but let there be discipline, with rules to follow.

To my shame, my stereotyped, narrow-minded view was wholly unfounded. Far from being undisciplined, the children were in the control of responsible, smartly-dressed teachers, whose instructions, when given, were adhered to without question. The children were even told to be quiet for the *tired hiker*, and when they passed me by in the corridor they smiled and said hello. They were from Redruth, a credit to their teachers and their parents. After supper, I was invited to join the teachers on their table for chocolate cake and coffee. As I only had a can of Irish stew to my name this was particularly welcome.

Later, when discussing blisters (everywhere I went I was asked about blisters, as though I was a leading authority with a Ph.D) one of the ladies asked to see me in private, whereupon she removed her trainers and socks and showed me her blisters. She asked me what she could do about them. I told her it was too late to do anything about them. She looked so let-down I thought she was going to ask me to hand the cake back.

*

That summer, under those indulgent skies,
Upon smooth Quantock's airy ridge we roved
Unchecked, or loitered mid her sylvan combes...

Thus wrote Wordsworth, who visited the Quantocks, his *other country*, with his sister, Dorothy. It's hardly surprising that he turned his pen to them.

I stepped outside, bound for I knew not where. Except that I would traverse the Quantock Hills, a long, continuous ridge reaching to over a thousand feet. That pleased me, although I didn't fancy the look of the country beyond – 'flat and uninspiring' I wrote in my notes. The weather looked uninspiring too. My constant companion, the sun, had deserted me. Instead, heavy cloud seemingly covered all Somerset, and the Quantocks, just a mile off, were lost in a grey shroud.

A narrow lane led straight up the hillside, reminiscent of Lakeland's fells in its steepness, though the similarity disappeared on sight of huge lorries emerging from an enormous quarry, cut deep into the hillside. Beyond, on top of the ridge, is the Triscombe Stone, *around which all kinds of superstitious tales have been woven about the Devil and death,* and the vastness of Great Wood. A good path through scrub and heather leads to an ordnance column at a place called Wills Neck, the scene of a battle between the Celts and the Saxons. At around 1,200 feet, this is a place for views – on a clear day. Instead, the distant fields of the country I had traversed were lost in uncertain greyness. The only landmark I could pick out was what appeared to be an enormous power station in the direction of the Bristol Channel.

On sunny, summer days, and especially at weekends, this must be a popular spot. I can just see dad, mum and the kids, out for a drive from Bridgwater or somewhere, going for a stroll on the Quantocks:

"Land of Quantock, long may your ridges and open heather spaces lie as they are now, preserved from the vulgarities of the unreflecting tourist, and from the profane aggressions of the enclosing owner, whether great or small, squire or squatter".

Thus wrote William Greswell. He didn't say anything about quarries.

Just yards from the path stood a white horse. She watched my every step, apparently reluctant to move away. The reason was soon evident, for at her feet lay a new-born foal. I ventured as close as I dared – not too close, in case mum became cross. She would not be keen on having a stranger for company, especially a human stranger. Animals don't trust us, and who can blame them?

A wide track led down the eastern flank of the Quantocks through Great Wood to Hawkridge reservoir, where my feet decided to remind me how tired they were. Strange, isn't it: on the hillside, no problem; on the road, they're tired. So I sat on a wall by the reservoir to give them a rest, and here fedupness crept in.

Fedupness is liable to come and go on any long distance walk. This is not to say you get fed up with the walk as a whole, but rather bits of it, which, for one reason or another, get you down. It could be the weather, the terrain, or you might be lost. Or there could be other factors: the football team you support might have lost (though as a lifelong follower of Newcastle United, I'm used to this), or your Aunt Ada in Aberystwyth might have died. Blisters are part of the experience, and do not qualify as a reason for fedupness. Today, my feet were throbbing, the day was cold and grey, the country ahead was flat and looked boring, and the prospect of having to walk it made me feel a bit down. It's at times like this a companion is to be desired, I suppose, although if he (or she) was also fed up then it would be fedupness times two, an even worse prospect. So, what you do is give yourself a pep-talk, and that's what I did now.

Great Wood   P 2001

First, it wasn't raining. Second, Bridgwater was just five miles away, a place for goodies – pubs, cafes – and where I could buy a towel. This latter point I mention because I had left the one I had at the youth hostel at Crowcombe Heathfield. Having thus given myself a renewed purpose in life, I moved on. I'd have moved on anyway, it was freezing cold sitting there.

The road led to Four Forks, where, in the 19th century, Henry Prince, also known as Brother Prince, an unfrocked curate, took money from wealthy, single females, whom he kissed – for religious reasons, of course. He declared himself the Messiah, a name by which he became known to the Post Office, who accepted *God* as his name and address. Brother Prince died in 1899, and to the best of anyone's knowledge hasn't been resurrected.

And so to Bridgwater where, having spent the entire morning alone, I entered a pub whose sole occupants were two massive women. They sat in a corner of the bar, competing with one another to see who could stuff the biggest chunks of cheese rolls into their mouths in any one go, a pastime they had been practising for years by the look of it. After five minutes as unofficial referee I decided it was a tie. If this is ever an Olympic event, I guarantee Britain will win gold, though whether either could climb the rostrum to claim a medal is debatable. Then I wandered the streets where there were shops selling everything except towels. By the time I found one my feet felt as though they had walked an extra ten miles.

Bridgwater takes its name from *Burgh Walter*, a Norman knight, and not Bridge Water, as I had supposed. By far the most striking feature is the unbelievably high sandstone spire of St Mary's parish church, which, though described as graceful, seems out of proportion to the church. But graceful it is, no doubt about that. The bronze statue of Robert Blake stands outside the market hall, with Blake pointing towards the River Parrett. Like Sir Francis Drake, he sorted the Spanish, sinking sixteen of their ships off Tenerife in 1657. Like Drake, he died at sea. Blake's statue formerly stood in Cornhill, and the locals were up in arms when they moved it. Poor Blake!

From his position on top of the church tower, James, Duke of Monmouth, saw the approaching Royalist army of his uncle, James II, which he engaged at the Battle of Sedgemoor in July, 1685. Monmouth lost, with 1,300 of his Rebel soldiers killed, miners and peasants mainly. People who died in battles in those days were often caught up in Royalist causes, rather than fighting for *just* causes – like fighting Fascism, say. Either that or it was over 'religion'. Here, the Duke claimed he, not his uncle, should rightly be James II, so ordinary folk died for his cause. He was executed for his trouble.

A dreary landscape lay beyond Bridgwater, begging the question: what was I doing here when the fells of Lakeland or the mountains of Scotland were going begging. I carried on, bored and footsore, two conditions guaranteed to bring about a third, depression. A quiet lane led alongside empty fields, with electricity pylons as far as the eye could see, a far cry from Cornwall's coast and Glorious Devon. When I trudged into a place called Bawdrip I called it a day. Not that it looked a likely place to find accommodation, yet in minutes I was knocking at the door of a 400-year old house, whose palatial interior was fit for a king. I was surprised the lady let me in, actually, for I had been walking eleven days and my sweat-soaked clothes had not seen a laundry. When she offered to wash them, it was unclear if her gesture was one of kindness or because she didn't want her house smelling like a shelter for dossers. Needless to say, I accepted.

My bedroom was enormous, beautifully furnished, a veritable bridal suite (without a bride). Having gleefully given up my walking apparel, I soaked in a luxury bath with as much Radox as I could pour in without disappearing without trace in a cloud of bubbles. I'd earned a pint, and was pleased to be told there was a pub by the main road, the Knowle Inn. If I thought it would be a quiet evening spent on my own, I was mistaken. A fellow my age entered the bar, wearing a uniform, as it turned out that of a bus driver. I was reminded of the smart bus drivers and conductors in the days when I was a lad. They wore blazers and peaked caps. So did postmen. There were standards then, and they've slipped badly. Except in Somerset, perhaps, at least as far as bus drivers are concerned. Anyway, as we were still the only people in the bar – it was barely six o' clock – we passed conversation, as you do, he offering something really original.

'This road carries all the traffic between the M5 and Gladstonbury.'

Well, blow me down and honk me horn, I thought, as more, equally stimulating conversation on this fascinating road ensued. Amazingly, I forget exactly what it was. Except my bus-driver friend did pass a meaningful observation.

'Not from this part of the world, are you?'

This astute perception (I've never really lost my Geordie accent, just had it watered down over the years) led me to explain the complexities of one who was born in Northumberland but now lived in Hertfordshire.

It transpired we had much in common, not least certain watering holes both in Hertfordshire and the North-East. The latter included my dad's workingmen's club, where as a kid I used to sneak around the back and collect empty bottles which I took to the front to hand in at threepence a go. As the exchange of information flowed, so did the booze. He said he was known as Flower, though he didn't say why. Then he told me he knew a local man who owned a racehorse called Pantechnicon.

'It's a great steeplechaser,' he assured me, one to watch out for next season.

I'm not one for betting on horses, save for a flutter on the National, but said I would, by which time our alcoholic-driven discourse at the bar was terminated by the sound of 'time please'. This, for Flower, posed a problem, as his car was parked outside. 'I'll get the wife to pick us up,' he declared, and made the phone call. When Mrs Flower arrived, one look at her husband was proof of her displeasure about his state of inebriation. One look at me was proof of her belief that it was my fault, but as I had doubts about successfully locating my lodgings again, she kindly agreed to drop me off. I mumbled an alcoholic 'goodnight' to my kind lady host and crashed out in my lovely clean, comfortable bed and slept the night through without so much as a stir.

I never saw Flower again, but I did keep an eye out for Pantechnicon. Sure enough, months later, the horse appeared on the morning racecard, and I invested £5 on his nose. He came 2nd. Not bad. I tried again. Nowhere. I tried again. Nowhere. I decided a pleasant evening with a bus driver in a pub in Somerset was no reason to persist with a lost cause and so, with reluctance, I gave up on poor old Pantechnicon. Needless to say, the horse then romped home to victory.

*

There was one other guest at breakfast, a middle-aged gent who looked like a rep. He was halfway through his breakfast as I made my appearance, but I repaired to the wings, as it were, choosing to eat alone. Okay, a bit anti-social, but I wanted to avoid the conversation I knew would follow. After the introductory 'good morning' and 'nice day/rain's forecast', etc, such encounters are entirely predictable.

'Passing through, are we', meaning who are you and what y'doin' here? ('We' means 'you' – old English colloquialism).

There's a brief pause till he gets to grips with the idea that someone's walking around here.

'Going far?'

'Dunnet Head.'

He wolfs down the last of his bubble and squeak.

'So where've y'walked from?'

'Lizard.'

'Lizard? In Cornwall? Went there with the missus once.' He's on to the toast and marmalade. 'Most southerly place in England, isn't it?'

Ten out of ten.

'Not a lot there, is there?'

I concur, knowing damn fine what's coming next.

'Where to again?'

'Dunnet Head.'

He's never heard of it, of course.

'Near John o' Groats.'

Ah, he's heard of John o' Groats. So why Dunnet Head? Cos it's the most northerly point in Britain, etc, etc. I avoid it all, let him go, just a brief nod as we pass at the entrance to the dining room. I eat alone, no stupid questions to answer. Then I take my leave, my clothes cleaned and even pressed, a veritable Prince Charming going to the ball (albeit on foot).

I had a quick look around Bawdrip, which I found to be a pleasing village, where old houses blend in with the new, and that can't be bad. In the churchyard, two magnificent yews stand astride the path leading to the church, St Michaels and All Angels. It's built of an unusually light-coloured stone, local I supposed. There was peace here, broken only the sound of children playing in the nearby schoolyard. It's a sound I love to hear.

I had decided to walk through Cheddar Gorge and visit the Mendip Hills, never having been. My destination today was Cheddar. The sun made an early appearance, and I headed north, for Woolavington, where I called at the church of St Mary the Virgin. It was locked. This came as a shock. I'd never known a church to be locked to the stranger. I rattled away at the door, but it was no good. Could have gone and asked for the key, but I didn't bother. One can only assume the church must have fallen prey to thieves, a sign of the times, I suppose. Once, stealing from churches was regarded as an especially serious crime, sacrilege, and the punishment meted out was severe. Now, it's indistinguishable from other crimes.

I'd noticed on the map there were many straight blue lines in this area (not to be confused with thin blue lines, i.e. those who should catch thieves who steal from churches). They represent irrigation channels, designed to drain water from land barely above sea-level, which can become flooded at high tides. These are the Somerset Levels, where man has been known to survive since as long ago as 5

BC. If you want a house built here, you have to sink concrete supports into the peat before they rest on solid rock. The Victorians pressed trees into the ground as foundations, so many of the buildings on the Levels lean at crazy angles today. Trackways made from timber and brushwood have been discovered, preserved by the soggy peat. One of them, the Sweet Track, is said to be the oldest road in the world.

I pressed on. As the sun got higher and I got hotter, salvation was found at Mark parish church, where the following notice was displayed in the porch: 'Visitors to Mark are welcome to this beautiful and ancient church. It is hoped that it's quiet and beauty may refresh those who pause here awhile'. I took this to include backpackers walking to Scotland, or anywhere else for that matter, so I rested, relieved to be out of the sun awhile. And to take in the splendour of the church, whose walls are built of small stones, square, rectangular, mis-shapen, whatever, all in light-grey. I wasn't the only one to be impressed: an entry in the visitors' book reads, *Love your walls*. A plaque by the door lists the *Incumbents of Mark parish church*, the first being one Richard de Dynam, in 1242. And there's a memorial plaque, dedicated to the men who fell in the Great War. I always find it moving to look at names on war memorials. Each was an individual; each went abroad and died for *us*. Now their names are immortalised. How many of us today, no matter what we achieve in our lives, will have his or her name forged on a bronze plate or set in stone? Precious few. But then, who of us earned it as they did?

Moving on, I crested a hill from where, in the haze, the Mendip Hills appeared in the distance, with Cheddar Gorge looking impressive, even from afar. Then I found myself by the River Yeo, with Cheddar directly ahead. The name is synonymous with two things: the famous gorge and the famous cheese.

Cheddar cheese dates back to the 17th century, when the milk from all the cows in the area was pooled to make one big cheese. Maybe it looked a bit like the ones in the Co-op in the old days, before pre-packaging, when they cut a piece off and weighed it for you. Now it's made as far away as New Zealand, although it's still *called* Cheddar cheese. It's down to the process; as long as its made in the Cheddar method it's Cheddar cheese. Cheddar was famous for its strawberries too, which were loaded on to railway wagons attached to passenger trains bound for London and beyond, a service known as the 'Strawberry Special'. Now the line is closed. A pity, and such a lovely name, too.

I bowled through Cheddar, a man in shorts and boots and carrying a rucksack, who merited the curious gaze of a long line of people at a bus stop. Then, I kid you not, a bloke stopped me and asked where he could catch a bus to somewhere. Scores of people at the bus stop and he asks a hiker. Not surprisingly, I wasn't able to help. At the youth hostel I met an aged Scot with a bike who told me he was cycling from Land's End to John o'Groats. He said he'd bought the bike just before setting off and the gears kept slipping. Should've tried it out first was all I could say, admittedly not a suggestion likely to promote good relations. Still, he was doing it alone and I respected him for that. Alternative company was a tabby cat, whose purring when you tickled its chin must have been audible in the gardens of nearby houses. But not as audible as the noise generated by a large group of schoolchildren, also staying at the hostel. They were from London, under the alleged control of teachers whose authority was non-existent. The kids were enjoying themselves, and that was good to see, but I cringed when a half-hearted instruction to do this or not to do that went totally unheeded. Still, I was compensated by the appearance of a lovely young thing called Angie, whose smile and natural charm I much preferred to the Scotsman with the bike, and the purring tabby for that matter.

Later, I wandered into town where, lo and behold, I encountered the aforementioned Angie. Pure coincidence, honest. She was with another young lass, Jenny, who was on her way to Lundy Island for some reason. The one thing we shared was revulsion of the screaming horde, so we bowled into a pub to seek refuge. It was soon apparent that Jenny hadn't two pennies to rub together, but I didn't mind buying her a drink. If I can help somebody as I go along, then my living will not be in vain. Sadly, once her intention to visit Lundy Island had been disclosed she had nothing else to say. In fact, she didn't seem able to string two sentences together.

Angie was staying in the youth hostel, not, as one might think, as a guest in the usual sense, but as a sort of inspector, in due course to report back to YHA head office on the quality of meals, hostel cleanliness, etc. Her visit was thus of a covert nature. She said she found it refreshing that she could confide in me, and trust me not to spill the beans. I told her I was a police inspector, whereupon she asked why I didn't lock the London kids up for the night. We got along like a house on fire, actually. I should add this is a true story, only the names have been changed.

Back at the hostel, the kids had settled for the night. Or, rather, part of the night. Little did I realise, as I crawled into my YHA sleeping bag, that what should have been a peaceful night's rest would be shattered long before dawn.

*

It started around 4 a.m., a thunder of hooves which grew louder until what became a stampede inevitably woke me from my dreams, whatever they were. They might have been about Angie or even Jenny. I'm narked at not being given the opportunity to remember. Who knows what I got up to?

It was the Bash Street Kids, jumping from their bunks. I was downstairs, they were upstairs. Great fun – for them. For us older, more sedate individuals below, it was hell. We prayed for the authoritative voice of a teacher, the official command for hostilities to cease. Alas, none came. And no wonder, for we were billeted in an annexe, whilst those who had the responsibility for discipline slept peacefully in the main building. Lucky them. It occurred to me that in the event of a fire, the responsibility of rescuing their charges would have fallen to total strangers. Definitely none out of ten. Those teachers from London should go to Redruth to learn about responsibility.

Angie spent the night in the main building too, so wasn't in a position to report on the noise that bleary-eyed males complained about at breakfast. You couldn't blame the YHA, it wasn't their fault; it was the teachers' fault. Anyway, I was cheered when Angie announced she would walk through Cheddar Gorge with me, and after a breakfast accompanied to the tumultuous din of the Bash Street Gang we wandered off together in the already-hot morning sun.

Cheddar Gorge is England's Grand Canyon. For over a mile, near-vertical limestone cliffs up to 1,000 feet high tower above the winding road, a dramatic scene unmatched anywhere else in Britain. There are underground caverns, which the Celts believed were occupied by fairies, though none have been discovered by cavers, some of whom have lost their lives in flash-floods. You wouldn't find me messing about in tunnels. I prefer to be above ground, where I can see the sky and breath fresh air.

Angie and I were too early for souvenirs, ice cream or even a cup of coffee. Clearly, tourists weren't expected in Cheddar until later in the morning. Right now the gorge belonged to a bloke with a rucksack, and a lass dressed in pretty clothes, two strangers sharing a one-off experience. Alas, all things come to an end: when the road turned away to the south, Angie declared she would make her way to her car, and I would take the West Mendip Way. She was a super companion.

Alone again, I climbed up on to the Mendips, hills of carboniferous limestone, except the highest tops are sandstone which afford pastures suited to sheep and cows, some of whom lazed on the grass across the path as I approached. I've had problems with cattle in my time. Cattle are more curious than malicious, but you can never tell with animals. Threatening cattle are best dealt with by chasing *them*, but don't sue me if you run at a bull and find yourself with a horn in an orifice. Not that cattle pose quite the risk of rhinoceros and wolves, which lived here before the last ice age, a mere 35,000 years ago. Today, as I approached, a cow got to her feet and stood astride the path with a 'what you gonna do about it' look. Then another got up, then another, as though offering support. I gave them the proverbial wide berth, hoped they wouldn't charge from behind. My fears were misplaced; when I glanced back not one was looking my way.

The path – the West Mendip Way – now led across an enormous meadow, bordered by trees and hedgerows. All was silent, save for the singing of unseen skylarks, the chirping of crickets. Back in Cheddar Gorge, the tourists would be gazing upwards, oblivious to the wonderful landscape above the rim of the cliff-tops. Would just a few of them venture up here to savour the work of Nature? I doubted it. Alone, I walked where the air was fresh and a balmy breeze brought respite from the sun. Then rich pastures gave way to rugged terrain at the Mendips' highest point, Beacon Batch, where a purply-blue haze of heather and bluebells stretched away to a hazy distance. The landscape was bisected by the narrow path leading over Black Down, with the lowlands of the north lost in the shimmering heat of a wonderful day. Alone every downhill step, I sang all the way until it all ended at the road above Burrington Combe. If, as they say, there is such a thing as a walk in heaven, this could be it.

It was *Quench* time again, but unlike my enforced period without a drink in Devon, Blagdon was convenient for the purchase of oranges. Then I walked the length of the dam at Blagdon Lake, a reservoir built at the turn of the century. Usually, man's creations fail hands down to match the beauty of Nature's own, but I was in for a surprise, for the path runs through woodland, where long grasses and millions of dandelion clocks bordered the lake, or reservoir if you will. After a half-mile, as I reluctantly turned from the lake-shore, I came upon a deep pool, where shrubs clustered thickly by its waters and the sun, barely able to penetrate the canopy above, glistened on overhanging, green foliage, a scene worthy of an artist's brush. Everything was so *still*. The final glory was the perfect reflection of all around in the waters below, beauty unsurpassed. I will never forget it.

Further on I took a by-road for Long Ashton, unfortunately along with half the population of Bristol who evidently use it as a short-cut when they drive home from work. Several times I was obliged to flatten myself into the hedge as motorists, who never think about anyone on foot, sped past. It seemed a question of what would happen first. Would I be caught up by somebody's wing mirror, and dragged to a ghastly doom? Or maybe a passing truck would flatten my toes, in which case, I would have no need to worry further about blisters. In any event, I ran the gauntlet unscathed, reaching the main road ahead, where the tall buildings of Bristol came into view, dominating the skyline.

Despite the fact that I was about to enter a great city, there was more good stuff ahead. Passing through the gateway of Ashton Court Estate, I found myself crossing lush meadows, where red and fallow deer wandered at will and a feeling of openness prevailed. A pretty girl wearing shorts and tee-shirt was, happily, the only candidate to enquire of the place; alas, she too was just passing through. In fact, the Estate was first enclosed by one Thomas de Lyons in 1391, and comprises some 800 acres of meadow and woodland. It's a gem.

Another mile or so led to Clifton Suspension Bridge. Designed by Isambard Kingdom Brunel, construction began in 1836, but was constantly held up due to lack of funding and even apathy. When the bridge opened in 1864, Brunel had been dead five years. With a single span of 708 feet, the bridge towers 250 feet above the Avon Gorge. Judging by the amount of commuter traffic using it now, it's a damn good thing they built it.

For 2p I was permitted to walk across the bridge. The most striking feature of it is its height, enhanced by the vertical walls of the gorge. It's like looking from an aeroplane a few minutes after take-off, the river a thin, brown thread, cars like toys on the road below. It shook alarmingly when a lorry trundled over, but reason made me keep my nerve. Notices displayed on the towers at each end invite anyone who feels the need to talk to the Samaritans in confidence. This is scarcely surprising, for lots of people have decided to end it all by jumping from the bridge, with a hundred percent success rate, you might think. Yet in 1885, Sarah Ann Henley, who'd had an argument with her lover, failed when the crinoline hoops of her petticoat acted as a parachute. She lived to 85. The gorge itself is a site of 'special scientific interest', where natural grasslands and rare plants thrive on the steep sides of the cliffs. Exploration is out of the question, unless you're into rock climbing.

Clifton means *Place of the cliffs*, hardly surprising, for parts of the village are perched right on the edge of the gorge. It developed and prospered in the mid-18th century, with the arrival of businessmen like Joseph Fry, who opened a chocolate factory, and the Wills family (tobacco). Today's magnificent Georgian and Regency streets are testament to the period. Clifton pleases greatly. For me, it was love at first sight. People were everywhere, going home from work, mainly, but whatever, they wore smiles, were smartly dressed. I was unable to prevent myself comparing Clifton to today's modern new towns. Truly, there is no contest.

I was wilting in the sun, yet finding accommodation proved far from easy. There didn't seem to by anywhere suitable for a man of the road. Finally, I accosted a group of students, one of whom came up with a likely suggestion and even handed me a map of Clifton. It wasn't long before I was knocking at the door of a bed and breakfast, catering, normally, for business people, but not turning away a footsore traveller nonetheless. I was put out when the lady proprietor requested payment in advance, but settled anyway, before taking the bus into Bristol where I whiled away the evening hobbling around the city centre. Walking day after day had undoubtedly improved my fitness, but my feet were in dire straits. When the sound of breaking glass heralded the inevitable lager louts, I caught a bus back to my lodgings in the knowledge that by this time tomorrow a significant point of my journey would be reached.

I'd be in Wales.

*

'What'll it be?'

'Weetabix,' I said, after due consideration, then watched mine host carefully select *one* from the carton and place it into a tiny bowl, along with a meagre portion of milk and a sprinkling of sugar. There followed a barely adequate breakfast and a minuscule cup of tea. Hardly sufficient to start me off on a long day's hike, and it's not as though he didn't know what I was about, for he decided to inform me at length of a walk *he* did once, a 200-mile journey on foot in Canada. What vestige of credibility he had vanished when he declared he'd got a lift for forty-odd miles. 'But I did it,' he concluded with pride. I refrained from mentioning he'd cheated as one fifth of his journey was completed on wheels. Perhaps he only had one Weetabix too.

My feet had recovered miraculously overnight, and soon after leaving my lodgings I found myself on a vast expanse of open space, Durdham Down. A thin trod led over short-cropped grass, with the main road running parallel. It was a busy Saturday morning, with much traffic, but on the common there were few people and I enjoyed the feeling only open spaces can give.

Bristol impressed me, with its fine stone buildings and wide streets. The name means, simply, *Bridging point*. The city dates back to the Saxons, who built a fort here. Bristol was once a major port, where wealthy traders became still more wealthy. In the 17ᵗʰ century ships sailed forth carrying another sort of cargo – people. Thousands departed these shores from Bristol: entire families, single men, refugees and fleeing nobility, fearing for their lives in the Civil Wars, and anyone else who was just plain ambitious, all bound for the New World. Yet Bristol's trading importance, with increased consumption leading to increased productivity and demand for labour led to its infamous reputation through the slave trade, when thousands of native Africans were shipped to the West Indies on Bristol ships, to work 'until death'. That's if they weren't dead by the time they got there. This 'industry' was financed by what was regarded as decent people. I believe Britain has a proud history, but the chapter on the slave trade does not qualify for inclusion. Actually, it's surprising that Bristol ever was a major port: it's seven miles from the sea, navigation being hazardous due to mudbanks and awkward tidal movements.

I found myself at Westbury, a smart suburb where the locals were shopping on a sunny Saturday morn. There was an atmosphere of decency about the place and the people. They *belonged* here, and were proud of it. Checking the map I saw that just off to the right, but unseen, lay Filton airfield, where, if my memory served me right, the world's first supersonic jet passenger aeroplane, Concord, was tested. Yes, Concord – without an 'e' (check your dictionary). Why do the

British always fall in with the rules and customs of foreign countries, in this case the French spelling of an English word? I passed beneath the M5, after which I intended to visit Northwick church. Alas, my intention was thwarted, not, on this occasion, because the doors were locked, but because there weren't any doors at all. The church is a ruin, even though the tower remains intact, proud sentinel to a few gravestones and trees; it still maintains its dignity. From the church, the tall towers of the Severn road bridge were discernible, just two miles away. The bridge is over two miles long, if you include the one across the Avon which continues directly on from the main bridge.

I took the right of way across the fields, bound for the bridge. Or, rather, I tried to, except the path (if there is one) disappeared among brambles and nettles and tangled hedgerows. In fact, progress was impossible, and I emerged on the road again with legs scratched and stinging. All part of the experience, I reminded myself, consoled at the proximity of the tall towers of the bridge, now looming up ahead in a grey mist. It was opened in 1966. The cost: £8m. A notice in the motorway services area informs anyone who wants to know that the suspension cables contain 18,000 miles of high tensile, galvanised steel, long enough to stretch to Sydney and back, the towers stand 450 feet above sea level, the total span is 5,400 feet, the equivalent of six Wembley stadiums, and it takes 56,000 gallons to paint the bridge. The first time I saw the bridge, I was accompanied by a Welsh prison officer. We were escorting a prisoner to Cardiff gaol. As we gazed in awe at the bridge, my Welsh friend, aware I was looking at it for the first time, was keen to milk the moment.

'Grand, isn't it though?' he asked, after allowing me a few moments to take in the majesty of the superstructure. I concurred. He allowed me a few more moments, before slowly nodding his head, a gesture meaning there was little need for any more words. 'Makes me proud to be Welsh,' he said, before turning his back and leaving to stand in wonderment, alone. It wasn't until later I discovered that his pride was misplaced, for the entire suspension bridge is in *England,* and it isn't until you cross it and move on to the bridge over the Wye you enter Wales, and then not until you're halfway over. I, not he, ought to have extolled the virtues of the bridge.

Long before the bridge, the Romans ran a ferry service here, around AD 50, and later, during the Civil Wars, sixty Parliamentary soldiers were drowned pursuing Charles I and his men who had just been ferried to the English shore. The Parliamentarians had demanded to be taken over too, but were deposited on a reef where the rising tide drowned them. No prizes for guessing which side the boatmen supported. Cromwell was so annoyed he closed the ferry service. Unlike the suspension bridge at Clifton, crossing the Severn was free. This didn't make sense: 708 feet costs 2p; 5,400 feet – zilch. Not that I was complaining. As traffic thundered past just feet away, I wondered if the bridge would shake, and it did. Halfway across I leaned over the parapet to gaze into the murky greyness of the Severn estuary, just as a heavy articulated lorry was passing. Not a good idea. When the bridge swung on those suspension cables, I got to know the meaning of vertigo better than any dictionary could explain. I didn't do it again. Then I continued over the spur of land betwixt Severn and Wye, which, according to the map, is part of Gloucestershire. There was a cricket match in progress, with tiny figures in white far below, no doubt oblivious to the towering feat of engineering they would be used to seeing. Then I crossed the Wye, here a murky, grey estuary, and nothing like the 'sylvan Wye' I would discover tomorrow. I was now in Wales: in the space of thirty minutes I had passed into another country and walked in three counties.

Chepstow youth hostel is situated at the top of a steep hill. Whoever decided to put it there is no friend of mine. I suppose it might have been the Sheriff of Monmouth, whose former home it was in the 18th century. Then again, he couldn't have known the old pad would be turned into a youth hostel, and that I'd be along a hundred or so years later with my aching feet and sweat-ridden clothes. But the good news was there was a washing line. So, my clothes got another laundering, and wouldn't have to be carried outside the sack to dry, a tactic I was loth to employ after the experience with the albatross at Mevagissey.

3

Wye Valley and Welsh Borders

First it was the Romans, then the Normans who saw the strategic advantage of Chepstow, at the lowest bridgehead of the Wye. But it was the Saxon name that stuck: *Cheapstow,* a market town. Work began in 1067 on Chepstow's first castle, built, of course, by the Normans – they didn't waste much time after Hastings – and a wall almost encircles the town, with the river completing defensive cover. It's said Chepstow was to be a base to invade Ireland, but it's the English Civil Wars where its greatest history lies. It was held for the King when Colonel Morgan of Gloucester laid siege with 300 cavalry and 400 infantry, though with a garrison of only 64 it was hardly surprising they gave up.

Sir Henry Marten was a co-signatory of the death warrant of Charles I. So, when Charles II took the throne he was incarcerated in Chepstow castle for his trouble. This poem, written by Marten, in the form of an acrostic, points out how he felt about his part is the King's death:

P 2001

Chepstow Castle

Here or elsewhere, all's one to you, or me,
Earth, air or water gripes my ghostless dust,
None knows how soon to be by fire set free.
Reader, if you an oft-tried rule will trust,
You'll gladly do and suffer what you must.
My life was spent with serving you and you,
And death's my pay, it seems, and welcome, too,
Revenge destroying but itself, while I
To birds of prey leave my old cage and fly.
Examples preach to the eye; care then (mine says)
Not how you end but how you spend your days.

Evidently, when Cromwell signed the warrant he accidentally
spurted ink across Marten's face. So Marten did the same to
Cromwell. Brave man.

Today, I was walking to Monmouth. It was one of those special spring days, when unseen birds sing in a cloudless, blue sky, and where you just *know* it's going to stay that way. It would be a day of hazy views, the first of which was of Chepstow Castle, backed by the town and tall trees, the Wye flowing serenely by. On this quiet, Sunday morning, I was looking at a still-life painting. Only the gently-rippling waters of the river betrayed the fantasy.

I crossed the Wye – into England again – into what was the former Kingdom of Mercia. The Saxon king, Offa, ruled Mercia from 757 until 796. It was Offa who gave us our currency, the pound, when he decreed that 240 coins would be 'struck from one pound of silver'. The silver coins were known as sterlings. Later, the Normans broke the pound down to shillings and pence, and later again (1971) it was all 'decimalised'. Anyway, for reasons best known to himself, but only speculated on today, Offa built a dyke from Chepstow to Prestatyn, a distance of 168 miles. Or, rather, had it built – no-one suggests he did all the work himself. The dyke was probably a line of demarcation, although there is a suggestion it was to stop those in the west (i.e. Wales) rustling the cattle of those in the east. Offa's Dyke *footpath* generally follows the line of the dyke, although, as I would discover, in many places it wanders through fields where lots of styles have to be negotiated. Signposts bear the inscription, *Llwybr Clawdd Offa*, the name of the path in Welsh.

Soon I was climbing steeply through woodland, high above the Wye, where Offa's path runs through sun-kissed glades, the perfect walk on a perfect Sunday morning, the only hint of the human race the distant sound of cars on an unseen road. Ah, what they miss, these motorists. They'd probably explore the tourist sites, but miss the best attraction, these woods, nature in all her splendour. For four miles I trod carpets of brown leaves, lying where they'd fallen in autumn. In truth, this was a walk for lovers, and I was saddened to savour it alone. I had everything but the girl.

The path followed the sweeping curves of the river, far below. Every now and then the browny waters of the Wye came fleetingly into view, but distant views were lost in early morning heat-haze. It didn't matter. These woods were my view, all I needed. I arrived at last at the Devil's Pulpit, a limestone tower six hundred feet above the river where the Devil reputedly preached bawdy sermons to the monks of Tintern Abbey to entice them from their work. Cheeky Devil!

A path led from the lofty ridge where, after getting into a muddle in the woods, I crossed a rickety old footbridge across the Wye – back into Wales. It had been necessary to forsake the woods. I could not have proceeded without taking in the splendid ruins of the abbey, founded in 1131 for the monks of the Cistercian Order by the Norman Lord of Chepstow, Walter fitz Richard de Clare. The Welsh called this place *yr anghyfaned*, meaning uninhabited, away from towns. It's still relatively uninhabited, except for the small village of Tintern, but easily accessible nowadays, thanks to the motor car and the road – in past times the only access to the abbey was by the river.

Today, the abbey stands roofless and windowless, a magnificent ruin, backed by the woods which adorn the hillside on the opposite side of the Wye. *All description must fall short of its awful grandeur*, wrote John Byng in 1781. The abbey was a tourist attraction even then, where beggars acted as guides for visitors, artists and poets. As I beheld the ruins from across the road, they somehow took second place to the magnificent backdrop of the woods beyond, atop the lofty cliffs on the opposite side of the river, a miniature *Mato Grosso*. As usual, nature's work proved superior to man's, but let not the splendour of Tintern be understated.

A couple whom I'd noticed at Chepstow youth hostel happened along. Last night we'd not spoken, but today, because we were 'out and about', we exchanged a greeting. They were walking the Wye Valley route, 'just taking our time', as they were at pains to point out. I knew what they meant. People seem to think a lone walker covers great distances in a day, and might look at their achievements with scorn. How mistaken they are. What matters, as I tell them, is not how fast and how far, but what you see, what you discover. Like the ruins at Tintern, which demanded us to linger, for what would be the point of passing them by?

Like me, Wordsworth walked by the Wye. Like me, he walked alone. He was just 23, a man with much on his mind, not least a Frenchwoman, Annette Vallon, whom he loved and who had given birth to their daughter, Caroline. The year was 1793, when France declared war on England, so forcing estrangement from his family. On this, his first visit to the Wye, he was greatly moved by the *steep and lofty cliffs* along the lower reaches of the river, and the abbey at Tintern, which drove away the worries of a man in torment.

I found myself at St Michaels church, close by the river. It stands on the site of an old Celtic church, a place of worship over 350 years before Tintern Abbey was thought of. With time to spare I sat in the cool of the church. Just along the road were the sightseers, the tourists, amassing in their cars and coaches, yet it was I who had discovered what was worth seeking: a place for reflection, a place for rest. I emerged into the hot sun to find the grey waters of the river curving away into a hazy distance, with the woods above, glorious country on a glorious day.

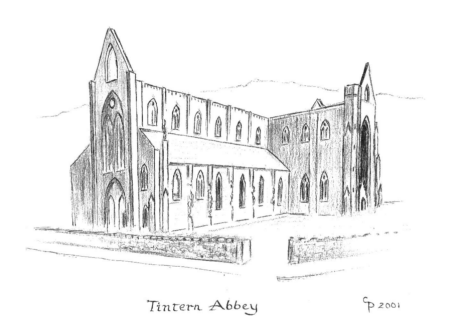

Tintern Abbey   ℗ 2001

On lush turf I followed the river, finally chugging into the former Tintern railway station alongside the old platform. It's a picnic site now. The railway was opened in 1876, principally to serve the needs of what was once an industrial valley. Trains carried timber, iron, wire, coal, paper, rope, glass and cider for export; timber, copper ore, linen, wines, beer and tobacco which were imported. (Why timber was exported *and* imported isn't clear; different sorts of timber, I suppose). Before the railway, most traffic along the valley used the river; the road, such as it became, was considered unsafe due to highwaymen. Many visitors were artists on the famous *Wye Tour*, arriving on boats fitted with a central table for eating, writing and sketching. Not everyone wanted the railway: those for said it would bring prosperity, those against said cows would run dry of their milk and hens wouldn't lay. Whether they were right isn't known. The railway continued until 1959, so presumably it was a success. Today, it's hard to imagine such activity, such industry.

Hunger spurred me on, and I crossed the river again at Brockweir where I found a pub. It was crowded: locals, possibly; motorists, certainly. No-one hiking. A sandwich and half a gallon of lemonade served my needs. I looked longingly at someone's bitter, but any alcohol on a day like this would have turned my legs to jelly. Emerging, I set off along the east bank of the river whose waters changed from grey to clear, due to this being the extent of the tidal reach. This is a lovely walk, across green meadows and through woodlands, always with the river as a companion. The afternoon was a scorcher; it was the sort of day to fall asleep and dream, or take a boat for a leisurely cruise, not to wear boots and carry a backpack. I eased down a gear, ignored the curious glances of those who through half-closed eyes watched my progress by the *sylvan Wye*. People were strewn everywhere, like corpses left by a victorious army. I longed to join them in their sweet repose, but resisted the urge. I had to press on for Monmouth.

Unexpectedly, I encountered two hikers, a couple walking Offa's Dyke, north to south. We met in some woods, pleased to chat the way like-minded people do. No sooner had we parted I spotted another two, this time bearing down on me from behind. They passed me by, two blokes carrying packs, obviously 'doing' the Dyke. They were Paul and Greg, whom I would encounter again in due course.

My next objective was Redbrook, four miles away, four miles in which I sweltered under the ever-increasing heat of the afternoon sun, feet, tired and swelling, and where I became hotter with every step. This path followed the route of the former railway – I had temporarily forsaken Offa's path – and was deserted. At a stile set amid a forest of nettles I removed boots and caressed my swollen feet: it was bliss, but not a good idea as I had to get them back into the boots again. How would I have fared with the backpack, I wondered, tent and all? And what purpose, what pleasure would there have been in carrying such a load? There could be no doubt that to jettison it had been the right decision. But, I wondered, when, if ever, would I have sight of the old railway bridge which carries the right of way across the river. At last it came into view, and I was greatly relieved, for I was by this time without anything left in my water canteen and there was nowhere to replenish it – except the river, I suppose.

Finally the right of way led to the old bridge which I crossed into Monmouth. I wasted no time in making my way to the youth hostel, situated in what was, until 1770, a school, which served a Benedictine priory. I lay on my bunk, shaking from the day's efforts, my feet swollen and aching. That evening, recovered, I explored Agincourt Square, where statues of Henry V, who was reputedly born in Monmouth castle, looks down from the 1724 Shire Hall, along with Sir Charles Rolls, who holds a model bi-plane, representative of his achievements at the turn of the century.

Henry and Charles were both heroes, albeit of different times. It was Henry who hammered the French at Agincourt, and even captured Normandy in his mission to claim the crown of France for England, whilst Charles Rolls was a pioneer of aviation, and he became the first person to fly the Channel both ways non-stop. Rolls' name is synonymous with quality; he bought his first car in 1895, being at that time one of only four people in the whole country to own one, and in 1904 he joined forces with Henry Royce, the start of a very successful partnership. Rolls was killed when his aircraft crashed in a spot-landing contest. Before my visit to Monmouth I never knew about his achievements. Perhaps he is an unsung hero.

*

As at Chepstow, the Normans wasted no time in building a castle at Monmouth. But the Romans were first on the scene as long ago as the first century AD. In the 14th century the town was all but abandoned, thanks to floods and, afterwards, the Black Death. In later years, Monmouth's identity became somewhat muddled, thanks to Henry VIII, who, after unification (1543) divided Wales into counties, adding Monmouthshire to England. So, when new legislation was passed at Westminster, they had to refer to Wales *and Monmouthshire* because folk still regarded it as being in Wales. Very confusing.

I would leave the Wye now, later to rejoin it briefly at Hay. The river had been a wonderful companion. Other visitors, apart from Wordsworth, were George Bernard Shaw, Lord Nelson and Charles Dickens. If, in later years, my name is included in such company (however unlikely that might be), I will be a happy man.

The route out of town crossed the famous Monnow bridge, with its massive 13th century gatehouse perched right in the centre. There's a small guardhouse above the arch in what is a unique building. Old pictures show it against a backdrop of old Monmouth; and there it is still, unchanged – except for the backdrop, of course. Where once there'd be the clip-clop of horses' hooves, now heavy lorries make their way carefully through the narrow archway. Crossing the bridge, I spied a young couple, well laden, on Offa's Dyke path. Unexpectedly, they walked up a side-street, lost before they'd even left town. I called them back and thus we made friends. Together with Paul and Greg, we would pass and re-pass one another for the rest of the day. My destination was uncertain; I'd take Offa's route, maybe as far as Pandy, a logical stopover before tackling the Black Mountains tomorrow.

The path led for a mile through the vast King's Wood, uphill every step. The day had started dull, but when I emerged from the wood the sun emerged from behind cloud. It was going to be another scorcher. As for the path, it was so well marked use of the map was unnecessary until, unexpectedly, the waymarking disappeared and all of us – Paul and Greg, the young couple, me –searched in vain to calculate where we were supposed to go. Whether we somehow missed one of those little yellow arrows or there weren't any where there ought to have been I will never know. But it seems to me if they're going to put direction arrows on fenceposts and gates and things they should put them everywhere or nowhere at all. Those who follow the arrows do so with such dedication that reference to the map is forsaken, so when one is missing they get into a muddle. Between us, we sorted it out in the end. Then, alone, I discovered a beautiful, isolated church that I hadn't noticed on the map. I checked it out. This was Llanvihangel-Ystern-Llewern. How I missed a name like that is a mystery. It means *St Michaels of the Fiery Meteor*. It's said that the church was founded by Ynyr, King of Gwent, who set foot on dry land after falling into a bog. There's a graveyard of tumbled gravestones and long grass, a scene unchanged for centuries. The young couple missed it completely. Maybe they didn't see it, maybe they weren't interested in what lay on Offa's route, although why anyone should undertake such a venture without being interested I cannot comprehend.

After the church I got into my second muddle of the day, ending up in fields and farmyards and, ultimately, Llantilio Crosseny where I went into the inn. Paul and Greg arrived. Where they'd got to, considering I'd whiled away the time in Ynyr's church and been lost, God only knows. Amiable conversation flowed, although I avoided alcohol for the usual reason. But we lingered at the inn, so aspirations of reaching Pandy were thwarted. Moving on, the sun bore down relentlessly, only now instead of the sylvan Wye I had green pastures and hedgerows and oak trees for company. The birds sang to my every step. I was a man in heaven. And my heart lifted at sight of the distant, dark ridge before me: the Black Mountains, tomorrow's objective, the highest ground on my journey.

And so to Llangattock Lingoed, where I found accommodation and a hot bath. Later, I wandered into what might be described as the centre of the village, although it isn't a village at all, more a *community*: a cottage or two, a lovely church, and the Hunter's Moon, where I had a pint or three and a superb meal. The pub was almost deserted. This pleased me at first, but after my meal, as the alcohol took hold, I thought it would be nice to have company for a change. It isn't always the case that I wish to be alone; there are times when it is good to share.

Reluctantly, I returned to my lodgings, the sun still beaming above the green canopy of the trees of the village. Little could I know that through the night the weather would break, that sheet lightning would illuminate my bedroom and deafening crashes wake me from my slumber, with rain lashing angrily against the window. Water at last! Now the air would be fresh, the ground dampened and the streams and rivers more lively!

*

The storm clouds were dispersing at breakfast, though a grey morning was in prospect. Not, perhaps, the best conditions for tackling the Black Mountains, but, as my lady host pointed out in her lilting Welsh: 'You just 'ave t'take what comes, you see.' She told me Captain Henry Morgan, the famous buccaneer, bane of the Spanish, is buried in the cemetery of St Cadog's church. I searched among the old gravestones but found no sign of him.

Continuing on Offa's Dyke path, this should have been an easy stroll, which it is, only I somehow contrived to get lost. Indeed, scarcely had I left Llangattock Lingoed and taken to the fields than I found myself off the path, wondering where I had gone wrong and how I could go right again. I became a trespasser, and might have become a hospital case when my endeavours to straddle a 5-barred gate almost ended in disaster when a log I stood on rolled at an inopportune moment. Under leaden skies I fumbled my way to a country road and back to the path again, annoyed at such a blundering performance but relieved I was still in the game of walking.

And so to Pandy. Or, rather, not quite, for the path turns west for the southern extremity of the Black Mountains. Low cloud was draped cold and grey over the ridge, now directly ahead, so it didn't look as though there would be anything doing in the way of views. Just my luck: after days of golden sunshine I reach high ground only to find the weather's closed and I won't see anything.

The Black Mountains are a 9-mile ridge, stretching from Pandy to Hay Bluff, rising to over 2,000 ft. The term *mountains* is, perhaps, an exaggeration, yet in contrast the surrounding country it may be appropriate to thus describe them, for they have to be climbed, in the sense that steep, uphill walking is needed to get on to the ridge. They are so-named because, seen from the lower ground, they appear black, whatever the weather. It is said that a woman sometimes appears hereabouts, at night or in the mist, and that she carries a pot or wooden cane, and walks in front of any wayfarer causing him to lose his way, even if he is familiar with the area. In the past, night travellers were advised to put a bowl of water at the foot of the maypole in a village, near Hay, to keep her away. They say she's scared of water, though if so, on the evidence of last night's storm, you'd never have thought she'd want to live here in the first place. I never saw her, anyway.

A steep, narrow lane led upward, past an iron gate, with a notice bearing the name of a farm: Little Llwygy. I tried to say it as I continued climbing. I managed *Little* OK, but got stuck on the Welsh bit. I tried again: *Llewgy*. No, that didn't seem right. Hang on, you're supposed to do something with your tongue when there's a double *l*. I tried again, but only succeeded in sounding like someone with a speech deformity. I kept climbing, until the lane ended at a track leading upward into the gloom. *Shlewgee*, I said. Nope, still didn't seem right. When at last I reached the ridge proper I still hadn't managed it.

Grassy slopes led to a forlorn ordnance survey column. I was pleased to see it, for it confirmed my navigation was accurate. Further on I came across Paul and Greg. They were lying on the ground, against their sacks. 'We're resting,' one of them explained, 'cos we're knackered.' Fair enough. Yet here, on the ridge, the going was easy now, with vast expanses of grass and outcrops of peat leading off in all directions as far as the eye could see. Which wasn't far, actually. Leaving Paul and Greg to their repose, I found myself alone in a world of silence and dank, clammy mist. The path followed the border. My left foot was in Wales, my right in England. The way was clear, better by far than the countless stiles, gates and muddled, off-route deviations of the farm pastures below. It is good to walk the meadows and country lanes; but, for me, there is nothing to compare with the high ground, the joys of the hills where clear space assures progress – even if it *isn't* clear! Just to make my day, the sun broke through, and I was able to see distant Welsh and English lowlands.

The further along the ridge, the worse the peat bogs became. They were wet and sticky, thanks to the overnight storm, but apart from being ankle deep in places, there was no problem. I walked in silence, save for the squelch of my boots in the peat and the puddles, and the cries of the birds and the bleating of distant sheep. There was nothing else, no wind, no people. I had the Black Mountains to myself, other than Paul and Greg, assuming they were following on behind.

The gradient rose almost imperceptibly to around 2,300 feet, with unhindered views to north, west and east. The remainder of the range, which form parallel ridges, lay bathed in sunshine. When I reached the ordnance column on Hay Bluff, at the northern extremity of the ridge, there were just four more miles to Hay (and I still couldn't say *Little Llwygy*). They say the apostles, St Peter and St Paul, once stood in the gap between Hay Bluff and Lord Hereford's Knob on a cold, grey day. I accept the bit about the weather, but the rest comes as rather difficult to believe. I mean, how did they get to Wales from the Holy Land, and how did they get home? Anyway, as their mission was to convert heathens to Christianity, the gap became known as *Bwlch-yr-Efengel*, meaning the Pass of the Evangelist, or the Gospel Pass.

I reclined against the ordnance column, looking over to Lord Hereford's Knob. Who was Lord Hereford, I wondered, and what attributes had he possessed to have a hill with such a name in his honour? I've known many peaks and pikes, and, in Scotland, *sgurrs, mealls* and *mullachs*. But never a knob. Perhaps, if he were alive, Lord Hereford could tell us something.

Life is a sweet thing when you can rest. Especially if there's no skin left on your heels and you've risen to the challenge and won the day. I lay content, wondering if at any minute Paul and Greg might appear, or if someone might be toiling up the hill to the place where I now lay. And I considered my journey to date. This was the seventeenth day from Lizard Point, and how far away and how long ago that seemed. If it hadn't been for that heavy pack at the start, I'd have been further than this by now; but no matter. I was here, at Hay Bluff, and the Black Mountains would soon be a memory, just as everywhere – and everything – is, once left behind. The sun had been an almost constant companion, and now, under its warm glow, I drifted among random reflections of Lakeland's fells: of heady days on grassy fellsides; of cold, wintry days, the rain and sleet lashing into my face, running down inside my collar; of Pillar, Gable, the Sca Fells; of my three favourite valleys, Borrowdale, Langdale, Wasdale. Today I was warm, and the larks seemed to be singing just for me. But somewhere above a persistent droning intruded my near-unconsciousness. It seemed threatening, and it was getting nearer...

I woke to see a strange winged creature high above, its dark shadow silhouetted against the sun. It hovered awhile, as though ready to swoop, then changed its mind and flew off north, no longer interested in its prey. I watched it go, one of those tiny micro-light things, its tinny engine fading into the hazy distance. Well, if nothing else, it woke me up. Best I got to Hay.

The descent from Hay Bluff was so steep that at the bottom my knees shook. I was still at around 1,500 feet, with glorious views to the north, over the Wye Valley, and now walking across turf so lush you could play bowls on it. Perfect for anyone with tired feet. There's a house by the path, backed by trees. In such an idyllic setting, it might be a place of dreams. And yet dreams, if there were any, must be shattered, for the house is derelict. I peered through a broken window to see rubble scattered on the floor of a cold, lifeless room, the old fireplace, once its heart, broken and cluttered. Oddments of family belongings lay unwanted on naked floorboards: an ornament, a teacup, bits and pieces of someone's lives. People had eaten and slept here, worked and lived here, were born here, had made love and died here. Now, only their ghosts remain, keeping silent vigil.

A country lane led to Hay. I walked it without seeing a soul. I was hot, I was tired and hungry, and I needed a bed. I knocked on the door of a B and B. The lady had no room, she said. No room! I'd seen no-one all day, save Paul and Greg; where was everyone? Anyway, she telephoned a friend who had, a helpful gesture, though it's all part of the 'I'll scratch your back if you'll scratch mine' routine, and it wasn't long before I was soaking in a hot bath. My feet were weary, but I was content.

There appears to be some confusion about the origins of the name, Hay-on-Wye. It may be derived from the Latin *La Hiai*, meaning 'the Hay', or the Norman, *Haye*, meaning an enclosure. In Welsh, it's *Y Gelli*. It's only been called Hay-on-Wye since 1947. In prehistoric times, primitive man occupied the high ground around where Hay now stands, and bears and wildcats roamed the forests by the Wye. When Henry's Act of Parliament 'incorporated Wales with the realm', Welshmen enjoyed the same political status as Englishmen (notice it's *men*, nothing about what women might or might not enjoy). The Norman castle was destroyed by King John. Henry III built another in 1233, but it was sacked by the Welsh. Henry's castle is still there, only now it's a bookshop; but then that isn't surprising, for in Hay-on-Wye there are bookshops *everywhere*!

The whole thing started in 1962 when Richard Booth opened a small bookshop at the former fire station. Then he bought the cinema with a view to founding the biggest second-hand bookshop in the world. (A change from the conversion of cinemas into Bingo halls). Then he acquired the castle, and after that, with so many more bookshops, he installed managers, and advertised on radio and t.v. To say his venture caught on would be an understatement. Today, bibliophiles everywhere make the pilgrimage to Hay for that one special book they need. Even tourists, your couch-potatoes who, when at home, are glued to *Coronation Street* and *Brookside*, who never open the cover of a book from one year's end to the next, can be seen thumbing through such titles as *Understanding Dentistry* and *Neoclassicism.*

In the 18th century, Henry Skryne, a renowned author of travel books (could you get one in Hay, I wonder?) stayed in Hay on his way home to Somerset from a tour of the north of Scotland. Wrote Skryne: 'We entered a romantic corner of South Wales near the Hay, where the broad and transparent River Wye emerges from its native mountains and approaches England through a broad and fertile vale. I was conducted in the course of my rides to several points of view that confirmed to me that we need not have gone to Scotland in search of the most striking beauties with which nature has endowed a country'.

Well said, sir! Hay deserves this accolade, for the town is a gem, with its clean, light-grey cottages, sometimes in orderly rows, sometimes scattered along the narrow roads of the haphazard collection of lanes. And, in the 17th century, for collecting 13s 3d (65p) towards the building of St Paul's Cathedral following the Great Fire of London. (Would the citizens of London have collected anything if Hay's church had suffered a similar fate, I wonder?).

I anticipated uninterrupted sleep that night, not unreasonably, you might think, in a quiet little town nestling in a quiet little valley. Unfortunately, my dreams of 5-barred gates, microlights and Lord Hereford's Knob were interrupted by the town clock, or, more accurately, its Westminster Chimes: at a quarter past the hour, the half hour, a quarter to the hour and on the hour. Every hour. All night. It wasn't that they were loud, just they were *there*, and once awake, I lay in restless slumber, unable to avoid, subconsciously, awaiting the next round, knowing in advance precisely what it would be.

At a quarter past: bong-bong-bong-bong.

At half past: bong-bong-bong-bong, bong-bong-bong-bong.

At quarter to: bong-bong-bong-bong, bong-bong-bong-bong, bong-bong-bong-bong.

And, of course, on the hour: bong-bong-bong-bong, bong-bong-bong-bong, bong-bong-bong-bong, bong-bong-bong-bong.

Then BONGGGG... the appropriate number of times.

I read somewhere once of a woman so demented by church bells she took a knife to the ropes and cut them, so preventing them being rung. Don't blame her. I've nothing against church bells and clock chimes. In fact, I like 'em, along with most other people. But through the night? I guess it was okay in the old days, before the stresses and strains of today's modern world. Then again, maybe in sleepy Hay-on-Wye there's not much stress. There wouldn't be if it weren't for those chimes.

*

Next morning, I looked out of the window to see the sun already high in the sky. I didn't know whether to be pleased, as might be expected, or disappointed, but the fact was my scalp was suffering from the effects of sunburn, thanks to losing my hat somewhere. I thought I'd buy a new one, although this was like closing the stable door after the horse had bolted. There was a shop, but the only hats they sold were white, a sensible colour, true enough, it's just that when I looked in the mirror with a large, white, floppy hat stuck on my cranium I looked ridiculous (as though I'd looked sensible wearing the old blue one). Anyway, I emerged from the shop hatless.

Today, I had a 14-mile tramp to Kington, a logical stopping place before going on to Knighton. Crossing the bridge out of Hay I met up with an elderly gent who clearly wanted a natter. A grand fellow he was, calling out a cheery 'good morning' on my approach. He spoke with a strong, Welsh accent, remarking on the glories of the Wye and enquiring of my journey. Mostly, though, he extolled the virtues of Wales, his country: Snowdonia, the Brecon Beacons, the Severn Bridge, of which I left him to his blissful ignorance. He retired to Hay, he said, for peace and contentment after a long career as a schoolteacher. Presumably he didn't live anywhere near the town clock.

I scribbled *Little Llwygy* on to a piece of paper and asked him to put me out of my misery. He looked at it intently for a moment, doubt clouding his face.

'Let's see,' he muttered, stroking his chin, 'it says *Little something...*'

Came the moment of truth.

'I don't know what it means,' he admitted. 'You see, I've spent most of my life in Hertfordshire.'

I should have known, for only about one fifth of the Welsh can speak their own language – though they may with some justification blame the English for that – and they are mainly in the north. So, I'd never be able to say *Llwygy*. There was nothing for it but to get on with my life. And my walk, here on the bridge at Hay. It was the scene of rioting in 1861, after one Richard Parry was granted 28-shillings towards the cost of an inscription in Hay church relating to the bridge. It's recorded in the churchwardens' accounts of 1799: '...the Commissioners by an Act of Parliament...granted the Wye bridge a lease of the toll thereof for 98 years from 1 October, 1763 and after the expiration thereof the bridge is to be free from toll'.

In July, 1861, another Richard Parry wrote a letter to the Hereford Times, reminding the people of Hay of the inscription (they would have needed reminding after nearly 100 years) that from 1st October that year there would no longer be a toll to pay when crossing the bridge. This would be well received by the populace: the tolls weren't cheap – 4 pence for a 'drawing beast', one penny for a horse 'not drawing', and half a penny per passenger. Notices were posted about town to ensure everyone knew of the imminent free right of passage across the bridge.

On 1st October, a crowd of around 300 gathered at each end of the bridge, expecting free passage. But the gatekeeper had other ideas – like refusing to let them pass without payment of the toll. So they did what any crowd would have done: tore down the gates and threw them into the river.

There followed a meeting in the town hall, which broke up with the crowd returning to the bridge, this time armed with iron bars and pickaxes. They removed the gate posts and besieged the toll house which evidently was in such a decrepit state one good push would have sent it into the river, along with the keeper and his wife and kids. The rioting continued for two days, then the gates were recovered from the river and re-erected, after which the townspeople of Hay were shown an Act of Parliament which empowered the Commissioners to continue charging a toll to pay for maintaining the bridge. They had to accept it and the tolls continued until 1933.

Crossing the bridge – it's a relatively new one built on thin, concrete pillars and looks as though a good puff of wind will blow it over – I found myself once again alongside the Wye. The old chap on the bridge had said he'd never seen the river so low, and no wonder, for there had been no rain to speak of – apart from the night before last – for weeks. Even so, the Wye was as lovely as ever this glorious spring morn, where it wanders through lush meadows, alongside tree-lined banks. I followed the river for a mile or so, before the path, such as it was, disappeared in a forest of nettles, leaving me hot and bothered in vain attempts to discover just where I was supposed to go. Looking up, I discovered Paul and Greg on the opposite side of a barbed wire fence, picking their way through nettles on their side. Then I left the Wye for good, where a path led up through a wood, which provided shade from the increasingly hot sun. Further on I became so thirsty I had to break my own rule about knocking on someone's door for a drink of water.

I had quickly become dehydrated, so much so that I simply had to have that drink. Dehydration makes you weak, turns legs to jelly. The woman who opened her door at that little cottage was only too happy to oblige, waving away my apologies in a kindly Welsh voice as I handed over my empty canteen. She returned with a smile, handed it back and closed her door. Ah, nectar! Cold, clear, sparkling, refreshing water. I poured it down my throat greedily, water spilling down my face and even running up my nose.

An unmetalled lane carries the border of Wales and England, so once again I had a foot in each country. Then I dropped down to Newchurch, passing below the magnificent stone church with old gravestones set high above the road. Rising ground to the right, Disgwylfa Hill, I knew was on the route and would have to be climbed. I crossed the River Arrow and set about the task, at the top of the hill discovering Paul and Greg were cheerfully marching off in the wrong direction. I checked my map to make sure there was no mistake, then called out at the top of my voice. They heard, and after visibly checking their own map retraced their steps. Good turn done for the day, I marched at speed for Gladestry, where the map indicated an 'inn'. I hoped it was still there, that it hadn't been turned into a private dwelling, which sometimes happens these days. I pressed on, sweat dripping from my forehead and arms, my throat longing for a drink, a drink with a kick this time. Reaching the inn at Gladestry became my sole purpose in life. *Please* let it still be there, and *please* let it be open. It is and it was.

Gladestry is a tiny place, even though it's name appears in bold letters on the map. The Royal Oak was deserted. I broke my own rules and downed a quick lager, just like John Mills in *Ice Cold in Alex*. Did you see the film? Some soldiers cross the desert in an ambulance during the war, and when they reach Alexandria they drink ice-cold beer. It's done so well you can almost taste it yourself. When Paul and Greg appeared I downed another, then another. I told myself I'd earned it and I was jolly-well going to have it. I gobbled up a banana split with ice cream, too, just for good measure. Incidentally, whilst the lager cooled my stomach, the top of my hatless head now burned so fiercely you could have boiled a kettle on it.

I had noticed Paul was always the one reading the map, Greg always following. That's how it seemed to me, anyway. Now, accepting that Paul's are natural leaders, it nevertheless irked me (though it was none of my business) that this should be so. Yet it is often the case that you see one person leading, others following. Those who follow rarely know where they are going or where they have been, and theirs is the loss. It's the same right across the spectrum of life: leaders and followers. Human nature, I suppose.

Four glorious miles to Kington remained. They included a traverse of Hergest Ridge, a straightforward climb to around 1,400 feet, all on grass, a surface fit for playing bowls (if it was level). I'd been on the ridge before, with two of my sons, when conditions were far different from today. Then, the day was dull and dank, with the entire ridge enshrouded in mist so thick we had to stick close together for fear of losing one another. Today, the sun blazed away as I climbed the grassy sward to the top of the ridge where, halfway along, I sank to the ground, exhausted, thanks to the combined effects of the heat and the lager and the banana split and the ice cream. I leaned back against my sack and drifted into a deep slumber. When I woke Paul and Greg were asleep beside me. For a time, we were three helpless corpses. Feeling groggy, I dragged myself and my burning scalp away, leaving them where they lay, my unsteady legs taking me down the hill into Kington, in England once more.

The town is said to derive from *Kingstown*, after Edward the Confessor, who sent an army into the area to avenge the sacking of Hereford by the Welsh. The people of Kington were probably Welsh, but they were driven off so now it's in England. St Mary's church contains the tomb of Thomas Vaughan and his wife, Ellen, otherwise known as Black Vaughan and Ellen the Terrible. They weren't the sort of people to fall out with. Vaughan was a tyrant, and Ellen is reputed to have avenged the murder of her brother by attending an archery contest dressed as a man. As soon as the tournament got under way she turned and fired an arrow through the heart of her brother's killer, then escaped in the confusion. Then again, maybe he deserved it. Black Vaughan was killed at the Battle of Banbury, in 1469, fighting for the Yorkists, after which, it is said, his ghost turned into a fly that tormented horses. Thereafter he haunted Kington as a bull. Twelve people tried to exorcise Vaughan's evil spirit by taking part in prayer. Eleven failed, but the twelfth somehow managed to reduce the spirit until it could be fitted into a snuff box which was then thrown into a pool. That put paid to Black Vaughan. Snuffed it, you might say.

An elderly woman opened her door and provided accommodation for the night. I think she took guests for the company rather than the money, and who could blame her? No sooner was I sorted than Paul and Greg arrived, and we drank the evening away in the Swan. Company for a change! It was raining by bedtime, and this pleased me, for the air was in dire need of freshening up. I even hoped it would rain tomorrow. To have carried my waterproofs nearly three hundred miles and not used them was galling.

Twelve miles to Knighton – *Tref-Y-Clawdd* – the Town on the
Dyke. The sun had deserted me, but instead of the hoped-for rain I
faced a dank, cold day, where low, clinging mist would mar views of
the lovely hills of old Radnorshire. Elgar wandered these hills,
probably taking inspiration for his music. He must have had better
weather.

Hereabouts the Wales-England border wanders hither and thither,
and after climbing Bradnor Hill (on a thither section) with its golf
course, one of the highest in the country, I crossed the border yet
again, back into Wales. This is – or was – Radnorshire, a much-to-be-
preferred name in my view to its replacement, Powys. I am not alone, I
know, in mourning the passing of some of the former names of our
counties, following the local government re-organisation of 1974.
Cumberland, Westmorland, Huntingdon, Middlesex, they all
disappeared.

The only time I've ever had anything to do with golf courses was
when my dad took me for country walks across one near our home. For
him, it was welcome relief after working down a hole in the ground in
the cold and dark, where he and his *marras* crawled around in
eighteen-inch seams, hacking out coal, a job he did for nearly fifty
years. Coal miners didn't play golf, which was the sport of the affluent
businessmen of Newcastle. I never heard my dad complain, but it
seemed to me if anyone should be out there swinging a club and taking
in the fresh air and exercise it was the miners. Anyway, now and again
he'd find a wayward golf ball and take pleasure in watching its owner
searching for it whilst he kept it in his coat pocket. Mam told him he
should give the balls back. 'They want the exercise,' he said, 'I'm just
seeing they get it.' He brought them all home – the balls, not the
golfers – except one, which he gave to me, a one-off gesture following
its immediate dispatch through someone's kitchen window. When he'd
collected a sackful he'd hand them in. He was honest. They all were,
the miners. They worked hard and knew the value of things.

Although I was close to the Radnor Hills, alas I saw nought of
them. In fact I could see little of anything, and had to check the
compass to ensure correct navigation in mist so thick you'd have
thought me at three thousand feet. I was in a world of my own, save
for the inevitable sheep. Strange, they are. They either scarper on your

approach, or the odd brave one will allow you to pass close by with apparent indifference, turning a head to watch your progress, as though to make sure you're not going to make a last-minute lunge. Then, when the head can turn no further, their eyeballs roll right into the corners, head and eyes now at a maximum looking-back angle. It's either panic or couldn't give a toss. But we humans shouldn't scorn the mentality of these woolly creatures: more than once I've questioned my sanity when, toiling uphill to reach the top of a mountain, I find the sheep already there, grazing in blissful contentment. Sheep usually walk around mountains, not up them, as the ancient sheep-tracks testify.

I was now walking right alongside Offa's Dyke, here a high-sided ditch whose presence more than compensated for the gooey conditions. I was thus following in the footsteps of Offa. Or, if he didn't actually walk it himself (and, let's face it, he probably didn't), in the footsteps of those who built his dyke. Even so, I left the official path near Discoed, preferring instead to aim for Whitton where, hopefully, there would be an inn. I had ample time; I fancied lunch and a wee drink, especially on such a miserable day. Sadly, at Whitton, there was no inn, so I passed the time by sitting on a bench where I heard children playing in the schoolyard opposite. Their happy chorus of laughter cheered me, reminded me of my own schooldays: sharpening lollypop sticks into make-believe daggers, playing marbles, swopping milktops. And, before secondary school, playing 'tag', or 'tuggy' as we little Geordie darlings called it. Kissing girls came later. But not that much later.

The weather lifted a little, at last permitting views of the rolling hills and deep valleys of this grand country. I moved on, rejoining the dyke for a grand finale, just two more miles to Knighton. This was the best section of dyke so far, a deep trough lined by fine trees. It all ended on the high ground above Knighton's glistening rooftops, barely visible in the mist which lay unmoving in the valley. In light drizzle I entered the town, and after taking tea with a young Canadian bloke with enormous feet and equally enormous boots (and we know what that means, don't we?) I strode purposefully to the town clock, the terminus of the first part of my journey.

4

Shropshire and Staffordshire

The Saxons called it *Scrobbesbyrigscir*, the Normans changed it to *Salopescira*, and later it became *Shropshire*. Then someone with a bent for modern-day culture but without a brain called it *Salop*, a name, not surprisingly, disliked by the natives. So, in 1980 it became Shropshire again. The county was occupied by the Saxons and Romans, colonised by the Celts, invaded by the Danes and the Normans. For 400 years, its border with Wales was the domain of the 'Marcher Lords', baronial allies who fought the Welsh and just as often each other. It was, and is again, a strictly agricultural land, yet it was in Shropshire where the world saw the birth of industry. It's quite a place, really.

On a brisk autumn day I marched boldly past the town clock in Knighton, and crossed the Teme onto English soil. Or, rather, English tarmacadam, on the quiet byroad that follows the River Teme, here wedged in below high, wooded hills, the sort of country which calls out for one to linger, to explore. But I was anxious to press on, to discover new horizons. Craven Arms and, beyond, Wenlock Edge, were my immediate goals. I had no idea where I would spend the night. It could be the youth hostel at Wilderhope Manor, a few miles beyond Wenlock Edge, or guesthouse accommodation. Or a ditch. As one whose life was geared to rules and timetables, the uncertainty appealed.

Yet I kept stopping along that country road. The cause was blackberries, growing in profusion in the hedgerows. Picking blackberries added to the feeling of living off the land, as it were. Still, mustn't get too carried away; it was hardly akin to, say, survival in the wild, or the equivalent of an SAS man behind the lines in Iraq or somewhere. Actually, I was surprised to find blackberries unpicked, so close to a town, but in an area of sparse population I guess there's more than enough to go around. Enough for a passing hiker, anyway. Ah, those were the days, when mum took me blackberrying. We had long sticks to push prickly brambles aside, and we filled jars and biscuit tins, all in the cause of blackberry jam and blackberry pie, which nowadays you buy in the supermarket, complete with E-numbers.

On that road I saw not one vehicle, the only sign of humanity being a lone fellow who returned my 'good morning' almost reluctantly. Seemed to, anyway. He had a strangely vacant expression, short of a full dozen, as it were. Or maybe he was just surprised at the sight of me, like him a lone fellow, but unlike him carrying a rucksack, wearing boots and a floppy hat. Thinking about it, he'd probably walked this road every day for twenty-five years and this was the first time he'd seen a hiker. As he passed me by I turned and watched him go, just in case he was about to strike me from behind with an unseen club. But he was just ambling along, minding his own business.

There were lots of dead rabbits on the road, flattened by passing cars – when there are passing cars. There's something about the human race and rabbits: we shoot them, snare them, infect them with horrible diseases, keep them in captivity, eat them. And any lucky enough to somehow survive we run over. All this after we brought them here from a foreign country. It's not as though they asked to come. I walked the rabbits' 'death row' for four miles before turning north at Bucknell. There was always the feeling of getting somewhere when I turned my face to the north. After all, the north was my ultimate goal. Yet for many a mile the overall direction on this part of my walk would be east, for I was bound for Dovedale and the

Pennines, so I'd have to traverse Shropshire and Staffordshire, counties not familiar to me. The countryside, though lovely, was largely unseen, as the hedgerows which border the roads are high; it was almost like walking through a long, roofless tunnel.

Today's modern road follows the course of a former Roman one to Craven Arms. The town is named after an inn, and came into being thanks to the Shrewsbury-Hereford railway. Prior to the railway it was an important venue for the drovers of old, taking their sheep from Wales to the English market. Presumably they took their refreshments at the inn, but today I took mine in a modern shopping precinct contained in what might aptly be described as an enormous shed. Then I wandered into a car park and, ignoring the curious gaze of shoppers, tended to newly-formed blisters. These came about thanks to an experiment, namely walking in trainers instead of boots. I read somewhere trainers are better. Whoever wrote it is mistaken, or perhaps a sadist. I discarded the trainers, but the damage was done. Anyway, sitting barefoot in the car park at Craven Arms merited the attention of a fat bloke about my age who could just about manage the journey, on foot, from the shops to his car. His advice, given in the tone of an older, worldly person, was forthright. 'Walking does you the world of good,' he wheezed, clearly whacked from the effort of walking forty yards. Well, it wasn't doing him much good by the look of it.

I headed north on the busy A49, stepping deftly on to the grass verge as cars and lorries roared past, over two miles of purgatory ending, mercifully, at a quiet country lane leading off in the direction of Wenlock, with the 900-ft high limestone escarpment of Wenlock Edge now towering on the right. The experts say it was formed by a coral reef 420 million years ago. Hard to believe, but what's the point of having experts if you doubt what they say? There were no people, no cars along this road. Two small communities, shown on the map in bold type, turned out to be little more than farmsteads, memorable only for their glorious isolation and snarling dogs. As the day wore on, my strength held up but my feet were suffering. A tempting bed and breakfast sign loomed up, but I kept going. Too soon yet to call a halt.

Presently, I arrived at a place with a lovely name: Wall under Heywood. Enough was enough. There were two guesthouses. Alas, both were full. There's an inn round the corner, I was told. But it was full too. Could the lady help? I asked. She racked her brains, telephoned other guesthouses, did her best to find a bed for the man of the road. But they were full, all of them. There was nothing for it but to press on. If nothing else turned up, I'd just have to try the youth hostel at Wilderhope Manor, but I wouldn't reach it before dark.

A mile and a half further I came upon a sign: 'Bed and Breakfast 500 yards'. A lane led off left. I considered the position. Did they have any room for a footsore traveller? If I walked down the lane to find they did not, that would be 500 + 500 = 1,000 yards, which I could do without. But the youth hostel was two miles away and, who knows, it might be full too. In gathering darkness I set off, arriving only just in time for, as I reclined in a hot bath, a knock at the door heralded the arrival of people whose custom would have proved more lucrative than the single male given a family room for the night. My hosts held no grudge as they entertained me with social dialogue and provided a good supper. All was well, save for my feet, which by now were utterly wrecked thanks to the experiment with the trainers.

*

Yesterday, I had walked below Wenlock Edge, had looked up longingly at its lovely woods, knew from the map of the paths that run along the graceful contours of the hillside. Then, the Edge had been a temptress, silently beckoning. But the need to secure accommodation had spurred me on below, where progress was rapid and where accommodation could be found. Today, a Sunday, with ample time, I could savour the joys of the Edge, and I would stay at the youth hostel at Ironbridge, just thirteen miles off, a logical stopover before going on to Eccleshall. I stepped outside to find the air refreshed by heavy overnight rain. I felt good, and better still when an attractive woman who was attending her garden smiled broadly and called out a cheery 'good morning.' I actually turned my head, looked behind. Yes, she was talking to me.

'Would you like a drink?' she asked, never mind I'd downed a gallon of fruit juice at breakfast. What had I done that's so right? I wondered, then realised she must have thought the bloke carrying the rucksack had been out all night in the rain and was probably wet through. So, whilst on the inside I felt good, to others I must have looked haggard. I declined her kind offer, but her warm smile and kind gesture made my day anyway.

At Longville in the Dale (another lovely name) I intended to take the course of the former railway, then climb into the woods.

Unfortunately, relax-mode was abruptly shattered by the sudden appearance of a huge dog. If, at the end of my journey, I was asked to allocate a special prize for 'worst dog', this fellow would win, paws down. I was wearing shorts, not the best raiment for instilling confidence at the hands – or jaws – of such a hostile creature. He meant business, it was obvious by his snarling and barking and growling and the saliva dripping from his mouth and his teeth and the hate in his eyes and his utterly fearful presence. Bravely, I stood my ground, adopted the nuisance dog procedure. Or, to put it another way, froze in abject fear, with his jaws inches from hands clasping the straps of my sack, my way of putting them somewhere out of reach of man's worst enemy. Unfortunately, other vulnerable bits had to remain in situ. I considered taking the initiative, like kicking him in the teeth, but rejected this on the grounds that I'd probably miss by a mile, and it would only provoke him. Ever the pragmatist.

He was seeing me off his territory, I guess, for as I moved slowly forward the sound of snarling faded. Eyes forward, I scampered up the hillside, onto the Edge, where I found myself alone on a long, straight forest road, the route of the old railway.

After the charge of yesterday it was a joy to walk the route of the old line. I had it to myself: the trees on the steep hillside above; below, Shropshire's fields, bathed in the autumn gold of an English landscape at harvest-time, and pale green meadows with ubiquitous cattle, tiny figures in black and white, reminiscent of those little toys we had as kids. Toy farms: how do they compare with today's computer games, understood by kids, beyond the comprehension of ordinary, adult mortals? Distant combines, too, were toys, the sound of their engines drifting faintly across the still morning air. As I walked, I reflected on the benefits breaking the journey up had brought, for where I had savoured the joys of the south-west in springtime, now it was autumn's turn. And what a good job she was making of it.

For three miles I followed the course of the old line. Here, once upon a day, trains carried fuel to the power station at Buildwas. What a journey it must have been. Imagine it, if you will, as you chug along, the smoke from the locomotive dispersing into the woods. And not that long ago either, for the line didn't close until 1962. Such a shame, with so many of today's children glued fast to television sets and those computer games; how grand it would be if they could ride the old railways. Could they be brought back? Is it too much to ask? If millions in lottery money can be spent on Royal Opera Houses for the benefit of the rich, and Millennium Domes in London for the benefit of politicians' egos, and monstrous statues for the benefit of nobody, surely we can afford things that people, especially children, would enjoy.

I saw no-one along the Edge, until I reached Much Wenlock. It's an ancient town, granted borough status by Edward IV in 1468, and famed for its 'harmonious architecture' and ruined priory, originally founded in the 7th century by a Mercian king. The priory fell into ruins and was replaced by another by the Normans, its rich, stone architecture proudly defying the ravages of time. The ruins are magnificent, which is more than can be said of many of today's structures. Doesn't bear thinking about, really.

I bought a Sunday newspaper, went for coffee and lazed around awhile. Then, with the early afternoon sun appearing, I sought out the old railway again. I hoped it would lead all the way to the Severn. It's clear enough on the map. Sadly, after a mile, the route was barred by dense undergrowth. There was nothing for it but to take to the road, which I was obliged to follow all the way to the Severn, two miles of dodgy bends, with approaching traffic obscured by hedgerows. I toiled away in the hot sun, meeting up with a woman with two kids and a horse, then arrived at Buildwas Abbey. It was founded in 1135 as a 'daughter house' of Furness Abbey, Cumbria. Today's ruins, standing proudly on close-cropped lawns, include a magnificent stone colonnade dating back to around 1200. They almost replicate those of Much Wenlock. Both are in safe hands now after stone was plundered in days gone by. Shropshire can be proud of its ancient buildings.

I crossed the Severn, renewing acquaintance with the river for the first time since crossing the Severn Bridge. Where before the river was wide and grey, here she was narrower, and, in the sunshine, she was in her Sunday best, a splendid sight and never mind the four giant cooling towers of a power station close by. In a quiet meadow, I gave up the ghost, took off my boots and lay on the grass, where I drifted into a contented slumber to the sound of distant clapping, wafting from a cricket match on the opposite side of the river. When, finally, I got moving again, I followed the river to Coalbrookdale, the birthplace of industry, where 'the course of civilisation was changed forever', and where artists came to paint the 'satanic mills' of the industrial revolution.

It started in the 18th century, when timber was our most important product: timber for houses and furniture, for windmills and ships, for fuel. Britain was a land of forests once, and the fact it is no longer is due largely to this demand over many years. But in an increasingly industrial world, demand for *iron* grew dramatically: iron for the new steam engines of England's rapidly-growing industries, for railway lines and locomotives, for new bridges, for guns in the endless wars against France and whoever else we were fighting.

Wood, as a fuel, produces charcoal, used for smelting iron ore, a method that was unsuitable due to a preponderance to make the finished iron brittle, and in any case could not possibly meet the needs of the increasing demand for iron. Coal replaced wood in the process of iron manufacture, thanks to Abraham Darby, who pioneered the technique of smelting iron ore with coke. Shropshire coal was of a suitable type, and the river itself was a natural channel for transporting materials into and out of the area. As a result of this improved technique, the production of iron increased by 3,000% over the next 100 years.

But there was a problem. The source of many raw materials for use in the manufacture of iron was at Broseley, on the opposite side of the Severn. This, and some of the manufactured produce, had to be ferried across the river, a laboriously slow and costly process. A new bridge was needed, so they built one, the first iron bridge in the world. It was completed in 1780 and it's still there, a monument to English industry and achievement. With the rest of the world still a sleepy, backward place, Coalbrookdale forged ahead – literally – in the production of iron, and today basks in the glory of a proud heritage, whose once-thriving blast-furnaces and ironworks are reminders of that time. There was full employment, although that is not to say the wealth thus created was evenly distributed – far from it. A few owners reaped the riches, while the workers who toiled long hours in the blast furnaces literally worked themselves to death. Children were employed in the mills from six in the morning until seven in the evening, summer and winter.

Standing on the iron bridge is a good place to reflect on what life must have been like here in those days, when the flames of the furnaces lit up the sky, 'a vision of hell', as someone wrote. In the bright sunshine of a lovely autumn afternoon it was hard to take in. Anyway, having thus made acquaintance with the birthplace of industry, I made my way to the youth hostel where I became the odd-one out among a horde of 16-year old schoolgirls. Well, I didn't mind if they didn't. Tomorrow would be an unplanned rest day, for a new rucksack I carried was doing my back in. There was nothing for it but to bus into Shrewsbury in the morning and buy another. All part of the experience.

Ironbridge   ᵠ 2001

*

I was eager to be on my way. Delay does not suit the long-distance walker.

Frankly, I anticipated a somewhat boring trek today. Twenty-odd miles to Eccleshall seemed to hold little of promise. Just a matter of pressing on for sweeter things, like Dovedale and, beyond, the distant Pennines. I was mistaken. Shropshire and Staffordshire would have much to offer someone on foot at this time of year.

I was in good spirits, and good shape, too, thanks to my enforced day off. I made good time in circumnavigating Telford, then taking a backroad to Shifnal. The town was once a staging post on the Holyhead road, and nowadays is bisected by the railway, which passes through the centre on a high viaduct. Many of the Irish navvies who did all the hard work in building the railway settled in the area. The Nell Gwyn, a large, timber-framed pub, is a classic, except nowadays it incorporates a Chinese takeaway. But it's St Andrew's church that takes the eye. It's cathedral-size, with a 700-year old tower, surrounded by huge, well-kept lawns. Sadly, coils of wire adorn part of the roof, the sort you expect to see around high, prison walls. It's there to foil lead thieves, I was told. How utterly sad.

Inside the nave there's a stone plaque. It tells of the deaths of two parishoners, whose combined age was 251 years. They were William Wakely, who died in 1714, aged 124, and Mary Yates, who 'died in the same century', aged 127. Supports the theory that women outlive men, I suppose. Another plaque, in the porch, says the interior was restored in memory of Peter Osborne by his family in 1379. They certainly made a good job of it.

Shifnal was a staging post for me, too. I located a cosy café where I ordered a cup of tea and a bacon roll, a rare treat. The café was almost deserted, save for two women seated in a corner. Settling into my newspaper, I could not help but hear them as they spoke, their unmistakable 'Midlands' accents proof of my progress northward. Changing accents were becoming an interesting feature of the walk; theirs was a far cry from those I heard in Cornwall, to be sure.

We were minding our own business, when another woman entered the café. A sort of witch-like creature in rags, she was recognised at once by the others, who gave her looks of mutual resentment. And no wonder. As she plonked herself down not too far from my table, I could have cut in half the pong she brought in with her. I looked at the waitress; surely she would ask her to leave. But no, she was accepted as part of the furniture. Which I suppose she was. I imagined her to be Meg Merrilies...

The two women tried to ignore her, but she wouldn't let them.

'Nice day, isn't it?' said Meg, a smile showing both her teeth.

The women glared.

'Town's quiet.'

That was ignored too. But Meg was nothing if not persistent.

'Isn't it, though?'

They had to speak to her in the end.

I left them to it, gratefully gulping in lungfuls of carbon monoxide outside, and took a byroad leading out of the village to a bridge across the M54, where the right of way led over a huge, recently cropped cornfield. I enjoyed that field, which I crossed beneath blue skies and fleecy white clouds. I felt free, as a man does when he has his liberty. Liberty is something to savour, to appreciate and not take for granted. Especially when one's footsteps lead unexpectedly to a place of beauty. A small lake, or mere, was indicated on the map. I crossed the roadside ditch, brushed aside the nettles and peeked over the hedge to find myself gazing on the still waters of a lovely pool. It was surrounded by mysterious wild flowers, weeds and nettles, a mishmash of this and that growing in wild profusion. Under a September sun, the scene somehow belonged to the day. It was a place for picnics, for lovers, for lying on the ground and dreaming. And for a long-distance walker, who, had he the time, might have taken due advantage. Alas, I could not, for I had lingered at Shifnal and there were many miles still to Eccleshall. I dragged myself away, and sang every step along the country road beyond. I felt so *alive*! But then, who wouldn't, on such a day, in such country, in such a mood? Shropshire served up tasty fare, to be sure.

After negotiating a 100-yard stretch of the A41, lorries and all, more byroads led to a brightly-painted blue sign by the roadside. Staffordshire, it proclaimed, as though to say 'now it's my turn', after the delights of Shropshire. It was a significant point, for the Dove is in Staffordshire, and the Dove was my goal. I followed the road to Orslow, a place of scattered houses, and rich, green meadows bordered by fine trees, a scene somehow reminiscent of Kentucky. Or South Fork, Texas, maybe. I looked around. A handsome American would appear, on a white stallion perhaps. J.R. Ewing himself, stetson and all, maybe. But no, there was just me. I pressed on, where the right of way led off across a big, open field – then disappeared. The field was prairie-size, one of those where hedgerows and fences have been removed. As I tried to work out which way it was to Walton Grange, a Toyota pick-up unexpectedly appeared directly ahead. It was driven by an old boy. He pulled up, looked questioningly through the open window. I guess a map and compass, held in the hand of a bloke wearing shorts and carrying a large rucksack, told its own tale. I thought I was in for a hostile reception, like 'get off my property', but I was mistaken. Instead he was smiling, looked helpful even.

I asked directions to Walton Grange, according to the map just two miles away. He declared he'd lived here for years but had never heard of it, and said I must be lost. I asked him if I was on the right of way.

He didn't know what I meant. Then he asked me where I was going. John o'Groats, I told him. He nodded knowingly and jerked his thumb over his shoulder and said I should head north. Then he said cheerio, and was off in a cloud of dust.

I should explain. Although I wasn't actually bound for John o'Groats, I had learned that when questioned about my mission, the name Dunnet Head always drew blank looks from enquirers. But it's *near* John O'Groats, so rather than repeatedly explaining the geography of the Scottish coast I'd just say John o'Groats, which made things simpler. Just as well in this case; if this guy hadn't heard of the next farm, I'd have had no chance with Dunnet Head.

The sound of farm machinery droned ahead, out of sight over a low ridge. It sounded like a German tank, reminiscent of those old war films. I crossed the ridge, saw a tractor and hoped its driver wouldn't mind a hiker walking all over his handiwork. I don't think he saw me. After negotiating nearly a mile of ploughed furrows – it's hard work, try it – I mercifully came to a by-road, where I opened the throttle, striding past Walton Grange – see, I wasn't lost – for Gnosall (pron. *Nozall*) after which I passed through the grounds of Ranton Abbey, which I couldn't get near for the 'keep out' notices. I was in marching mode now, bound for Ellenhall. Just before the village it was time for the latest escapade with the canine fraternity. I was getting used to these skirmishes, but this time the aggressor was a pit-bull terrier.

He emerged from an open gateway, and despite the laws of England and Wales wasn't wearing a muzzle. As I prepared to be torn to shreds, his master's voice commanded his return. And, fair do's, he obeyed without so much as a snarl. Just as well. You can't argue with a pit-bull, can you? I'd have been reduced to a mangled heap in minutes, identified only by my police i/d and an old wasp-sting on my forearm. Continuing, I wondered if I should carry a gun in one of those upside-down holsters, Kojak-style, just to bump off hostile dogs – which was all dogs. In fact, I had just about had my fill of dogs. But I shouldn't complain. Imagine meeting up with a lion face to face.

Ellenhall came and went, no more than a blur as I passed through in top gear. Two more miles and I was striding down the hill into Eccleshall, 'a quaint episcopal town' of Georgian houses, guest-houses, pubs, restaurants and hotels. I was weary, footsore and hungry. Enough was enough. It was time to call a halt, to bathe and eat and relax. Alas, Eccleshall had everything for the weary traveller except somewhere to put his head. Eccleshall was full.

I went into the Kings Arms, only to be told the last room had just been let. Nothing to do with me being a 'single', or being a sweat-stained hiker, of course. But the man was helpful. He telephoned a friend who knew someone who had a bed at Croxton, 'a couple of miles up the road'. I checked the map; the couple of miles were 3½, and off-route at that. There was nothing for it but to press on. I was weary, yet I felt fit; my legs were pistons, mechanical, untiring, able to pump away without respite. Those extra miles didn't matter, although I was disappointed not to have the opportunity to explore Eccleshall. Just the same, it was with great relief when, in Croxton, where no street lamps burned, I checked into my lodgings, then kicked off my boots and groped my way to the pub for a well-earned supper.

*

I ate breakfast to the accompaniment of heavy rain lashing against the window. Luckily, by the time I stepped outside, it had stopped, leaving clearing yet uncertain skies, and wet tarmacadam glistening under a million puddles. I splish-splashed my way along country lanes to Standon, where my arrival at All Saint's Church coincided with the appearance of the sun. It beamed brightly on church and churchyard, as though inviting me to explore. So I did.

'Surely the Lord is in this place,' said the sign in the porch. Locked in, presumably, for here was another church barred to the traveller. I explored the churchyard instead, where, on the tall, red sandstone war memorial, the faded names of the war dead, worn almost smooth with time, are reproduced on a more recent slate tablet below. 'Their name liveth for evermore,' it says, and the tablet proves it. Church, churchyard and memorial are quite superb, an unexpected jewel of discovery on my journey.

I came to the 'wooded, park country' of Swynnerton, an estate village, in days long past in the hands of the Swynnerton family but since 1562 the Fitzherberts. There's the 18th century Hall, a fine building of light-coloured stone, which backs on to two churches. In St Mary's, the visitors' book dates back to 13th December, 1953; and there's a 13th century, 7-ft high statue of Christ, in the chapel – sadly locked away to Joe Public. It seems it was probably buried during the Reformation, and unearthed later. So, whilst they saved it for posterity, no-one's allowed to see it. Still, I enjoyed my visit to St

Mary's, which is more than can be said for the nearby Our Lady of the Assumption – locked, of course.

Swynnerton was a treat-in-store, another unexpected discovery, the only intrusion the faint sound of traffic on the distant M6 motorway, gradually increasing as I trod the rights of way across country. Nearing the motorway, the traffic noise took second place to another, familiar sound: it was time for yet another brush with canine warriors, a large, wolf-like creature and a terrier that might have been directly responsible for the expression 'barking mad'. It was as though, in the knowledge that other dogs had had their turn, they were damn-well going to have theirs. So, while the wolf snarled and ran around in ever decreasing circles, the terrier snapped at my heels and tried one or two speculative leaps, pawing at my shirt. If it hadn't been for the wolf I'd have kicked its head in. Oh for that gun!

They followed for a hundred yards or so, then got bored and sloped off. It occurred to me that I might have lured them across the motorway, a pied piper leading dogs instead of children, under the wheels of a passing artic.

I had traversed grand country this morning, but after crossing the M6 I joined the busy A34 trunk road where the Darlaston Inn came into view. Lunch beckoned. The inn was quiet, save for a smattering of business folk, who probably use it as a regular watering hole, and a couple, he in his forties, she a bright-eyed young thing, late twenties. They skulked in a corner, held hands beneath the table, forbidden love simmering across empty plates and half-filled cups of coffee. There was no-one else with a rucksack. I sat in a corner, where old newspaper cuttings adorned the wall. One, dated 24th November, 1939, took my fancy:

"Mr Justice Brown told Miss Ella Rankin, 25, at Belfast City Commission: 'You are as charming and attractive a girl as ever appeared in this dock'.

"Of her employer, who had accused Miss Rankin of stealing £50, the judge said: 'No jury with any brains would believe the evidence of this man. The lowest skunk in Belfast would be ashamed to have contact with him after the evidence he has given'. Miss Rankin was discharged."

Charming and attractive, eh? Did that make her innocent?

I ordered a ploughman's, and occupied myself by covertly observing Darby and Joan. His wife didn't understand, it was obvious. Somehow, they were the antithesis of the honeymooning couple I saw on the little ferry in Cornwall: they were in love, and their love was for the world to witness; whatever Darby and Joan had wasn't for anyone to witness. (Still, let he who is without sin and all that...). Suddenly, he picked up his car keys and they were gone, probably in search of the nearest lay-by. The sole focus of interest thus removed, I turned to the map; it was a fair hike still to Dimmingsdale. Best I got going.

I crossed the Trent and Mersey Canal, built in the 18th century as part of the growing canal system. Josiah Wedgwood, of Wedgwood pottery fame, cut the first sod in 1776. Then, the canals were needed to transport goods; now it's holidaymakers who hire longboats for a week or so. There were none to see today. Perhaps too many choose the summer months. It seemed I had the canal to myself. I had the road to myself, too, or so I thought until a lunatic in a Mini almost wiped me out. Fortunately, a sprightly leap onto the verge as he roared past was sufficient – just – to ensure I went on living. How thin the line of fate: in that moment, I was able to resume my journey as though nothing had happened, or I was a corpse. I carried on, uphill, arriving at an ordnance column in the middle of a huge field, 600 feet above sea level, with grand views of distant fields and woodlands looking further below than they actually were. I never knew you got views like this in Staffordshire. Further on, at Fulford, I called at the village shop for refreshments.

'Going far?' asked the man, curious at the presence of a backpacker. And no wonder; I hadn't seen a single person carrying a rucksack since leaving Knighton.

'John o'Groats,' I replied, as casually as possible.

'You've a fair way yet,' he ventured, also as casually as possible, either unimpressed or indifferent to my undertaking. Or maybe, in casual conversation, he didn't really hear what I'd said in reply to his polite query. He was just going through the ritual of attending to a customer, I suppose. If I'd said, 'mind your own business, you snout-nosed son of a wart hog,' he probably wouldn't have taken the slightest notice.

I route-marched to the top of the map, the 13th of my journey, and I would walk further on it than on any other, for I had entered this map at the bottom left-hand corner and would traverse it diagonally, leaving it at the top right. Small achievements, like moving on to the next map were important. As a matter of fact, I had devised the ingenious idea of posting maps home once I'd done with them, partly to lighten my load, partly to just get rid. I looked forward to posting this one home more than any of the others. For those who walk long distances and copy this idea, just remember who thought of it.

I mentioned Dimmingsdale. I was bound for the youth hostel there, a significant point on my journey, for the Dales were, effectively, the termination of the Shropshire-Staffordshire traverse. Beyond lay Dovedale and the Pennines, the 'backbone of England', my schoolteacher said. As the day wore on, I became increasingly concerned about finding a bed the hostel. What if it was full? I could see nowhere else on the map likely to offer accommodation. My concern grew so much that when I chanced upon a telephone kiosk still four miles from my goal I called the warden and said I'd be there in just over an hour, and was there room for a weary hiker? 'Probably,' she said. Probably! I stepped up a gear then, closing in on country I knew from the map was special, that the green pastures and cornfields would give way to hills and woodlands, deep valleys and rivers. I had targeted the Dales, walked many miles to be there, and never mind the overall south to north direction walking the length of Britain demanded.

I joined the Staffordshire Way, which led through lovely woods to the youth hostel. It's situated in a clearing, Canadian-like in appearance, a great place to wind up a long day's trek. It's a 'simple' grade, the sort usually frequented by walkers and cyclists. My worries about securing a bed were unfounded, the only other occupants being a young couple who gave me a friendly reception, much appreciated after a long day on my own. Youth hostel rules being youth hostel rules, he had to spend the night in the male dorm, of course. Pity about that, I thought, until, after lights-out, he crept quietly out, evidently preferring his sweetheart's company to mine. Fine by me. I just hoped I was in for a quiet night.

*

Beans on toast! Self catering at Dimmingsdale youth hostel meant, at least, a change from the mandatory bacon and eggs. My young friends gathered their belongings and skipped breakfast altogether. They were nice people: polite, friendly, considerate. I was pleased to have their company; without it my night at Dimmingsdale would have been spent utterly alone.

The Dove! I'd never been. Heard about it a thousand times over from walkers everywhere, read about it in books, seen pictures on the telly. Now I would see it for myself, arriving in the best possible way – on foot, from afar, alone.

It was a beautiful morning. No, I lie: a *wonderful* morning, as I rejoined the Staffordshire Way, bound for the River Churnet. When in my life I walked a better half mile I do not know. Many are they who have never experienced the joy that was mine that morn. Everything was perfect: a bright autumn sun, a blue, cloudless sky, a fine path leading through glorious woodland, and birdsong to accompany my every step. What privilege was mine just to be here, to be free to walk here. With deliberate slowness I walked those woods, drank in the moment. It all ended by the still waters of a deep pool, a sylvan setting of peace and utter loveliness. If I die tomorrow, life will have been worthwhile for this hour.

And not a soul seen. This walk, the length of Britain, has its highlights, and it is not possible to place them in order of merit, for they are all different. They depend on circumstance: the time, the weather, the terrain. On another day I might have walked this very path and enjoyed it, yes, but the moment would probably have passed unnoticed. But on this day it was a walk in heaven. Others will walk the path and never know what it was like for me that morning.

And so to the Churnet, where the river runs through a steep-sided, wooded glen. A railway once ran here, and I sought out the course of the old line. But what were those strange noises that echoed from above? The mating cries of some unseen monster, perhaps, or the sound of men at work, quarrying for ore? Wrong on both counts. It was the fun-rides at Alton Towers amusement park, on the hillside above. It all started in 1814, when the 15th Earl of Shrewsbury, impressed with the beauty of Alton and the Churnet Valley, laid out gardens here, and extended an existing lodge in a 'Gothic manner'. Later, his nephew, the 16th Earl, completed the 'folly palace'. Then, in 1924, the whole was sold to a company that had been formed for the sole purpose of saving the gardens for the public. The rest, as they say, is history.

Sadly, after a couple of miles, I had to leave the Churnet behind, forsaking the railway for complicated country lanes and then striking out across country to Ellastone where, with time to spare on a relatively short day, I stopped over at the pub for lunch. The only other occupants were two elderly couples, friends on a day's outing. I kept my own company, but one of the old boys, I could tell, was just dying to know what I was about. As they were leaving the pub, he paused, unable to contain his curiosity any longer. 'Where y'bound?' he asked. 'John o'Groats,' I replied. I should've said Ilam or something, but it just came out. He remarked on the weather before following his companions outside. I watched them through the window. 'That fellow's walkin' Lands End to John o'Groats,' he confided, and faces turned. Well, fancy that! Then they were off on their own walk, to live out the remainder of their lives in the belief that I reached John o'Groats a few days later.

I checked the map. The Dove was close now, only half a mile away. I emerged from the pub to find the sun had disappeared, and the day turned cold. I strode forth for the river and there it was, flowing serenely by, after its journey through the gorge, a few miles upstream. I enjoyed the pastoral delights of the meadows on its banks, complied with the instructions on a home-made notice board: 'Please do not play in the grass'. There are so many signs in our lives, aren't there? Do this. Don't do that. I suppose, in this case, people on the right of way must, on occasion, stray on to the grass close by the path – dads playing footy with their 4-year old sons, perhaps, or little girls running off and falling to the ground in fits of giggles. Tut-tut.

But there were no mums and dads and children. Only cattle and I occupied those quiet meadows, and the former showed no interest in doing anything at all, let alone playing in the grass. I bowled along the riverbank, the Dove a noble companion close by. I looked forward with eager anticipation to the morrow, where I would walk *Dove Dale* proper. Incidentally, the name of the river evidently derives from a Celtic word, meaning 'black', possibly because the Dove flows below shadowy cliffs through Dovedale. Silver might be more appropriate.

I came to Mayfield, where I rested awhile before being driven on by the cold. Was it really this very morning, and not so many miles ago, that I had savoured the joys of the Staffordshire Way? Indeed it was. Fickle autumn! Moving on, I headed through the grounds of Okeover Hall, where I crossed the river into Derbyshire, then, further on, recrossed it back into Staffs. Then I found myself by another river, the Manifold, which I followed to Ilam, a grand village of light grey stone buildings, including the splendid Ilam Hall.

Ilam was bought in the early 19th century by Jesse Watts Russell, a wealthy manufacturer, who had the Hall rebuilt in a Gothic battlement style to keep up with the Jones's of the day, i.e. the Earl of Shrewsbury, who built Alton Towers. He also had an 'Eleanor Cross' erected in the village to commemorate his wife. Was he copying Richard I, I wonder, who, when his wife, Eleanor, died near Lincoln, had her body taken to London, and had an 'Eleanor Cross' erected at every overnight stopping place along the way? Or would Mr Russell have had a Cross erected, no matter what his wife's name? A Maud Cross, perhaps, or an Ada Cross? Anyway, nowadays, the Hall houses a high-grade youth hostel with laundry facilities, so I could wash my clothes. About time too.

5

The Pennines

'Better that the Pennine Way had been given the glorious entry to the hills provided by charming Dovedale,' wrote Alfred Wainwright (instead of Kinder Scout, presumably). Now it was time to go and see if he was right. I walked in warm autumn sunshine under a clear autumn sky. I was fit and good spirits, except my toes were suffering. No matter. I could live with that, and would have to – a 25-mile hike to Buxton was on the agenda today.

By Dovedale, of course, I mean the four glorious miles where the Dove flows through the deep limestone gorge, whose walls reach up to 500 feet above the river. I approached it eagerly, praying not to feel let down, as one sometimes is when something comes recommended. I need not have worried; Dovedale was all it was cracked out to be, and more. The route follows the river, on the Derbyshire side, and trees clothe both sides of the gorge: ash, sycamore and beech. I had expected crowds, even early in the day, yet there was no-one, not a soul. The sun shone on the river, but not on me, for the sun was not yet high enough to reach the path. No matter. This is a theatre of beauty whatever the weather, and I intended to soak in each moment. I walked slowly, for it does not do to hurry by when all is good. At Lin Dale, a secret valley, I encountered a woman. She was standing on the path, looking at her husband on the opposite side of the river, which he'd just crossed by means of stepping-stones. It was a lovely spot, we agreed. A lovely day too. Would they be going on to explore the gorge, I enquired? She shook her head. 'He can't walk far these days,' she said, with more than a hint of sadness, and not taking her eyes off her old man. Then she looked at me with pained resignation.

'Heart attack.'

Says it all, doesn't it? I mean, here I was, fit and free, doing my thing on a wonderful day in a wonderful place; and there was her husband, objective achieved for the day, no doubt. At least he was making the most of it. I moved on, almost feeling guilty about my good fortune, if, as it seemed, my health was good enough to allow me to proceed.

The gorge became even narrower, with tall, limestone pillars of harder rock left exposed by erosion of softer rocks, a simple geological process over time. They stood phallic-like against a backdrop of green and blue, the ever-present river in between, its bubbling surface glistening in the sun – an artist's paradise without an artist. Where were they on such a morning in such a place, with their canvas and paints? Photographers, too, where were they? They would turn up later in the day, probably, when the light would be different, when people would be wandering aimlessly. Such wasted opportunity!

The path runs below Lover's Leap, where, it is said, a young woman who, 'for unrequited love', threw herself from the cliff above, yet survived, her fall broken by the undergrowth below. Further on I passed by Dove Holes, two enormous caverns formed as a result of erosion. Hereabouts I rested, and encountered the second person of the day, a skinhead bloke wearing black boots. I'd noticed him the previous evening at Ilam youth hostel. Typical yob, I'd concluded at the time, and here he was again, in Dovedale. He passed me by with a polite greeting and a smile, proving you should never judge anyone by appearance. By the time I reached Milldale, the woman I'd seen earlier and Skinhead were the only two people seen in three miles' walking through the gorge.

Milldale is a tiny hamlet, a smattering of buildings of light grey stone that blend perfectly against the backdrop of green fields behind. There's an old packhorse bridge, Viator's Bridge, referred to in Izaak Walton's *The Compleat Angler*, (1676 edition). Walton was a writer, Staffordshire born, a man who loved fishing. His book contains descriptions of fishes, rivers, ponds, rods and reels, idyllic glimpses of country life and even dialogue. He must have loved Dovedale to write so. Milldale has a 'touristy' feel, but no matter; it's a gem, along with its bridge. I met up again with Skinhead, and we joined forces for tea and Eccles cakes in the little café. Café, bridge, gorge: we had them all to ourselves. Lucky us, we agreed, before he set off for Ilam, whilst I continued north. Dovedale had lived up to its reputation; Wolfscote Dale, with no reputation I'd heard of, was next. It turned out to be similar to Dovedale, except the valley opens out a bit and the trees are fewer. Whilst it may be second in beauty to its neighbour, Wolfscote Dale is lovely nonetheless, and worthy of a visit in its own right. And, in Wolfscote Dale, I came upon people. About thirty, all in all, in small groups, and twos and threes. Everyone had a 'hello' or 'lovely day', along with a smile to match their mood. So I smiled and said 'hello' and 'lovely day' times thirty. Strangely, everyone I saw was heading in the opposite direction to me, an exodus from some unknown place ahead. I was marching apace now; I had lingered in Dovedale, idled my time with Skinhead, but there was many a mile still to Buxton.

Marching mode ended in Beresford Dale, where a path led uphill and over superb limestone country to Hartington, a fine stone village. I had lunch in a pub, before moving on again along a gated country road. Here, the Dove occupies a wide valley, where the river is bordered by rough pasture. Higher up the valley, the road turns away, and the right of way continues to the ruined motte and bailey of what was Pilsbury Castle, recorded in the Domesday Book as *Pilesburie*. This is wild country, and it's easy to imagine the scene all those years before when the castle guarded the upper reaches of the valley.

I pressed on, joining a quiet road that led steeply away from the river to Earl Sterndale. The pub in the village is The Quiet Woman, whose sign shows a picture of a woman who would be quiet because she doesn't have a head. She was 'Chattering Charteris', who evidently made her husband's life a misery by continually scolding him. He might have been able to live with that – as many husbands do

(I'm told) – but when she began to talk in her sleep too he chopped her head off. That would be enough to stop anyone chattering. The locals must've had more than their fair share of her, for they bought a headstone for her grave, which was inscribed with a suitable warning to chatterboxes. I wish I knew where it was.

Four more miles to Buxton. I marched forth, full speed, eager to secure a bunk in the youth hostel, and to shower and relax. Youth hostels usually open at five o'clock; I made the front door at three minutes to, third in line behind a smiling young lass and an old boy, the latter cycling from Lands End to John o'Groats. We chatted, as you do, until, at five on the nail, the warden opened the door and, after admitting the others, proclaimed the hostel full.

Full? What, even for the man who'd just tramped 25-miles? Yes, full, he said, indicating the cars in the car park. Ah, full of people who'd booked in advance and had come by car. That sort of full. Why didn't I book in advance, you may ask? Because I had long lived in the belief that no matter what, there's always room in a youth hostel for the backpacker, who more than anyone needs a bed. Other wardens keep a spare bed or two for those who travel on foot, who can never be certain how far they will get, or even which route they might take. But not the warden at Buxton, now giving me a 'well-you-might-as-well-bugger-off' look. I wondered, though, if he might still prove to be of some use to a weary walker: could he recommend alternative accommodation? He could, he said, whereupon, being the helpful chap he was he told me where I could locate the town's bed and breakfasts, pointing out cheerfully that it was a conference weekend and that everywhere was 'pretty-well full'. Resisting the temptation to insert my youth hostel membership card into his throat (sideways), I picked up my sack and headed into town, resolving that in my next life on this planet I will become a warden at a youth hostel and I will spend my days looking out for this sod, and if he ever turns up for a bed there won't be one, so there.

In the street of a thousand guesthouses I tried every one, being turned away on the basis that (a) I was a 'single', (b) I was a sweaty hiker, (c) it was full, or (d) a combination of two or more of these. But I *had* to find somewhere, and when the woman at the last chance saloon looked me up and down and declared there'd be a supplement to pay but I could have a twin room to myself, I was in. Don't think for a moment she took pity on me; it was getting late and it was either me or the room would stay empty. Just the same, if my feet could have spoken they'd have thanked her.

Having thus secured a bed, I went out for a look around Buxton. It's a fine, bustling town, England's highest. Later, after well-earned pint, I treated myself to a Chinese meal, then called it a night. I was tempted to return to the youth hostel to sort the warden, but I'd forgotten where it was exactly. Just as well, I suppose.

*

As I shovelled the last of the inevitable bacon and eggs into the eager hole in my face, I looked yet again at the woman who sat in the far corner of the dining room. I'd barely been able to take my eyes off her all through breakfast, and even now, with only the toast and marmalade to go, I was transfixed.

It was her specs. Truly, they were the biggest I had ever seen. They were ice-blue, made from a plastic material and covered, literally, the whole of the upper part of her face. They were intended, no doubt, to appear chic, but they did not help her appearance in the slightest. They were the 'bottle-end' variety, so that where her jaw, nose and upper forehead were of natural proportions, her eyes and cheeks were magnified to such an extent she took on the appearance of a grotesque alien just landed on planet earth and now taking breakfast in Buxton. Hammer Films would have signed her up then and there.

Buxton is a place to linger. That was my conclusion the next morning as I prepared to do the opposite. They say the Druids settled here, and the Romans certainly did. The attraction was – and is – the water, which emerges from deep within the earth. The Romans called their town Aquae Arnemetiae.

Spa water, or thermal water, is defined as 'waters at the point of emergence having the same or a greater temperature than the mean average for the surrounding air', although whether the Druids or the Romans actually thought of it that way is doubtful. Anyway, by the Middle Ages, Buxton, thanks to its spa water, had become a sort of Lourdes of Derbyshire, where invalids came to seek healing. Included among them was Mary, Queen of Scots, who, as a prisoner, sought a cure for her rheumatism, and reputedly scratched an appropriate message on a window at the Old Hall:

Buxtona Quae Calidae Celebraris Nomine Lymphae
Forte Mihi Poste Hac Non Adeunda Vale.

Which, translated, means

> Buxton, whose fame thy milk-warm waters tell
> Whom I, perhaps, no more shall see... farewell

I guess she knew what fate had in store.

Buxton still has its water. It flows from St Anne's Well at a constant temperature of 82 degrees Fahrenheit (that's 28 degrees Celsius for anyone under 35). You can buy it at Sainsbury's and Tesco's, still or sparkling, as the labels say.

The road out of town, appropriately named Long Hill, was a long, uphill pull which, with ever-improving fitness and in glorious sunshine, I scarcely even noticed. It led to a lane running along the top of a high ridge above deep valleys, absolutely super country. Here was freedom. I could see for miles across the dales, a sweeping panorama of green and purple. A fresh breeze blew gently into my face, and all was good with me that morning. How could it have been otherwise? Even my feet were improving. I was bound for Glossop, beyond which, not too far away, lay my next objective: the high Pennines. Or, if you will, the Pennine Way. Identifying objectives had become an established routine: just as Plymouth had been at the start, just as Dovedale had been more recently. But the Pennines also instilled feelings of progress. I'd started my journey at Lizard; soon the Backbone of England would be joined.

I breasted a hill, roared down the other side to a little village called Comb. It isn't always possible to anticipate what a place will be like. Checking the map, I saw that Comb was on a quiet crossroads, close to a railway line. Maybe it would be pretty, maybe not. In the sunshine of this autumn morn, Comb turned out to be picture postcard material, where trees cast their shadows onto an empty road, where birds sang and there was no-one save the solitary hiker. I was thirsty, but the inn, clearly marked on the map, was closed. Well, there was a change. Never mind, further on, at a place rejoicing in the name of Cockyard, there was another one that was open. I gorged myself with crisps and lemonade. This was the life!

Moving on, I chanced upon two young women by the side of the road. They were five minutes' walking time apart, and I experienced totally different reactions to their encounter with a single male in the middle of nowhere.

As number one approached I gave her a cheery 'hi' and a friendly, even exaggerated smile, both in keeping with my mood and, perhaps subconsciously, to reassure her that the stranger was OK. The reaction: exactly the same – a cheery 'hi' and a friendly smile (her smile might have been a tad prettier than mine). Five minutes later, number two. Cheery 'hi' and a friendly smile. The reaction: a steely glare and silence. Why? Was she acquainted with number one, and if so had they had a tiff of some kind and was she in a strop? Or did she consider the stranger could not be trusted? I felt offended, yet there was nothing I could do. I couldn't chase after her and demand she smile and say 'hi'; once we'd passed one another by we were history. Sad, isn't it?

I continued north, on to the sixteenth map of my journey, one with familiar names: Edale, Kinder Scout, Featherbed Moss, Longdendale, Black Hill, White Moss. Pennine Wayfarers, eat your hearts out! I walked the Pennine Way in 1986, after a long, wet winter. The millstone grit boglands of those first 2-3 days I will never forget – quagmires of naked, black, filthy peat. In a couple of days I would again join the Way, but this time I would cheerfully omit the horrors of the Dark Peak, as it is, and join it further on at Standedge. Not that it guaranteed missing out the bog altogether, but I saw no point in wallowing needlessly in black ooze.

The best of the day's walking was behind me now, as main roads and, here and there, unmetalled byways, led to Hayfield, a sizeable village astride the A624. Clear in view above the village you can see the high moors, miles of coarse grasses and peat-hags where once, long ago, anyone who fancied could wander at will. But when a few men made their fortunes, thanks to the industrial revolution, and turned grouse-shooting into their exclusive pastime, they claimed the moors for themselves, and the commoner found himself barred, his freedom to roam taken away. Here, at Hayfield, in the 1930's, came the acts of 'mass trespass', and the fight for the right to roam. 'The vast population, confined to their slag heaps,' proclaimed the Ramblers' Handbook in 1924. In other words, people were denied the right to walk when they, more than anyone, and certainly more than rich landowners who wanted to shoot birds for sport, needed the fresh air.

The Ramblers' Handbook had more to say on the subject, notably about a fellow ironically named Walker:

"The champion of anti-access is Mr Henry Walker, to whom all things of the town are an anathema. His cunning argument is that the rare wild life of the moors is the priceless treasure of those who have spent thousands of pounds in purchase, fencing, cultivation of heather and enhancing the beauty of the moors, and maintaining the many species of wild bird life there which would otherwise be non-existent. The truth is there is not room in these islands for two such interests as private preserves and reasonable public enjoyment of mountains and moorland. The sporting 'fans' will not yield one iota of their unscrupulously obtained 'rights' ".

In other words, Joe Public was barred from the moors, where the rich man took his pleasure. But things changed in April, 1932, when one Bernard Rothman, a mechanic, organised a party of 600-800 ramblers and set off from Hayfield to climb Kinder Scout. Despite being attacked by gamekeepers wielding sticks, they achieved their objective, and in full view of the police – who were present in numbers – Joe Public walked on terrain where he had not walked for a hundred years.

It seemed the ramblers had support from no less a personage than Ramsey Macdonald, the first Labour Prime Minister, who declared himself 'committed' to their cause – then failed to provide facilities to discuss a bill for rights of access. Typical politician: populist statement, followed by no action! But with or without Macdonald, Joe Public was on a winner, for the ramblers realised that if they turned up in sufficient numbers the landowners could not stop them all. The *Manchester Evening News* was only too happy to publish a warning of a planned 'mass trespass', and leaflets were distributed, with the message: 'it is a crime for workers to put their feet where Lord Big Bug and Little Lady Flea do their annual shooting'.

The police were waiting, some even hiding in a local cinema at Hayfield. Undaunted, the ramblers stormed the hillside, and what a sight it must have been, with out-of-condition bobbies huffing and puffing up the steep slopes trying to catch them. (It would be the same today). The ramblers were attacked by gamekeepers wielding sticks, but offered no violence in return. Some were arrested and sent to prison – the ramblers, not the gamekeepers – but more mass trespass followed and today we can walk on Kinder Scout.

I was eager to reach Glossop, and decided to take the main road. This was a mistake: first, rights of way are always to be preferred, and second, the next hour of my journey was a nightmare. The A624 crosses high ground, and has many twists and turns. But its worst feature, for anyone walking it anyway, is its narrowness, with drystone walls encroaching right up the edge of the carriageway. As the road climbed and wound its tortuous way northward, I was obliged to squeeze close up to the wall, and even turn my feet sideways to prevent them being squashed under the wheels of cars and coaches as they thundered by. As vehicles approached, unseen, from behind, many had to give way if, as was often the case, something was approaching from the front. I could hear their engines ticking over behind me, imagined irritated drivers tapping their steering wheels, their progress barred by the hiker, and irritated further still perhaps by their kids, asking how long till they got to grannies? Motor vehicles are the hiker's worst enemy, or, rather, their drivers are. Give me wasps, recalcitrant schoolchildren and swaying suspension bridges any day.

Mercifully, a wide grass verge appeared and with relief I stepped from tarmacadam. Still on high ground, I spied a big lay-by, complete with mobile café, and went over for a well-earned cuppa. A gusty wind now blew from the west, and I somehow held on to the hot, paper cup without burning my fingers – as you do – and sheltered under the flimsy canopy of the cafe from the wind. Rain looked certain. Yet, far from finding my spirits dulled at the prospect, instead they were lifted, for the imminent storm somehow belonged, as though synonymous with the town with a name like Glossop. 'Dark' and 'Satanic'. Never were better adjectives contrived.

The man in the mobile café said I'd find accommodation at the Commercial Inn. 'It's just at the bottom of the hill,' he explained, as though a five-minute stroll would find me at the door. In fact, it was a long half an hour, downhill all the way, with the grey buildings of Glossop nestling in the valley, cowering in expectation of the gathering storm. I sang every step of that hill. It's easy to sing walking downhill, and I often do, at the top of my voice (especially in a gale when no-one can hear). When I saw the Commercial Inn I didn't fancy it, and continued into town where I didn't fancy anywhere else, so finished up at the Commercial Inn again, thus adding an extra two miles to the day's walking. If only my feet could have spoken!

Luckily, the rain held off until I was indoors, then the heavens opened with a vengeance. At least I was spared a soaking.

There was nothing wrong with the Commercial Inn anyway (later The Whitely Nab). I was given a warm reception, there was a t.v. in my bedroom, and I had an excellent meal with excellent beer which I drank to the sound of Derbyshire accents in the company of the barmaid and a woman customer, both of whom were dolled up to the nines and clearly intent on clubbing the night away somewhere, though whether this would actually be in Glossop seemed doubtful. Another woman, whom I might chivalrously describe as mature, also dressed to the nines but with an extra ton of eye-shadow applied for good measure, kept eyeing me up, possibly wondering who I was, possibly wondering if there was any chance of a liaison. She did look a bit desperate. Alas, after my meal, I wasn't fit for anything except climbing the stairs to my room, and even that was a struggle.

*

One of the great things about 'bed and breakfast', at least for anyone out walking, is the smell of bacon and eggs as you make your way downstairs for your 'full English'. Consequently, the smell of a sizzling fry-up was music to my nose on the stairs of the Commercial Inn on a Sunday morning where, outside, the streets were damp after the overnight storm, and the sky was Glossop-grey. Sadly, the reception by the nice lady with the frying pan was not quite what I expected. The look of surprise in her face said it all as I entered the room, where a middle-aged couple sat scoffing their brekkies.

'I wasn't told there was anyone else,' she said apologetically, as though not being informed of the unexpected guest was her fault.

'Well, I'm definitely here,' I replied with a smile exclusively designed to win her favour, or, to put it another way, to ensure she did me a fry-up too.

I needn't have worried. Emilia assured me breakfast was coming up. It would take a little while, but no matter. Although I had to cross high moors today, there was ample time to reach Globe Farm, and anyway I felt like taking it easy for a change. In fact, I'd pop out for a Sunday newspaper, a simple chore, you might think, except the nearest newsagents was in town and once again I found myself walking the streets of Glossop. I was certainly getting to know my way around. Back at the Commercial Inn, Emilia was serving up breakfast. I was in for a treat. No, not the food, perfect though that was. The treat was Emilia.

She was thirty-ish, pretty, an unexpected surprise at the start of what I knew would be a lonesome day. She lived in the town, and worked part-time at the pub. On a journey of changing accents, where I might have expected hers to be Derbyshire, instead I could discern a foreign tone, although I could not quite identify it. Just as I was about to embark upon a round-the-world guessing tour of accents, she put me out of my misery: Emilia is from Brazil.

A Brazilian in Glossop! Images of near-naked lovelies in thongs, dancing the Samba on white, sandy beaches, didn't seem to belong to grey-walled factories, satanic skies and heavy lorries clattering past the Commercial Inn.

'Sorry I can't speak Portugese,' I said. Not very original, I know, but it won me brownie-points anyway. 'You must be the first person I have met in England who knows my language,' said Emilia. I knew what she meant: many people think Brazilians speak Spanish.

Naturally, Emilia wanted to know what I was doing, and seemed strangely surprised when I told her. 'What are the moors?' she asked, a remarkable question from someone living in Glossop, I thought. When I told her she could see the moors from anywhere in town she realised what I meant, and expressed astonishment that I could consider venturing into such territory. Coming from the land of sun, sea and the Samba I could hardly blame her. More than anyone, Emilia seemed genuinely interested in my venture. We left the Commercial Inn together, shook hands and said goodbye. How nice it would be to start every day with an Emilia, I thought. Fry-up was perfect, too.

For the third time, I walked to Glossop town centre. Having walked so many of its streets in my short stay, a word about the town wouldn't go amiss. First, the name means 'Glot's Valley', although I haven't a clue who Glot actually was. A Saxon king, I shouldn't wonder. Glossop was a prosperous cotton town once, but the mills closed in the 1930's. Today, Glossop is grey and gaunt, a ghost of its former self, a living museum where the only thing missing is the opportunity to step back in time to its heyday, to see the workers heading for the mills for their day's toil for little money – people, including women and children, born into poverty.

From *The Factory Child*:

My mother, O my mother, is not my labour o'er?
My head is weak and giddy, my hands can work no more:
'Tis finished now, and I may rest – O mother may I not?"
Alas she could but turn away, and mourn her infant's lot.
'I cannot help thee, hapless boy,' thus bitterly she said,
' 'Twere better you had ne'er been born; far best that you were dead'.

The good old days, eh? I had calculated that Glossop was around the halfway point of my journey, that beyond Glossop I was on the 'home straight'. In a sense this cheered me, yet it was reminder that all things must come to an end. I pressed on; there was still a long way to go (especially as Glossop isn't halfway at all!).

It was a cold morn, to be sure. I wore shorts, as I had done all the way from Knighton. But with the prospect of high ground ahead, if it was cold in town I reckoned I might be perishing on the 'tops', so I went into the gents where I changed into breeches. Then, climbing the hill out of town, the rain came, so on went the cag and leggings too. It was the sort of Sunday morning where you just want to sit in front of a fire and read your Sunday newspaper. Well, I had my newspaper, but it was in my sack where it had to stay.

The map told its own story. Ahead lay a few scattered villages, a reservoir or two then the high moors, topped by a place named on the map as, simply, 'Wilderness', along with the Derbyshire-Greater Manchester county boundary. Or Lancashire, as I prefer (as do its citizens, I suspect). As I turned for Padfield, I glanced up at Bleaklow, now brooding under thick cloud. Below, youngsters played football, watched by eager parents, dads shouting encouragement – if 'pass t'bloody ball, y'silly bugger' can be deemed so. Typical Sunday, could've been anywhere. After Padfield came Hadfield, a postman's nightmare, I would have thought, places so close together with such similar names. At Tintwistle, I sat on a wall and rested awhile.

And there they were, your Sunday morning slouches, pulling up in their cars at the newsagents for their Sunday papers. Not for them a walk of three hundred yards for their *News of the World*. They were all at it: getting out of the car and slamming the door, into the shop, out of the shop, into the car and slamming the door and home. There were so many they could hardly find room to park. One or two looked at me, probably pitied the hiker on such a morning. But I pitied them, and held my head high as I crossed the A57 and headed for rising ground and darkening skies directly ahead.

I crossed the Ogden Brook into Lancashire. A good path led uphill – and, thanks to lots of twists and turns, back into Derbyshire again. It was wild country now: open moors, lonely streams, the cries of unseen birds. I reached the watershed, the aforementioned Wilderness, where I again crossed into Lancashire. Over these three miles of ascent I saw one person, a local chap I supposed. I wondered if he might be calling at the newsagents.

I had entered the Peak District National Park, England's first. It was officially designated in December, 1950. Much of it is desolate country, 'an unspoilt oasis in a desert of industrialisation'. It is estimated that up to half of the population of England live within 50 miles of the Peak, a quite remarkable statistic. There are two distinct areas: the Dark Peak and the White Peak.

The Dark Peak is the land of the bogs I mentioned, where the millstone grit lies sixty feet deep, and where 'edges' run along the perimeter of the high plateaux. Here are rocky tors, heather and cotton grass; here is the haunt of the red grouse and the curlew. On the higher ground are the dreaded bogs and mosses, and deep, black trenches known as 'cloughs'. In the main it is untouched by man, save for numerous reservoirs – the water companies have taken over from the privileged landowners – and, in places, shooting butts, where people with guns hide in the in their quest to shoot birds from the sky. The White Peak, to the north, is altogether gentler country: rolling grasslands split by dramatic valleys, with surrounding hills around 1,000 feet high.

The Wilderness is a good place to get the feel of the Dark Peak, and never was a place more aptly named; there is nought here but grasses and black, oozy peat – the *Peat* District, if you like. Hereabouts, by way of a change, there were people, around twenty or so, a ramblers' outing by the look of it. They wore brightly-coloured cagoules and gaiters, and huddled in groups, peering at maps. They all smiled for the lone hiker. I said 'hello' twenty times and left them in the Wilderness, heading for Chew Reservoir from where the trail would lead down to the next valley. Here, atop the watershed, a fresh wind blew into my face and a feeling of fitness was about me. I felt good in the Wilderness.

Two miles of steep descent led to Dove Stone Reservoir. It turned out, surprisingly, to be a sort of picnic site, complete with ice cream

"The Wilderness" Cp 2001

and trannie music and families out for a walk. I rested here, in the shadow of Saddleworth Moor, where the so-called Moors Murderers buried their poor victims. Then I crossed the A635 for Uppermill where, just before the church, the wind moaned, scattering autumn's fallen leaves across the road. It reminded me of my childhood when Miss Stevenson, our schoolteacher, took her class on a Nature Trail. It was a short walk from the school, but I've always remembered the wind blowing in the hedgerow, as the procession of thirty or so children marched dutifully behind their teacher. I rested here, by the Church Inn, a four-storey building that might have been a mill once. The huge, dark grey stone-built church completed a picture unchanged for generations.

Ahead now were scattered houses and fields, quarries and narrow lanes, spread out below in a deep valley, with high ground rising on the opposite side in uncertain greyness. 'Drab' is the adjective most suitable to describe the scene. I took to the lanes, and once again the rain came as I climbed up to the A62. I saw no-one on this two-mile traverse. I might have been the last person left on the planet.

You'd never know it, but directly below the A62 are three parallel tunnels. Through tunnel one runs the Huddersfield Narrow Canal, at nearly 3¼ miles the longest canal tunnel in the country – it took 17 years to build and was opened in 1811. Tunnel two houses a single-track railway, and tunnel three a double track railway (Leeds-Manchester line). If you're wondering why they didn't put the road in a tunnel too, the answer is obvious: cars and lorries and coaches can climb hills, longboats cannot, and trains can only climb long gradients. Just thought I'd mention it. I know people who don't even know why canals have locks.

Globe Farm bunkhouse, as many a Pennine Wayfarer will tell you, is the only accommodation for miles around. I stayed here when I walked the Way in 1986, when I had to wash all my clothes after slithering waist-deep into the mire on the slopes of Black Hill (after washing them the previous night at Crowden youth hostel, having sank thigh deep on Featherbed Moss). If I'd had a long, lonely day, I was in for a long, lonely night, as I was the sole occupant at Globe Farm this time around. I was welcomed as a long lost friend, then left to my own devices, and contented myself by reading my newspaper – I'd carried it far enough – and looking out of the window at the twinkling lights of Diggle, far below. How snug it felt, on a beast of a night, as the wind howled and the rain lashed against the window. It was cold in the bunkhouse, not least because of the considerable drafts, so I turned in early, in the knowledge that, as the sole occupant, I would enjoy uninterrupted sleep in my cosy nest.

Like hell! As dreamy thoughts drifted through my sleepy brain, possibly of a Brazilian lady, I was brought sharply back to life by the sudden clatter of the fire alarm bell, which, for reasons best known to itself, went off in my earhole. Being a man of action, I fled dutifully for the door, which I reached in total darkness and in safety, a not inconsiderable feat. Standing naked at the side of the A62, in driving rain and a cold wind – for Diggle, read perishing – I looked for the flames which would envelope the bunkhouse, and when there were none I went inside where I dressed in the unceasing din. When I knocked at mine host's door it was opened by a young lass in her nightie who smiled knowingly and said her parents, who were the only people on the planet who knew how to turn the alarm off, were out for the evening, but never mind they'd be home soon. So I repaired to the bunkhouse, where, mercifully, I'd not long to wait before normal service was resumed, to wit, silence, total and absolute.

Now, where was I? Oh, yes, that Brazilian lady. In my dreams...

*

The Pennine Way, the first 'official' long distance footpath in this country, was the inspiration of Tom Stephenson, a former Secretary of the Ramblers' Association, who, in a newspaper article in 1935, suggested a 'Pennine Way'. Three years later the Pennine Way Association was formed. It was agreed that 'the wide, health-giving moorlands and high places of solitude, the features of natural beauty and the places of historical interest along the Pennine Way give this route a special character which should be available for all time as a natural heritage of the youth of the country, and of all who feel the call of the hills and lonely places'.

There were many obstacles to overcome to create the Way, not least the reluctance of landowners who didn't want anyone walking across their property, a not unreasonable standpoint, except there are very few landowners and lots of people who would just like a little space to go for a walk. Fortunately, reason prevailed, and after unforeseen delay, thanks to the war, the authority to walk this or that footpath was ultimately secured and the Pennine Way was declared open at a ceremony on Malham Moor in 1965 (except the short section encroaching into Scotland, opened in 1977). Despite his achievement, Stephenson expressly wished that no monument should be erected to his memory, and there is none. That's a pity: thousands of hard-working people have enjoyed walking the Pennine Way, or parts of it, and there would be many who'd like to pay their respects to someone who worked so hard on their account.

That said, it isn't really a 'Pennine Way' at all. As Alfred Wainwright observes in his *Pennine Way Companion,* it's a 'Pennine and Cheviot Way' i.e. it traverses most but not all of the Pennine range – the so-called backbone of England – and part of the Cheviot Hills, on the England-Scotland border. As Wainwright points out, a truer Pennine Way might have started at Dovedale and ended, say, at the Roman wall, in Northumberland. As it is, it runs, south to north, from Edale, Derbyshire, to Kirk Yetholm, in the Borders Region, Scotland, a distance of 270 miles.

I walked the Pennine Way after a long, wet winter, when the peat bog country of the Dark Peak, Great Shunner Fell in Yorkshire and the Cheviots, were filthy, black swamps. Yet those who have walked the Way in late summer have encountered dry, almost dusty conditions. One thing is certain: after years of walking by determined Wayfarers, large sections of the Way have been seriously eroded, this being a major problem with long distance routes, where one and all place their size ten Zamberlans in the same place, day in, day out. Just as it had been on the coast path in Cornwall. Today, my walk the length of Britain would take me onto the Pennine Way. But because I wasn't actually 'walking the Way', I considered myself free to leave it and rejoin it anywhere I chose. Nevertheless, I intended to follow its general course, on and off, as far as Byrness, in Northumberland, after which I would leave it and continue north into the border country of Scotland.

Breakfast at Globe Farm was one of those awkward situations where the man alone sits with others, in this case a couple in their late fifties. (They had stayed in the B and B part of Globe farm, not the bunkhouse, thus missing out on the fun and games with the fire alarm). I say awkward because whilst neither party might give a damn about the other, just the same you feel you have to say *something*. That is, after 'Stormy night, wasn't it?' and, in this case, 'Are you walking the Pennine Way?' the latter asked in such a manner that it is presumed you are and if you aren't what the hell are you doing in a godforsaken place like this? But the man on the other side of the cornflakes caught me cold.

'Could you tell me the way to York?' he asked, as though the location of a city on the opposite side of the Pennines which I'd visited just once before in my life when I was fourteen could possibly have anything to do with my visit to Globe Farm. Still, instead of saying 'No', I did my best to be of assistance. 'Head east, into Yorkshire,' I said, stressing the first half of the name – *York*, upon which he and his lady wife nodded slowly, the penny having dropped that that the county of that name was where a city with the name of York must be. Only later did I realise that I failed to point out that Yorkshire is, in fact, three counties – North, South and West – and I had omitted to tell them the name of the one with York in it. They probably ended up in Bradford.

After more stimulating conversation, and having been informed by mine host that a woman Wayfarer doing the route north to south was due at Globe Farm this eve, I took my leave – making a mental note that it would be a treat to meet a woman, even if she was going in the opposite direction. I headed for the Pennine Way, and soon I was standing at the Ammon Wrigley memorial, a huge rock to which are affixed several plaques, one of which bears the following inscription:

> Winds of the Pennines fresh and free,
> You were ever good friends to me.
> Out on the moors from morn 'til eve,
> Happy with you and loth to leave.

Those words, surely, speak for someone who truly loved these hills. I remembered Wrigley's poem from my first visit here. It's one of my favourites.

Despite the 'fresh and free' winds of the Pennines, dank mist was clinging to the ridge as far as the eye could see – which wasn't very far, admittedly. But the ground was firm, the path well cairned and the walking easy in this world of solitude. I headed for a place called Northern Rotcher, where I was determined to get my navigation right, for here the path makes a marked turn to the right, a detail I had failed to notice in 1986 when I continued straight on to find myself lost in a labyrinth of fields and strange grassy hollows. It's easy to miss things when you're bowling along merrily, lost in your own world of contentment. This time, at Northern Rotcher, despite the murky conditions, I got it right, and followed the line of cairns. That's why they put 'em there!

Suddenly, out of the gloom, appeared one of the trans-Pennine roads, the A640. One or two vehicles sped past, emerging from the mist like strange, beady-eyed creatures from a Dracula movie. Strangely, there was no sound in their passing, so they must have been farther off than it appeared. Their drivers were travelling too fast for the conditions, in my view – the only view I had of anything. Maybe they were looking for a multi-pile up. Once across the road, traces of civilisation disappeared promptly, except that unexpectedly I came across two fellows with backpacks, Pennine Wayfarers for certain. They were taking a rest by a rocky outcrop. We acknowledged each other as I passed them by, but I knew I'd see them again sooner or later. That's what happens on long distance walks; you pass and re-pass, just like cars on the motorway.

Indeed, a motorway, the M62, was my next objective. It traverses the Pennines and cuts right across the Pennine Way footpath. Fortunately, being an 'official' long distance route, they had to build a footbridge especially for the likes of me. You *must* ensure correct navigation, for to miss the bridge would mean having to run the gauntlet of motorway traffic, where you'd have as much chance as a deaf hedgehog wearing a blindfold. Of great assistance in locating the bridge is a tall wireless mast which stands close by, or it would be if you could see it, which, in ever-thickening pea-soup I could not. Just the same I was relieved to see the mast, or pylon if you will, rising so high the top was lost in the fog. Motorway crossed, I could look forward to my next objective, Redmires.

Redmires, as any Pennine Wayfarer who has had to negotiate this special piece of England after a wet winter would tell you, is a ghastly, black quagmire of naked peat. You don't walk through this sort of terrain: you *plodge* (a Geordie word). There's a song that might have been especially written about Redmires and the other ghastly swamps hereabouts. You know the one: 'You put your left foot in, your left foot out, in-out-in-out and shake it all about'. Hoaky-Coaky! And there it was, a black, evil sludge. But wait! What was this? A *footpath*! Across Redmires? Indeed it was. Rough concrete, just thrown down, a firm base nevertheless, on which to walk dryshod. Redmires is a doddle now.

I pressed on for Blackstone Edge, a high, rocky escarpment affording extensive views to the north, where Stoodley Pike monument can be seen in the distance, and the town of Littleborough below. When it isn't misty, that is. But the mist was set to stay, it was obvious, a lurking presence among the peat hags creating an eerie, almost surreal atmosphere. If there's a hell on earth, it's right here. But there were no problems: I just followed the cairns, traversing Blackstone Edge, with the unseen Stoodley Pike in the distance. Here, the Way crosses a cobbled road, possibly Roman in origin but more likely an 18th century packhorse route. The ground is so gooey they had to construct a firm, cobbled base. It was either that or beasts of burden sinking without trace into the mire. The old road is wide, with a central drainage channel and is in excellent condition. It's rather wide for packhorses, unless there were hoses pulling carts too. Or chariots...

Suddenly, I encountered the woman I mentioned, an apparition dressed in glistening waterproofs, her hair lank from the clammy mist. She was late fifties, and she had walked here, alone, from Scotland. It had to be her, there could be no-one else, not here, not today. When she saw me her smile said it all. As I suspected, I was the only person she'd seen since breakfast. Not for her the concern of the woman alone, meeting the stranger in the middle of nowhere. She was walking the Pennine Way, and as far as she was concerned so was I. Nothing else mattered. We chatted awhile, during which she admitted some concern about navigation, understandably in the circumstances. Still, she'd got this far, she'd be okay. She confirmed she was staying at Globe Farm. I told her she'd probably not see anyone there either, adding she could sleep sound in her bed knowing she wouldn't burn to death. Then we parted, ships in the night, strangers who met briefly in hell. In fact, she and the two fellows I mentioned were to be the only other people I would encounter on the entire Pennine Way, at least the sections I would walk it this time around. Who says it's crowded?

At the Halifax road, light drizzle was falling as I made a beeline for The White House, an isolated pub, with the still unseen Stoodley Pike in the distance. Time for coffee and a sandwich providing, considering my appearance, they let me in. Despite the nice new concrete path, I was a bit of a peaty mess. In fact, I thought I might change my name to Pete; it seemed appropriate. Anyway, I was allowed to take refreshment in peace. Emerging, the next three miles led past a series of huge reservoirs, with the even this close unseen Stoodley Pike in the distance. The reservoirs were originally constructed as feeders for the canal system, but they're the property of the water companies now. I was astonished to find them almost empty of water where before they had brimmed full. At the side of one was a sign: *No Swimming*, despite the entire area being no more than grey, slimy ooze. At the exotically-named Warland Drain, a concrete waterway, I came upon another sign, a sort of home-made one: *Bus Stop*, it said. Someone with a fantastic sense of humour was here before me. Either that or buses hereabouts run on caterpillar tracks:

'Return to Redmires, please.'

'You can only get a single to Redmires.'

'Oh? And why is that, pray?'

'Because from Redmires there can be no return.'

Somewhere ahead, about five feet, according to the map, was the incredible-as-though-it-may-seem-unseen Stoodley Pike. You can't miss it. It stands on top of the ridge, and is 120 feet high. I kept straining to see what, after all, is a massive obelisk. I almost walked into it, this giant Cleopatra's Needle in the middle of nowhere. I huddled at the entrance, seeking respite from the rain. It wasn't very cosy, especially as the entrance faced the direction of the prevailing wind (who the hell designed this place?). A dark staircase leads up to a balcony, but I didn't bother climbing up. Instead, sheltering from the elements, I wondered... Just what is Stoodley Pike *for*?

In fact, it was built by public subscription to commemorate the Peace of Ghent and the abdication of Napoleon in 1814. (You remember the Peace of Ghent, surely). It collapsed in 1854 – who says old buildings were built to last? Incredibly, they rebuilt it, a little farther from the edge of the ridge, just to be on the safe side.

Incidentally, if you're wondering why I didn't climb to the balcony, I'll tell you: dark passages always remind me of the brick air-raid shelters near my school which, as kids, we used as toilets for number two's (what are little boys made of...?). That was before we discovered girls, after which they were used for other reasons. I had no wish to be reminded of the risks walking in the dark on Stoodley Pike's staircase.

The day was a stinker now: mist, rain, a cold, cold wind. I pressed on, loving it all, until a path zig-zagged its way endlessly down to the Calder Valley, a place desecrated by man, with a dirty canal, a railway and a busy road all competing with the river for the narrow space between steep hillsides. On such a day, with heavy lorries charging past, throwing spray into my face, it was no place for a lover of the open countryside to linger. In fact, having got down to the valley, I motored straight on up the opposite side, and climbed without pause to the top of the next ridge, at around a thousand feet. Here, the route became complicated, with lots of fields and stiles, little ins-and-outs between walls and fences. Picking my way through was difficult in fading light under heavy skies. Belatedly, I realised I hadn't thought about where I would spend the night. The rain was falling steadily, the sky was darkening; in fact, it looked as though all hell would be let loose. It didn't look like the sort of night to spend star-gazing. Panic grew within. I left the path, descending to lower ground, and ended up at a place with the unlikely name of Jack Bridge, where I discovered an inn with the equally unlikely name of the New Delight. To my great relief, the man said I could have the upstairs room. By this he meant the solitary room above the pub, to which access was gained by an outside staircase.

How best to describe the room. There was a fold-up bed in the middle of the floor, a washbasin and an electric light. Not the Ritz then, but the good news was I could be in the bar in twenty seconds, so who was complaining? Not me, especially in the knowledge that after a meal and a few drinks to replenish lost fluids I had no more to do than climb the stairs. The chap who ran the place had also walked the Pennine Way 'before they made those concrete paths'. He too had wallowed in peat bogs, and we agreed it was easier now, because of the paths. But we also agreed 'something had to be done' to deal with erosion caused by the endless procession of boots in the summer months, so maybe concrete paths are necessary. The two blokes I'd seen earlier came in. They were camping nearby, they said. It would have been good to share dialogue, but after four pints and a feed I'd had it. I climbed the stairs to my room, and was soon fast asleep on my shaky bed.

Through the night, I was awakened by the deafening clatter of thunder, a raging wind, and rain lashing against the window. I crawled from my cosy nest and looked outside where sheet lightning illuminated the dark, night sky, and thunder crashed again as the storm raged overhead, and unseen dustbin lids and other objects clanked and crashed alarmingly into walls and each other. Somewhere among the cacophony of noise the faint wailing of cat was audible. I went back to my bed, snuggled down among the sheets and thanked the Almighty for safe deliverance.

*

For the moors! For the moors! Where the short grass
Like velvet beneath us should lie!
For the moors! For the moors! Where the high pass
Rose sunny against the clear sky.

Bronte country. The Mecca of literary pilgrims. It would be tough, seventeen miles over rough country to Lothersdale, in North Yorkshire. Now that's what I call north. Nearly, anyway.

The storm had passed. I opened the door of my New Delight Penthouse to a bracing wind and breathed in fresh, fresh air. It felt good. Not so good was the stale, musty smell of cigarettes in the bar where I would take breakfast, but no matter. My stay here had been memorable, not least because without the sanctuary of the New Delight I would by now be a wet, bedraggled, sponge-like creature, or just as likely suffered death by drowning, hypothermia or electrocution.

I climbed a steep, narrow trod, back on to the Pennine Way, which here crosses Heptonstall Moor, a vast, open landscape where the breeze blows unhindered straight into your face. There were no fences or gates here, no forbidding signposts, no hazards of any shape or form. Just endless rolling moorland and wide, light-grey skies. My spirits soared as I bowled along, a man at peace, a man alive. For an hour I walked so, before it all ended at a row of reservoir cottages, where I paused and glanced back, my way of acknowledging the joy the Moor had provided, before proceeding over the Graining Water and heading for the land of reservoirs beyond.

There are three of them, the Lower, Middle and Upper Walshaw Dean Reservoirs. The route crosses a dam between the first two, then takes to rising moorland beyond, where anyone with a literary interest will find the pulse quickening, especially on sight of the ruinous cottage, known as Top Withens, now in view. This is, reputedly, Wuthering Heights, and these moors were the haunt of the three sisters who found literary fame: Charlotte, Emily and Anne Bronte.

The ruin stands alone and deserted on the open moor, guarded by two trees. If, as Emily says in her book, 'Wuthering' is 'a significant provincial adjective, descriptive of atmospheric tumult to which its station is exposed in stormy weather', then she named the house well. It's a forlorn place, where people once lived (Heathcliff, in fiction anyway) and, presumably, worked once upon a day. It's crumbling walls defy the ravages of wind and weather, although surely will come the day when they will collapse and fall, dust to dust as they say.

Literary pilgrims come from far and wide to visit this place. Yet today I had Wuthering Heights to myself. I lingered, looking over the sweeping moors, reflecting on the house and whatever its true purpose might have been. Here, people slept and worked. Within these now-crumbled walls they ate their meals after long days on the moors, where they tended sheep I suppose, for what other work could there be in such a desolate place? In this cold and tumbledown room, now roofless and open to the heavens, a man and a woman and perhaps their children would have spent their everyday lives. What did they do during long, winter evenings? There was no t.v., remember – imagine it! And how did they get food and supplies to the house?

And I was the stranger who didn't belong, just a bloke who'd walked here from somewhere or other. The occupants of the house wouldn't have understood how anyone would have the time, would never have seen the point. Never mind Emily Bronte, never mind her novel. This place is real: the people who lived here were real. People like me are passing through, that's all. That's what it's all about, isn't it? Whatever the occasion, the situation, we're all just passing through. If this ruin hadn't happened to stand astride the Pennine Way I wouldn't be here. Life's like that.

It was never Wuthering Heights anyway. As a plaque on the wall says: 'The buildings, even when complete, bore no resemblance to the house she (Emily) described, but the situation may have been in her mind when she wrote of the moorland setting of the heights'. It was the *location* she had in mind for the setting of her fictitious house, Wuthering Heights, and somehow this old ruin fitted the bill. No matter; I'm sure she would approve. Anyway, I could not pass through Bronte country without mention of the sisters and at least a part of their background. That would be like visiting Buckingham Palace without seeing the Queen. A potted history, then.

Charlotte, Emily and Anne Bronte were three of the six children born to Patrick Bronte (or, more likely, Prunty), a clergyman of Irish descent, and Maria, his Cornish wife. After the birth of their last child, Mr and Mrs Bronte moved to the now-famous parsonage, at Haworth (a few miles from Withins), where Mr Bronte became rector. Soon after, Mrs Bronte died of cancer, and her sister took up residence to look after the children, two of whom died in infancy – disease in the village was rife, probably due to poor sanitation – leaving the three girls and their brother, Branwell, to spend their days together, often out on the moors above Haworth.

The first literary venture by the girls was a joint enterprise, a small collection of poems that sold just two copies. Thereafter, each of sisters wrote a full-length novel. Charlotte wrote *The Professor*, which was not published until after her death, and later the acclaimed *Jane Eyre*, published in 1847; Emily wrote *Wuthering Heights*, also in 1847; and Anne wrote *Agnes Grey* and *The Tenant of Wildfell Hall*. Emily died of consumption in 1848, aged 30. Anne, after a long illness, died at Scarborough the following year, aged 29. Charlotte, who achieved celebrity status and married in 1854, died during pregnancy the following year after catching a chill walking on the moors which, unlike her sisters (who loved the moors) she reputedly hated. She lived to the ripe old age of 39.

I enjoyed my sojourn to Top Withens, or Wuthering Heights if you will, but time and hunger drove me onward. The walking was easy, all the way down to the Ponden Valley, still Bronte country, for here is

Ponden Hall, a 17th century farmhouse, a solid building of stone with oak beams, reputedly Thrushcross Grange in *Wuthering Heights*. Beyond, there was another hillside to climb, and more moorland to cross, Ickornshaw Moor, which reaches 1,400 feet, a rough, tough traverse of coarse grasses and heather. On this wild, untamed place you could be forgiven for not noticing that near a rocky outcrop called Wolf Stones, you cross an invisible boundary into North Yorkshire, England's largest county. If the name changes, the terrain does not, and it seems endless before the path finally descends steeply to Cowling, a village made up, strangely, of two separate hamlets, Ickornshaw and Middleton. Hopes of a cup of tea were quickly dashed, and I passed through without pause. There was another valley to traverse, another hillside to climb before a country lane led down into Lothersdale.

It's a lovely name, don't you think? Evidently it derives from the Old English *Loddere*, meaning Vagabond's Valley. A vagabond is a person of no fixed home. Could've been me, I suppose, especially as I was staying in a bunkhouse tonight – just like one of those cowpokes who turn up at the Ponderosa to drive the herd to Abilene. 'Y'can stay in the bunkhouse, an' keep yer hands off my gal.' It comprised a few outbuildings containing small bedrooms, toilets, etc., with breakfast taken in the main guesthouse the following morning (and no gal). The lady showed me to a room with four bunks. 'Take your pick,' she said, 'it's very quiet, as you can see.' Fine by me.

I showered and went off exploring the nooks and crannies of the vagabond's valley, finding it to be a lovely old place of fine houses with a tall mill chimney thrown in. But long distance walking leaves you tired and cold, so I repaired to my room before venturing out again for a meal at the pub. Lo and behold, who should turn up but the two blokes I'd seen earlier. They weren't camping tonight, they said, they would use the bunkhouse instead. Fair enough, only now three of the four bunks would be occupied in what was a small room, whilst the other rooms stayed empty. They asked politely if I minded, and of course I said I didn't. What else could I say? Yes, I do mind, so get the hell outta here? Anyway, they seemed good types, and after a pleasant exchange, which included the news that one of them 'snored a bit', we were all pals together.

I headed off for the pub, promising to ensure there was food aplenty for my new-found mates when they arrived. So it was we enjoyed a few pints after our meals. The lads were late thirties, from

Leicester, both unemployed and were doing their best to make ends meet on their Pennine Way adventure. Good luck to 'em.

Back in the bunkhouse, we retired to our respective bunks. I was tired, but a third consecutive night's sleep was about to be disturbed. Somewhere in the dead of night, I was awakened by a harsh, reverberating noise. Was it a motorcycle, revving just outside the window? A farm tractor, perhaps, with its engine running? Nope, it was the promised snoring of one of my companions, the guy in the top bunk, just six feet from where I lay. I've heard snoring before, but this guy was international status. Anyone passing on the street would have heard it. Suffice to say it was loud and it was continuous, and there was no way of closing one's ears to it. I willed it to cease, prayed that he would awaken and that would be that. But no, it continued mercilessly; and, unlike the snorer's companion, fast asleep below – used to it, of course – I could not shut it out.

Nor was it the only sound to emanate from this creature. Now and again he would snort, and stop snoring for about ten seconds as he turned in his creaking bunk. During each brief period of blissful silence I lay awake in the vain hope that it was over, that peace would return; but no, there'd be another half an hour of purgatory until it was turn-over time again, when the entire process was repeated. There were other interruptions too: grunting, groaning, wheezing, indecipherable mutterings. And, every now and then, the moment when everything, even his breathing, would stop, preparatory to an explosive release of wind, followed by a deep sigh of relief as the creature took its rest whilst I, in despair, could only grin and share it.

In desperation, I fled into the cold night where I tried to gain access to another of the rooms. Sadly, in vain, for every door was locked to me, every hope of escape from this living nightmare barred. And, just to round off the night, my body heat – what there was left of it, outside, naked under a quilt in the middle of the night in Yorkshire – triggered off one of those security lights, and the entire compound was bathed in a blaze of light, revealing a strangely-clad figure in his bare-feet, a burglar perhaps, or, more likely, a madman escaped from the local asylum. There was nothing for it but to return to the bunkhouse, where the snoring prevailed, muffled slightly, but only slightly, by the door to the room where the monster lay. Resigned to my fate, I wrapped myself in my quilt and sank to the annexe floor where I spent the remainder of the night, and where my dear companions found me next morning.

I gave the cause of my location on the floor as sleepwalking, but the snoring monster knew the real reason, and said so. Apologies were gratefully received, whilst I said his companion deserved a medal for the occasions he shared a tent with him. Then we went for brekkie, which was excellent, though I fear the lady will probably never know why her nice clean quilt ended up rather mucky. I threw it onto the snoring monster's bed so he'd get the blame. It was his fault anyway.

6

The Yorkshire Dales

Today the sun was shining. Any thoughts of tiredness after my sleepless nights were quickly dispatched as I eagerly took to fields of rich-green, bound or Malham. The boglands of the South Pennines, the mist and rain, noisy fire alarms and thunderstorms and snoring monsters were history now; the future was limestone.

Limestone country provides walking, *par excellence*: springy turf, gentle, rolling hills, rivers and streams or, just as likely, no rivers and streams where there should be. From Lothersdale I climbed easily to the top of Pinhaw Beacon, where the landscape to the north opened up before me, and Airedale awaited my arrival.

I followed the Pennine Way a short distance, to where it leads off west for Thornton, but that was not my chosen route today. Instead, I headed north along a quiet byroad for Broughton. This route provided me with the bonus of seeing Broughton Church, of fine, light-grey stone, awash in lovely autumn sunshine. The sheep appreciated it too, or rather the churchyard, where they grazed contentedly among the headstones. One way of keeping the grass in trim, I suppose. I pressed on, finally crossing the Aire into Gargrave, a long, straggling village which cars and coaches thunder through on their way to somewhere else. But I didn't care about them. What I did care about was fish and chips. Am I alone in saying there are times I find myself with a desperate need of our national dish? It is our national dish, isn't it? I mean, you couldn't go to Vladivostok or Volgograd and ask for haddock and chips with scrunchings, could you? Anyway, compared with the other villages I'd passed through on the Pennines, such as they were, Gargrave was more like a city, a cert for the desired fare. Sure enough, I found a small café to indulge my palate, pot of tea and bread and butter (2 slices) thrown in. Such treats are earned, as anyone who's walked the Pennine Way will testify. With ample time, I hung about Gargrave, the unofficial 'gateway' to the Yorkshire Dales. I saw no other walkers, but there were a few cyclists, dressed in their crash helmets and those strange shoes they wear. Some of them were women, a species of the human race rapidly becoming a fading memory to me. It came as no surprise – seeing cyclists, I mean – for the Dales is superb cycling territory, with hills not too unkind on the legs, and lots of watering holes to aim for.

I wandered into a shop to buy a film, only to be informed, in good-natured tones, that I was not allowed to leave until I signed a book and entered details of my venture. Sure enough, when I looked, it contained the names of other pilgrims, walkers and cyclists, presumably. I signed dutifully. Then I made the mistake, in conversation, of telling the nice people who run the place that I was old bill. Smiles turned to scowls. 'They should bring back hanging,' declared one. Oh, dear, touched a nerved there. There's a lot of feeling in the rural community about crime and punishment, especially the hanging issue. To these law-abiding people in a village in North Yorkshire, 'punishment' means capital punishment. Maybe they're right, but I don't think so. It's not that I care tuppence about the fate of child killers or terrorists – although I'm not convinced that putting a rope around someone's neck, standing them on a trapdoor and pulling a lever is an appropriate way for civilised people to behave – but until someone invents a system of guaranteeing that the person accused is guilty, I can't see how we can justify taking life. There's no bringing back an innocent person if you've killed him or her, in which case we become murderers ourselves. But I digress...

I had rejoined the Pennine Way, and soon I was crossing the Leeds-Liverpool canal, one of the first to be contrived (1770), yet one of the last to become operative (1816). And no wonder, considering that it had to traverse England's 'backbone'. They had to construct many locks, and dig a tunnel nearly a mile long through which children propelled barges in total darkness by pushing against the roof with their legs. I bet they never had the opportunity to walk the Pennine Way, or anywhere else for that matter. I confess such things were far from my mind as I crossed the official Yorkshire Dales National Park boundary, and climbed onto Eshton Moor where contented cows and sheep grazed in peaceful meadows, and where the sky was a white and blue canvas, stretching to far horizons.

This is superb country, where, I feel, the cyclists have got it wrong. Up here, among these fields, there was no traffic to concern me; up here, I could soak in the views at my leisure. The joys of freedom were mine, unrestricted and free of worry. You don't get that riding a bike, but each to his own I suppose. The path led once again to the Aire, where, in the distance, the towering cliffs of Malham Cove came into view. But that was for tomorrow. Today, I followed the river to Aire Head Springs. This is usually regarded as the river's source, although the water emerging from the earth here has made an underground journey of some miles from the strange but appropriately named Water Sinks, having left Malham Tarn to the north, so maybe that's the true source of the river.

And so to Malham, the tourists' Mecca, with its huge car park, information centre, youth hostel and two inns. But where Malham can be overrun with people, still it loses none of its charm, and today I mingled with the sightseers as they perused the postcards and licked away at their ice creams. It was hardly surprising to find it so popular, for the village was awash in the early evening sunshine. I stayed at Eastwood House, not far from the bridge over the Malham Beck, and spent the evening hanging around with everyone else.

*

The woman guest in the dining room was in full flow. She'd been to Blackpool, 'but we thought we'd just drop by to see the Yorkshire Dales,' she said, 'we' meaning she and her as yet unseen husband. Blackpool had clearly made a favourable impact, and she was going to tell me about it whether I liked it or not. As I've said before, that's the trouble when you're eating your 'full English', you're stuck with the company.

Soon nothing of Lancashire's famous seaside resort would be a mystery to me: the Tower, the Pleasure Beach, 'Seven Miles' of Golden Sands, piers, evening entertainment and, of course, the illuminations. She was describing the trams that go along the prom-prom-prom, where the brass bands play, tiddley-om-pom-pom, when her old man entered the room, on sight of whom she abruptly reached the tram terminus, as it were, for the poor man was bleeding from a wound on his face. Unfortunately, once it was established that it was the result of shaving, and realising he wasn't in imminent danger of death, we were back in Blackpool again. Gamely, hubby tackled breakfast, as he tried unsuccessfully to check the blood-flow. As I wolfed down the last remnants of toast and home-made marmalade, she was reminiscing about Reg Dixon – 'him with the lovely organ' – whilst her husband, for all I know, bled to death and may now be buried among the Norse invaders, once of this parish. If ever they dig him up, they'll presume he died in battle, or, just as likely, that he was executed for the murder of his wife.

The invading Norsemen came to Malham, and no wonder, for such territory was just up their street, so to speak. Later, in the 12th and 13th centuries, the area passed into ownership of two powerful monasteries, Fountains Abbey and Bolton Priory. But man was here long before, as the Iron Age settlements to the north of the village testify. In fact, Malham dates back 330 million years, give or take, to the carboniferous period when the main rock, limestone, was deposited. Later, ice age glaciers tore at the landscape, and then in warming conditions acid rainwater dissolved some of the limestone to create subterranean tunnels. Today, Malham Dale is a patchwork of walled enclosures and stone barns, or *laithes*, introduced by man, years ago – but only yesterday, if you think about it in real terms. Unlike most other changes he made to mother earth, man has done a good job at Malham.

The morning was cold but dry as I took the Pennine Way across Malham Moor. Here it was that thousands turned out for the opening ceremony of the Way in 1965. Today I had Malham Moor to myself. It wasn't long before I reached the great amphitheatre, Malham Cove, where a 250-feet high cliff towers above the Malham Beck, which seeps from its base. The cliff was formed as a result of the Middle Craven Fault, a major fracture in the base-rock, where rocks to the south dropped below those to the north during the aforementioned carboniferous period. The cliff seen today is the result of erosion by glacial meltwaters; it's set ¼-mile back from where it started at the original site of the fracture. It's hard to imagine, but evidently as recently as the 16th century a spectacular waterfall poured over this cliff. Nowadays the water disappears into fissures, and runs underground, leaving the dry, cliff face to birds and strange people who hang from it on ropes.

Stone steps lead to the limestone 'pavement', on the cliff-top. It's made up of blocks of limestone (clints) separated by deep cracks (grykes), the home of wild plants and creepy-crawlies. Once again, we have ice to thank for this wonderful phenomenon, the most recent ice age, in fact, which left the limestone exposed, and acid rainwater did the rest (not to be confused with 'acid rain', resulting from today's industrial blight). You have to watch your step crossing the 'pavement', where some of the stones are loose. This is broken ankle territory.

I lingered here, dreaming of Blackpool, then moved on to the nearby 'dry valley', where once the river flowed. The Pennine Way goes up the hillside opposite, and this is a mistake, for a much better option is to walk along the dry valley itself, where an excellent path follows the drystone wall. This I did, again having it to myself until I encountered a party of thirty or so schoolgirls and their two women teachers, all of whom stood back in line to allow me to pass. Smiles and hellos all round. I believe the children were being given a lesson in geology, and that pleased me. It's good to see youngsters learning, better still when you can see they want to learn.

I rejoined the Pennine Way at Malham Tarn, an extensive lake, a rarity hereabouts where, as I have described, water is renowned for sinking into the ground. The tarn, half a mile across, lies on an impervious bed of rock, hence its existence. Here, reputedly, is the setting for Charles Kingsley's *Water Babies*. I'd read about the water babies as a kid, and looked out for them now. Alas, I saw none. Life's full of disappointments, isn't it?

Walking by the tarn, I came upon a lone fellow to whom I gave the usual 'good morning'. Whilst I do not advocate greeting every Tom, Dick and Harriet met on the trail, there are times when it surely must be courtesy to speak. Without another human being in sight at Malham Tarn might be such a time. Anyway, this chap seemed torn between returning my greeting and ignoring me, and in the end he did neither, for whilst I distinctly saw his mouth move into an unmistakable 'good morning', no sound passed from his lips. He *mimed* it! Better than nothing, I suppose.

Again I left the Pennine Way, heading north-east towards Arncliffe and my ultimate destination of the day, Buckden. Here, in a maze of drystone walls I went astray, ending up in a field which contained the world record number of rabbits seen at any one time. I tried counting them, being thwarted in this endeavour by the fact that they would not stay still. I made it 1,593,462, although I might have counted the same one twice. How loveable they are, with their floppy ears and little white bobtails. Watching them, I realised that in spite of their reputation for 'breeding like rabbits', I've never once seen any 'at it'. Not even in this field. Someone – he or she was anonymous – was once inspired to write:

> The rabbit has a charming face;
> Its private life is a disgrace.

Anyway, having contrived to get lost, it wasn't long before I'd completed a full circle and finished up where I started, so at least I knew where I wasn't. Finally I located the path above Yew Cougar Scar, a deep valley, and followed it 3-miles down to Arncliffe. This is a grand, high-level route, with fine views across the Skirfare valley ahead. Needless to say, I saw no-one.

I'd been to Arncliffe before, when the village green was infested with people lying in the sun, drinking lager and wearing tee-shirts with meaningful messages: 'Smile if you had it last night', 'Elvis lives OK', and pictures of Blackpool Tower. Today, Arncliffe was as deserted as the paths around it. This is a lovely village, with its stone cottages and village green, church with tower, the Skirfare running serenely by. It was too cold to linger, and soon I was crossing the river and climbing the steep-sided Old Cote Moor, the second main ridge of the day at around 1,500 feet. Beyond is Wharfedale, but Buckden was a long four miles still. Approaching the ridge, I heard the unmistakable sound of a shotgun being discharged, directly ahead and not too far off. Then I heard it again, and then again. I couldn't see who was blasting away, which meant whoever it was couldn't see me either. This wasn't an arrangement I found pleasing. I scanned the moor, and moved on with caution, meeting two people, a man and woman, who were as concerned as me about our immediate wellbeing.

Atop the ridge, we saw the men with guns.

There were four of them, walking slowly abreast, across our line of vision. Each carried a shotgun, and carried a sack across his shoulder. The sacks were clearly empty. As we looked, one of the men would shoulder his gun and let fly at something ahead, what at first I could not tell, but then it was clear they were shooting rabbits. Or, I should say, shooting *at* rabbits, for as each man fired at the little white bobtail directly ahead, their quarry scampered off, apparently uninjured, with a 100% success rate over the gunmen who sought to destroy them. At first I felt sorry for the rabbits, but then I felt sorry for the men with the guns, for I realised they must be blind, or nearly so; never have I witnessed such ineptitude.

On the crest of the ridge we waited, the couple and I, as the men passed before us, banging away at thin air, outwitted and outmanoeuvred by rabbits. Not a single bunny suffered so much as a scratch, and each sack stayed as empty as it had been when they started. I carried on, wondering how such dolts could be allowed out in public with loaded weapons. And on a right of way, too. Freedom to roam, sure. But is it safe?

Below was the Wharfe; above, darkening skies. I knew there'd be rain before I reached Buckden. So it proved. Nearing the river I found myself in a world of rabbits again, dozens of 'em, country cousins of the ones seen earlier. The place was infested. Those fools with the guns were in the wrong place. Even a blind man couldn't have missed, not here, where to put a shotgun to your shoulder and let fly would have guaranteed hitting half a dozen at one time. I was pleased for the rabbits, but I have to admit they do ruin the ground with their unsightly holes, which in time collapse, causing the destruction of plants and crops.

I walked along the valley floor through woodland, in pouring rain. It was stimulating, the rain. There are times when it is good to feel it in your face, and this was such a time. I'd not far to go now, and I could relax, for I had unusually taken the trouble to telephone in advance and reserve a bed at Buckden. Two miles to go, and the light was fading fast. One mile. I followed the river, where the path led over rough pasture, through more woodland and wild undergrowth. The ground was rapidly turning muddy, with cowpats to negotiate, not easy to see in gathering dusk, especially when the rain turns everything into a muddy-brown texture. I pressed on, sadly not doing justice to what is a lovely riverside walk. I reached Buckden in darkness, a happy man. My accommodation turned out to be a big stone house, where a fire roared in the grate. Lovely! After a luxurious bath I hurried through the rain to the nearby Buck Inn for a well-earned supper. It was crowded, but I found a table next to a couple of businessmen. One, the elder, retired to his bed after his meal, whilst his companion remained at the table. He was 'not a well man', he said. 'Trouble with the liver,' he explained. I presumed this must be down to misfortune, but after losing count of the number of brandies he downed, a total I subconsciously tried to commit to memory but which proved as difficult as counting rabbits, I put 'trouble with the liver' down to alcohol poisoning. Finally, he gave up the ghost and staggered off to his bed. Or, just as likely, the nearest mortuary.

With nothing to do but 'people-watch', I looked idly about me. There was a good crowd in the Buck, people on holiday, a local or two perhaps. One of the gathered throng was a fellow to whom I paid little heed, until he stood up and walked to the bar, at which point I became transfixed by his, shall we say, unusual appearance. He was tall, around six feet six, a giant of a man, yet with a head so small it looked higher from the floor than it actually was. He was an American 'doing' Britain, and he was into museums. He reeled off a few: the British Museum, the Victoria and Albert, Madam Tussauds, the Houses of Parliament. He reminded me of Bluto in *Popeye*. But then I was looking through eyes blighted by Yorkshire Bitter. Time to go, I thought, before his missus took on the appearance of Olive Oil. I ran through the rain to my lodgings, and went straight to bed. My final thoughts of the day were about rabbits, or, more specifically, their nocturnal activities. Even now, the little blighters would be at it in their burrows, whilst I lay alone in my bed. I'll never feel sorry for rabbits again.

*

Once again, there were two main ridges to climb today, the first to Wensleydale, the second to Swaledale. I stepped outside with sprits high, in anticipation of what lay in store: superb walking country, including a 'green road', and afterwards arrival at Muker.

Wharfedale is lovely, a place to savour, whatever the time of year, whatever the weather – today grey and damp after the overnight rain.

My route led along a high terrace above the Wharfe, known as Buckden Rake, an old Roman road. It was a stiff climb up, with views improving with every step. Every now and then I kept looking back to see Buckden, nestling cosily by the river below green hillsides. To the left lay Langstrothdale, and the tiny hamlet of Hubberholme (with, let it be said, my favourite church in all England); to the right, Buckden Pike towered above. There's so much to see from this lofty terrace, a view I shared with three other people on its traverse of a mile or so before it ran down to the road again.

Soon I left tarmacadam behind me, and took to the 'green road', a 4-mile trek to Bainbridge. Green roads are ancient byways that run between drystone walls. Where others over the years have been converted into motor roads, today's green roads remain unchanged; they follow the easiest routes over ridges, and provide superlative walking territory. So it was for me now, and I strode forth, a man in heaven. I would see no-one these four miles, although, unexpectedly, I came upon a Morris Minor pickup, unattended, in the middle of nowhere, a farmer's presumably.

Atop Kidstones Fell, new horizons opened up: rolling hills cut asunder by deep valleys, typical 'dales' country. Included among those in view were Great Shunner Fell and a hill called Lovely Seat, which I'd climbed years before. After two miles, the road diverges, one going down to Semer Water, an extensive lake. There's supposed to be a city beneath the surface, where a beggar once asked for shelter, only to be refused by everyone except a poor couple who lived in a cottage. Next morning, the beggar had vanished and the city had disappeared into the lake. Evidently, passers-by can sometimes see the rooftops of the city just below the surface. I wondered if I might go down to see the city, but I decided on the direct route to Bainbridge instead, having become disillusioned with lakes after the failure to see any water babies at Malham Tarn.

It was grand, walking that 'road': the air was fresh after the overnight rain, the skies, although heavy with cloud, were high and wide, and there were shades of green in all directions. On top of the world, I sang all the way, until the green road ended and followed a country lane down to Bainbridge, in Wensleydale. The Bain is surprisingly wide considering it's the shortest river in England; it flows a mere two miles from its source to the River Ure.

At Bainbridge I'd anticipated a cup of tea, but there was nowhere. So, what was new? I sat on a bench by the enormous village green, until a cold wind drove me on to another upland climb, this time across Askrigg Common. I picked my way through fields and by a stream, then joined the motor road, which crosses the Common. A few cars were parked on the summit, their occupants doubtless walking to the beacon on Oxnop, a couple of miles off. With time to spare I considered going over to the beacon, but chose instead to press on, as the road wound its tenuous way among limestone outcrops all the way down to Swaledale. Halfheartedly, I tried to find a right of way which, according to the map, crosses the fields, but failed to locate it. So I took the road for the last mile, and crossed the stone bridge over the Swale into Muker.

The name Muker derives from the Norse, meaning meadow, but to me it means stone houses and a fine, grey church. St Mary's once had a thatched roof and a wooden platform where musicians played harmonium, fiddle and clarinet. If only they still did. And Muker has a pub, The Farmers Arms, where I ate a meal seated by a barrel that passed for a small table, so close to the fire I was almost roasted alive. The clientele that evening were locals, farmers mainly. The kindness of Yorkshire folk manifested itself on my return to my lodgings, where my progress up the stairs to bed was interrupted by the lady of the house, Mrs Peacock, who invited me to join her and her family at their fireside for tea and biscuits. I was a stranger, but I was a guest, which meant I was a friend.

*

Being the sole guest, I breakfasted alone. Which is not to say I *was* alone, for as I ate Mrs P sat by the fire, pleased at having company, perhaps, but in any case eager to voice her opinions on diverse matters, mainly current affairs. She had a knack of putting together short sentences that carried sufficient information to make her point – the very antithesis of your common-or-garden politician. Unlike the wretched woman at Malham, who had driven me almost to distraction over Blackpool, I was pleased to listen to someone worth listening to.

The morning was dull, with a sullen sky. It mattered not, rather it was better that way, for here, in Swaledale, the river winds its way lazily across the wide, green valley floor, where high ground rises on either side, and where the ghosts of the old lead mines may linger yet. Brooding skies seemed appropriate. I was alone, and that seemed appropriate too. It was not by chance that I had come this way; I had deliberately sought out Muker and the Swale, had looked forward to this section of my journey, and the riverside walk to Keld.

℘ 2001

Muker

I lingered awhile, breathing in fresh Yorkshire air. Oh, that you could bottle it! But Muker is worthy of one's time, not least to dwell on thoughts of what life must have been like here not so long ago, when miners with picks and shovels crawled about in tunnels in water and damp. Is it any surprise they suffered from consumption, with an average lifespan of only 46? Lead was responsible for the growth of Muker, and the demise of that industry led to its depopulation. The fine, stone buildings remain, testimony to those times, but visitors would do well to remember the miners, indeed will be bound to remember them as they pass by the now derelict smelt mills on the nearby hillsides.

It wasn't long before the rain came. It was in for the day, it was obvious. I put on my waterproofs, and headed north – and on to map 20 of my journey, the one with County Durham on it. Wow! I followed the river, finally climbing the hillside above Keld. I was tempted to go down to this isolated village, but resisted. First, there were many miles ahead of me today; and second, with the knowledge that I had to cross featureless moorland, I needed to allow as much time as possible to locate Baldersdale youth hostel. There was a possibility of getting lost, especially if, as seemed likely, the moors would be covered in mist. Again on the Pennine Way, I took the trail above Stonesdale. Here, the transformation is absolute, for where Swaledale is wild and lovely, Stonesdale is wild and stark, certainly not welcoming. There was absolutely not another soul as I tramped my way north, bound for Tan Hill and England's highest pub, at 1,732 feet.

It's three miles to the inn. Three miles where the rain got heavier and the mist closed in like a shroud. The path, at first clear on the ground, became indistinct. I checked the map, checked the compass. There are times in such conditions when one's sense of direction plays tricks, and the compass seems incorrect. You feel certain you should bear right, maybe, yet the compass needle unfailingly says it's to the left you must go. One must always obey the compass, for it is never wrong. What would be the point of carrying it if it were otherwise?

I didn't want to miss the inn, not only because it would provide well-earned refreshment (if it was open), but to do so would mean ending up a lost soul on Sleightholme Moor, beyond, perhaps never again to return to civilisation. There were peat hags and soggy patches of ground, but no sign of any path, never mind I was on the much-tramped Pennine Way (wasn't I?). I peered through the gloom, straining for a glimpse of the inn. Feelings of desperation mounted with every forlorn step. For all I knew, I had passed it by and was now heading for – where *was* I heading for? But wait! There it was, a tiny speck, dead ahead. It had to be the inn, for there is no other building for miles. It couldn't be a mirage; you only get them in places like the Sahara, which this most certainly was not.

Yet the inn is an oasis, and if it is the highest in England, today the lonely moorland road on which it stands was the bleakest. Many a Pennine Wayfarer must have arrived at its welcoming portal with feelings of relief – as I did today. The inn dates back to the days when coal was mined hereabouts, when its customers were the miners, and it served also as a stopping-off place for drovers taking livestock to local markets, and passing tinkers. All this has ended: the coal was poor quality and mining it here was not a long-term success, livestock is taken by road nowadays, and tinkers don't bother with Tan Hill when they can tink elsewhere. That would have been that, as far as the inn at Tan Hill is concerned, but nowadays people have cars, so they can drive out here for a drink and a meal and drive home again afterwards. The inn, or rather its windows, did feature once upon a time in a famous t.v. advert. You have to admit if double-glazing works at Tan Hill, it will work anywhere.

Oh, to step back in time here, to see the miners, the drovers, the tinkers, knocking back their beer. When men were men, eh? Aye, and they were too, to work here, to drink here. As I prepared to leave I wondered if the weather might have changed. It had. The wind was now a roaring gale, and the rain was falling as stair-rods at an angle of 45 degrees.

From Tan Hill the Pennine Way cuts across Sleightholme Moor, a ghastly moonscape of oxbow streams and the inevitable bog. Many Wayfarers opt out of the Moor, choosing the road instead. Can't blame 'em really, especially on a day like this. I crossed the Moor on my Pennine Way expedition, but today I chose the road. I was always going to. There would be two miles on tarmacadam, followed by another two on a farm road to Sleightholme, an isolated farmstead.

The stair-rods were angled straight at me as I set off along the road. There was nothing for it but to snuggle as best I could into my cag and get on with it, eyes down, yet somehow peering forward through the gloom to ensure I saw any oncoming vehicles before they ran me over. The last thing motorists would be thinking about would be an approaching pedestrian. The rain, the mist, the wind, the grey, gloomy, cold moors, all came together as a package, and my spirits soared to meet the challenge. I wouldn't have missed it for the world. Finally, I located the farm road to Sleightholme, where I forced myself between listless cattle barring the way at the farm gate. On the Pennine Way again, I pressed on across Bowes Moor for the A66, the trunk road that traverses the Stainmore Gap. It follows the course of a Roman road, and hereabouts in AD954, at the Battle of Stainmore, Eric Bloodaxe, the last Viking King of Northumbria, was slain. With a name like that his enemies must have been well chuffed.

It was time to tackle the day's last objective, Cotherstone Moor, a cert for getting lost in misty conditions. Well, not quite featureless, for there is Ravock Castle, but before you start planning a day's outing to it, it's best I point out it's no more than a pile of stones, scarcely enough in number to build a bungalow let alone a castle. (It was once a shepherd's hut). Other than this sad pile of rubble the moor is, well – a featureless wilderness. The rain stopped, leaving heavy skies with good visibility. I was greatly relieved by this. In fact, I could see for miles and this was important, for even the Pennine Way path disappears on the moor. Finally, breasting higher ground at Race Yate – there's nothing there, just more moor – the scattering of buildings ahead I identified as Baldersdale, and I knew I'd won the day.

To be honest, Baldersdale youth hostel, although ideally situated, doesn't feel like the most welcoming of places. It's just that, having had such a lonesome trek across such wild terrain, you might expect something cosy. The hostel was almost deserted, which might have given it that 'cold' feel. But I was pleased to reach it after what had, to some extent, been a race against time in appalling conditions over difficult terrain.

I contented myself indoors, as outside the wind moaned, and heavy clouds hung fast in a darkening sky. There was nowhere to go, and no-one to talk to except a bloke from Gateshead who'd brought his son here to 'do a bit of walking'. The lad was about twelve. It reminded me of the days when I too lived in Gateshead and took my children walking, good days that I've not forgotten and I know they haven't. This fellow was doing the right thing, for himself and his son. After purchasing a quantity of tinned food from the warden, and entering the enormous kitchen-cum-dining room to cook and eat, I must have walked another three miles at least between the cooking area and dining table. Back and forth, back and forth. Forgetting a spoon requires a major expedition at Baldersdale if you want to stir your tea. If you aren't fit when you arrive, you will be when you leave. Either that or knackered.

*

Baldersdale, perhaps more than anywhere, makes the Pennine Wayfarer and long distance walker ask themselves the question: why am I doing this? This is a bleak, windswept place, but so are many others, and anyway, isn't that what you are about – taking on the wild, remote places? Yet, for those on the Pennine Way, Baldersdale at least offers the comforting thought that you have reached half way, and having got this far you will surely be confident about completing the journey. For me today, it was one short stop from the end of this part of my journey, a mere five miles from Middleton-in-Teesdale. Allowing three miles' walking to cook and eat breakfast, and wash up afterwards, only eight miles for the day.

County Durham is – or was – the 'land of the Prince Bishops'. It all dates back to William the Conqueror, who realised such a far-off land would be difficult if not impossible to administer from faraway London, and just as likely had little interest in such a place (has anything changed?). So William granted authority to rule to the bishops, and Durham became known as the County Palatine. The bishops had their own council, courts and judges, minted their own coins, and even commanded their own armed forces. This suited the king, who would never have his ultimate authority threatened, as bishops have no heirs (just airs and graces); and it suited the bishops, who could live comfortably on their grand estates. Thus, where most of England was ruled by the sword, Durham was ruled by the mitre.

The bishops were unelected, the 'fat cats' of their day. As well as enjoying nice, cushy lifestyles, they had exclusive rights to hunt and shoot game, and were to a large extent above the law. Ordinary people could starve, never mind they worked hard, paid their taxes and served their 'masters' for measly pay. This is what happens when a privileged few hold high position without responsibility or accountability: they greedily take what they can, knowing there is nothing anyone can do about it. That sort of thing couldn't happen today – could it?

I headed north, where the Balder, then Lune, are the rivers of the dammed, Balderhead and Selset Reservoirs the result. For the record I passed close to Birk Hat Farm, one-time home of Hannah Hauxwell. If you've not heard of her don't worry about it. The Baldershead Reservoir dam is the biggest earth dam in England – over 3,000 feet long and 157 feet high, it holds back four million gallons of water (18,200,000 litres). I hope my maths is right. Thought I'd best convert to metric when in our so-called free society it's a criminal offence to sell bananas in pounds nowadays. Anyway, I hoped the dam wouldn't burst just as I was passing below, in which event I'd probably next be sighted somewhere off Hartlepool. Man has changed things at Baldersdale. Where before the River Balder flowed freely from its source at Stainmore Common, high in the Pennines, now the river is controlled, first by the dam itself, then by tunnels. As Alfred Wainwright remarks, 'the river had flowery banks where there are now concrete walls'. Amazingly, sheep graze in contentment right up to and even on the steep wall of the earth-dam. And, to be fair, the scene is a tidy one. If they had to build the dam, they did a good job.

Here, the Pennine Way leads to a quiet by-road. No sooner had I turned for Mickleton than a car pulled up with two blokes on board, and I was asked where they could park to go fishing in the reservoir. For some reason – copper's intuition I suppose, not that it's guaranteed to be right – I thought they might be poachers. They did look a bit sussy. I seriously considered asking them to open the boot, but my shrewd detective's mind calculated it wasn't much good doing that before they'd caught anything. So, I had a choice: forget it, or forget it. I told them I couldn't help them about parking (why do people persist in asking me directions when I'm carrying a rucksack?) and reluctantly let them go.

I walked the length of Grassholme Reservoir (how many reservoirs do they need?) across which I spied a familiar landmark, a hill called Kirkcarrion, topped by its clump of trees. Evidently it's an ancient burial site – haunted, of course. At Mickleton, on this cold Sunday morning, newspaper-buying motorists were whizzing into and out of the village in their unfailing quest for 'the Sunday papers'. Further on I crossed the Tees and entered Middleton.

Pre-19th century, Middleton was no more than an 'agricultural settlement'. Then lead mining, and the arrival of the London Lead Company in 1815, turned Middleton into the Klondyke of the north. The 'Quaker Company', as it became known, was the first in Britain to introduce a 5-day working week – this, in the 19th century – and it encouraged miners to grow their own food and thereby ensure a healthy diet – miners' health being of benefit to employee and miner alike. In 1877, the miners, at their own expense, erected a drinking fountain in the square to commemorate a respected superintendent of the company. Today's employers and unions, take note.

Middleton is a natural stopover for Pennine Wayfarers, seeking accommodation or just paying a visit. I once met a fellow who told me he had set off on the Pennine Way the previous year, only to fall at a stile hereabouts when he broke an ankle. That put paid to his mission, but only temporarily, for didn't he return to that very stile the following year and continue on his journey. So much for those who forever ask the question, 'how long did it take you to walk the Pennine Way?' Time taken, as I've so often said, is of no consequence. Unless, that is, you're an electricity meter reader from Staffordshire, for whom time was of the essence. So much so, he ran the 270 miles from Edale to Kirk Yetholm in 2 days, 17 hours, 20 minutes. He went through 5 pairs of boots and 27 pairs of socks. Forget 'how long'; you couldn't compete with that – could you?

7

Northern England and the Borders

I was going home. To Northumberland, my native county. But first, there were three ridges to climb on a 20-mile walk to Blanchland, the first, over Swinhope Head, reaching almost 2,000 feet. Morning brought an overcast sky with more than a hint of drizzle. Having temporarily forsaken my detective inspector's role, I wouldn't have cared if a hurricane had raged.

Breakfast was taken in company of a middle-aged couple from Yorkshire, and an elderly Dutch couple. The latter are regular visitors to the north, they said, and today they were off to explore some old mines in the Alston area. 'You're never too old to learn', was their motto, and their knowledge of the area put all present, including me, to shame. Breakfast over and I was off, soon on the Pennine Way again which here runs alongside the Tees, a grand walk. Just by the path I encountered a wee rabbit. He was hopping about aimlessly, instead of trying to flee his natural enemy. The reason for his indifference was soon apparent: the poor blighter had myxomatosis, or some similar disease. For him, a long, lingering death was in prospect. I wished I could end his misery, but I possessed neither a gun nor the expertise to kill him humanely. Are unsightly, destructive rabbit holes sufficient cause for the murder of these hapless creatures? If they have to be killed this seems the only way. Those fellows with the guns near Buckden couldn't hit a barn door from ten yards.

The Tees is lovely, at least in its wide, upper reaches. Sadly, it ends ignominiously at industrial Teesside, a place of chemicals and gas. At Low Force, the river negotiates narrow channels between unyielding dolomite rock, and does so angrily, before resuming its journey calmly, as though relieved that a hurdle has been overcome. Once, thousands of salmon fought their way through the waters of Low Force on their return to spawning grounds upriver, but chemicals polluted the water, preventing the salmon getting through. Maybe things have improved. I hope so.

Leaving the Pennine Way, I crossed Wynch suspension bridge, reputedly the oldest of its type in Europe. It looks like the ones you see in jungle movies, and sways alarmingly. I paused to look again at Low Force: the falls, and beyond, where the river winds between trees, wild and magnificent under a gloomy, rain-filled sky. Then a right of way led off across quiet fields, occupied by dejected-looking cows. I wanted to tell them they were the lucky ones. Not for them the demands of a detective inspector who has to travel miles and then only on rare occasions to be in country like this; they *live* here. Yet they might not be around to enjoy their freedom for long. Indeed, for all I knew I could be eating one of them before my journey was over. Not a whole one, of course.

A long, uphill gradient led into thick mist which seemed to cling to the heather – and my bare legs. At Swinhope Head, I turned to look back over Teesdale, but the entire valley was lost in the gloom. Ahead, Weardale was no different. I followed the river to Westgate, so-named after the *West Gate* of the Bishop of Durham's 16th century deerpark. In the old days there was food was a-plenty – for the bishops – but the moorhen wasn't available for ordinary mining folk. In 1818, when a group of miners was caught poaching the moorhen, they were taken to nearby Stanhope and locked up in the Black Bull by the bishop's keepers...

You brave lads of Weardale, I pray lend an ear,
The account of a battle you quickly shall hear,
That was fought by the miners, so well you may ken,
By claiming a right to their bonny moorhen.
Oh, this bonny moorhen, as it plainly appears,
She belongs to their fathers some hundreds of years;
But the miners of Weardale are all valiant men,
They will fight till they die for the bonny moorhen.

Fellow-miners forced their way into the pub, beat up the keepers and released their comrades. Strangely, none was charged. Equally strangely, no-one knows who wrote the poem.

The narrow road climbed steeply out Weardale, passing a bright yellow sign bearing the words *Veni, Vidi, Vici* – 'I came, I saw, I conquered'. Inspiring words, considering the task at hand. It's not that I'm acquainted with Latin; rather my knowledge comes down to a record of that title by a guy called Ronnie Hilton in the fifties. Heading down towards Lintzgarth, I came across twenty or so parked cars in what with justification may be called the middle of nowhere. Then people appeared, fathers and sons, wives and girlfriends, one big, happy throng whose one thing in common was the shotguns they carried. I had happened along just as they were ending a day of shooting. Shooting what? Grouse? Rabbits? Anything that moved? To me it was okay for the miners of Weardale to poach the moorhen two hundred years ago; they had to feed starving families. Today man shoots birds and calls it sport. I do not consider it so. Sport is supposed to be a contest. There is little chance of shotgun pellets missing hapless targets.

After Lintzgarth the road climbed again to the third and final ridge of the day, beyond which Northumberland came into spectacular view, a limitless landscape of wild moors, stretching to infinity. Wrote George Macaulay Trevelyan (1876-1962) of Northumberland: 'We walk all day on long ridges, high enough to give far views of moor and valley and the sense of solitude above the world below. It is the land of the far horizons'. Atop the ridge, a row of shooting butts stood not far from the roadside. I was dying to pee and took great pleasure in relieving myself in one, just where a brave homo sapien would crouch next time he – or she – was intent on murdering a grouse. (I'm not saying which one).

Three more miles led to Hunstanworth. The name is Anglo-Saxon, meaning *the worth or enclosure of Hunstan*. The church dates back to 1862, when it was rebuilt – and paid for – by the Rev. John Capper. The architect, Samuel Teulon, designed the church and the nearby schoolhouse in a Burgundian style, with light and dark tiles forming diamond shaped patterns on the roof. The old school, now a private house, has a large chimney with the school bell set in the centre between two chimney pots. An elderly lady told me she has lived there all her life. 'Hunstanworth hasn't changed,' she said with a smile. Ahead, the Derwent valley was a glorious contrast to the coldness of Weardale. I trod a golden carpet of leaves through the woods just south of the river, another half mile in gathering darkness leading to the bridge which crosses the river into Blanchland. I had reached Northumberland.

That night I had dinner in the Lord Crewe Arms. The inn is named after a former Bishop of Durham who, in 1699, married Dorothy Forster. At the time of the marriage, Lord Crewe was 67, his bride only 24. He had proposed to Dorothy nine years before, but she turned him down – hardly surprising – and he married someone else. When his wife died he tried again, and this time Dorothy accepted.

Dorothy's nephew was Thomas Forster, who had a sister, also called Dorothy. Thomas was a general in the Jacobite army during the Rising of 1715, but surrendered to government troops without a fight. He was imprisoned at Newgate, and indicted for high treason. Dorothy, his sister, disguised as a servant, smuggled duplicate keys to her brother who, naturally, was pleased to vacate his cell, locking the governor in behind him for good measure. Thomas escaped to France, but romantics believe he returned to the Lord Crewe, where he hid in a medieval priest's hole behind a fireplace. Today, it is said, Dorothy's ghost haunts the hotel in the vain hope she will find her brother. There was neither sight nor sound of them as I staggered back to my lodgings and a cosy bed. It's as well it wasn't far. My feet were killing me.

*

Sunday morning. Blanchland was deserted, the trees swaying gently in the grounds of the abbey, splendid in their autumn gold, and flowers spilling from the window boxes of stone cottages around the square. Blanchland lies beneath the high moors and is almost

145

surrounded by woods, so that it is unseen on approach until the last moment. Blanchland is a gem.

The village is probably named after the white-robed monks of the Premonstratensian Order, founded in the 12th century by a canon who dreamt that a band of monks were moving in procession in a chapel in Premontre, France. They were driven away by the Dissolution. Blanchland would have looked much the same a hundred or so years ago, except cars were parked outside the Lord Crewe, and the longer I looked at them the more I wanted them to disappear. If only people could be compelled to park outside the village – there is a large car park about three whole minutes walk away – leaving it free of the horseless carriage.

A quiet lane bordered by fine trees led to Blanchland Moor, which was deserted. I scanned the horizon, a million emotions passing through me: of pride in Northumberland, of the pleasures of today, of uncertainty of the future. Beyond, a good path led through Slaley forest, downhill now, a reminder that the moor I had crossed is over a thousand feet above sea level. The path became a lane, which I followed to Dilston. The name means 'the Homestead on the Devil's Water'. In 1710, James Radcliffe, Third Earl of Derwentwater, lived at Dilston. Four years later he and his brother, Charles, took up the Jacobite cause when George of Hanover was crowned. They were taken prisoner: James to the Tower, Charles to Newgate.

James was offered his life if he would conform to the Established Church and accept the House of Hanover. He refused. After his execution, his remains were buried with his ancestors in Dilston Chapel (from where his lead coffin was later stolen). It is claimed that on the night after his execution – he was beheaded – there was a vivid display of the Aurora Borealis, which thereafter became known locally as 'Lord Derwentwater's Lights', that the gutters of Dilston filled with blood and that his ghost still haunts the woods around the Devil's Water. Meanwhile, Charles escaped and fled to France where he remained in exile until 1745, when he joined the rebels under Bonnie Prince Charlie. This time Charles was captured and executed.

Today's Dilston Hall belongs to MENCAP. Notwithstanding the grounds are private, I bowled up to the entrance where I sat on the steps and tended to newly-formed blisters. My antics were witnessed by a group of mentally handicapped youngsters, every one of whom smiled and said hello. They wouldn't have known, as I knew, that previously the Hall was a maternity hospital, where, during the war I became a statistic. It was for this reason I decided to tarry, and think awhile about my parents, both now dead. I had always intended to visit my birthplace, and here, probably more than anywhere and at any other time, I wished I could see mum and dad again. Am I alone in concluding that after the death of one's parents, there's so much that went unsaid, and that now it is too late to say it?

I made my way to the A695 where I was reminded of that dangerous animal, the motorist. It was a shock to the system after Blanchland Moor and the quiet, country lanes around Dilston. Cars, lorries, coaches. There was no time to lose, not for anyone behind a steering wheel, even on a quiet Northumbrian Sunday. Every journey was a life-or-death issue. How more people aren't killed and maimed I do not know.

Ahead were road works, with temporary traffic lights. Before my eyes the generator chugged to a halt and the traffic lights went out. Now traffic approached from both directions with no signals to control the flow, and no workmen to turn those STOP-GO signs you see. They dig the road up and leave it in Northumberland like everywhere else. By some miracle I was spared the sound of metal striking metal, the cries of the injured. As I threaded my way carefully alongside the chariots of death, I wished I could be back on Blanchland Moor.

And so to Hexham, in Saxon times possibly *Hagustaldes Ham*, meaning 'batchelor's homestead', *Hagustald* being a younger son not inheriting part of a noble's estate. In 1296 the Scots burned the town to the ground. They even blocked the doors of a school with the scholars trapped inside. In 1771, there was a riot in Hexham, and 250 troops of the North York militia were sent to sort things out. They stood in front of the town hall and read the Riot Act, and when the crowd refused to disperse the soldiers opened fire, killing over forty people. Thereafter, the North York militia were known as the 'Hexham Butchers'.

The original Saxon church at Hexham was founded by Wilfrid as a Benedictine abbey, and was destroyed by Halfdene the Dane in 875, and after it was rebuilt, as an Augustinian priory, the Scots did much the same thing, in 1297. The present Abbey, dates back to 1170-1250, although parts were rebuilt later. Until the Dissolution, anyone within a mile around the pillory – marked by crosses at equal points of the compass – was able to claim sanctuary.

I once sang in the school choir at Hexham, in the Forum, when it was a cinema. Now it's a pub. We sang 'Nymphs and Shepherd's', and a song with a strange name, 'Ca' Hacky':

Hexham   P 2001

Ca' Hacky, Ca' Hacky,
Ca' Hacky through the watter,
Hacky is a sweer beast,
An' Hacky winna wae the watter.

For anyone not knowing the meaning of the above – most of the human race outside Northumberland, presumably, and even many of those within it – the words translate to a stubborn cow which wouldn't wade through a stream. Mum was tickled pink when I told her we came second in the competition. I can still hear her telling the neighbours. I never had the heart to tell her there were only two entrants.

148

Hexham on a Sunday proved no place to be if you wanted a cup of coffee. I concluded that the population must remain confined to their homes on Sundays. Or maybe they go walking. If so, they weren't on Blanchland Moor. A gate permitted access to the Carlisle-Newcastle railway line, which I crossed *very* carefully, after checking no trains were hurtling towards me. Not that they do hurtle hereabouts. They trundle, that's what they do. If one had appeared I'd probably have overtaken it.

Once, the Tyne at Hexham was crossed by ferries, operating at the aptly-named West Boat and East Boat, at either end of the town. As better roads were built a bridge was needed, but bridging the Tyne proved to be an undertaking dogged by ill-luck and disaster.

A new bridge was completed in 1770, but the following year the Great Flood washed it away. In 1774 they tried again, but work had to be abandoned when quicksand was discovered. They tried again, but the piers, only half completed, were washed away by another flood. Snow and floods and hurricane-force winds put paid to yet another attempt. Finally, they built a bridge so solid it's still there.

I crossed the river at West Boat – on a bridge built in 1904 – where a by-road lined by tall hedges led to Warden. The name derives from the Old English, *weard dun,* meaning 'watch hill'. Warden Hill, at 587 feet, towers above the green fields and trees below. The hill is topped by a prehistoric settlement. I considered going up, but there were four more miles to Humshaugh and time was pressing. Anyway, I wanted to explore Warden church. St Michaels stands in graceful solitude behind a clump of firs. The Anglo-Saxon tower dates back to the 11th century, and is partly built of Roman stone taken from Hadrian's Wall, just three miles away. The present church was added to the tower in 1764-5, thanks to monies raised by an increase in rents on the larger properties of the parish. The one-legged ghost of a murdered man called Joe the Quilter allegedly frequents the lanes hereabouts. Evidently he lost one of his clogs in trying to escape his murderer. Why he needed two in the first place is beyond me.

In the two miles to Walwick Grange just one motor car passed me by, driven in sedate fashion by an elderly chap who appeared as timeless as this valley. The only other indication of life came from the skylarks, whose singing was a fitting accompaniment to my trek north. Finally came the B6318, better known as the Military Road, built by General Wade during the wars against the Jacobites to facilitate rapid deployment of troops and artillery. Sadly, the section between Heddon and Brunton was built on Hadrian's Wall, and for this reason none of this section of Wall can be seen today. Wade may have been a great road builder, but he gets no marks for conservation. As for his Military Road, it was never needed for military purposes.

As young lads, we cycled the Military Road. You could really get up speed on the long, straight bits. The problem was, of course, for every downhill section, an equally long uphill stretch would follow. Just like the ups and downs of life: good, enjoyable bits followed by tough going. Our bikes had three-speed Sturmey-Archer gears, with a little lever you flicked on the crossbar. Nearing the tops of those hills, you'd stand on the pedals, straining as hard as possible – only for the gears to slip, and you'd land sharply and painfully on to the crossbar, an experience not to be recommended to your worst enemy. I always thought *ladies* bikes should have the crossbars; but no, they're on the gents. Who worked that one out? I bet it was a woman.

This is Roman Wall country.

Hadrian's Wall was built by Roman 'legions' – fighters, engineers, builders (yes, Roman, not local labour as I had long believed) – and garrisoned by 'auxiliaries', possibly as a defence against marauding tribes of the north, or possibly as a line of demarcation. No-one knows for certain. It did not, as many believe, form the boundary between England and Scotland. Nor was it the furthest the Romans got during their occupation: before the Wall, they made it all the way to the north of Scotland, building roads and forts to ensure good communication. But, by AD 105, they retreated from all Scotland and most of what is now Northumberland. Thereafter, for nearly three hundred years, the wall was the northern frontier of Roman Britain.

Hadrian had a bit of a cheek, though, if he was responsible for having the Wall named after him. Having conceived his plan he left Britain and the actual work was carried out under Aulus Platorius Nepos, legate for Britain. So, maybe it should be Nepos's Wall, although that doesn't sound right somehow. After the Wall was completed the locals lived in harmony with the Romans in and around their settlements. But why *did* they build the Wall? It covered vast tracts of uninhabited territory (it's still uninhabited), and it could not possibly have kept out anyone wanting to climb over it.

Now I crossed the place where the Wall once ran. Fortunately, Wade let this section be, diverting his road to the north, presumably to bridge the North Tyne at a more suitable location. Even so, no part of the Wall was visible to me. Yet there was still the *feel* of being in a place of history, for here Roman soldiers patrolled the Wall. What did they think of their posting to this outpost of Empire, far away from their own lands? What, did they wonder, was the purpose of their being here at all?

One of the forts on the Wall was Chesters (*Cilurnum*) which, thanks to Wade's decision to divert his road to the north, was spared – although all that remain are the excavated ruins of a stone-built barracks with stables, and a well-preserved bath-house, situated between the fort and the river. The Romans bathed *outside* the fort. You'd think they'd have extended the outer wall to the river, but the baths had underfloor heating, and the risk of fire spreading to the entire fort was too great. In the latrines, wooden seats were suspended over a deep channel, which carried effluent directly into the river. The Romans were polluting the Tyne long before anyone.

I was hungry and footsore when, at last, I turned up at the Crown, at Humshaugh, where Geordie voices booming across the bar got louder as the evening progressed. *Geordie* allegedly derives from George Stephenson, who, as well as reputedly inventing the world's first locomotive, designed a miners lamp around the time Sir Humphrey Davy invented his more famous version of the same for the tinners of Cornwall. I guess the Geordies wanted their own.

*

I breakfasted alone in the Crown, served by a waitress who asked where I was walking to today. Byrness, I said, thinking she'd be impressed. She'd never heard of it. But Byrness is nearly thirty miles away, over one of the most sparsely populated areas in England, so perhaps its anonymity wasn't surprising.

On a dank morning I took a narrow trod across fields. The path was muddy, but the walking was an early morning joy, with trees and hedgerows against misty backdrops, giving the North Tyne valley an eerie quality more akin to a Dracula film. There was no sound, just the soft squelch of boots on wet, sticky ground. I enjoyed that half-mile. It was one of those experiences you cannot anticipate and which, when it happens, you never forget. I walked briskly, in part to keep warm, but also with some feelings of anxiety about reaching Byrness before darkness. When I reached tarmacadam again, I opened the throttle.

The road was not without its quota of curious motorists. Some gave the hint of a smile, others actually turned their heads as they passed by, as though sight of a walker was as unusual as someone riding a camel. Perhaps in rural Northumberland it is. So, in part to satisfy a warped sense of grievance, and in part to amuse myself, I pulled a face into what I perceived as their expression. A vicar merited a righteous appearance, a scowl for anyone who appeared to be in a bad mood. It all went wrong when an attractive young woman gave me a dazzling smile. Somehow, trying to mimic her sexy, feminine appearance didn't work. Mercifully, no-one witnessed my efforts.

Further north, I rejoined the Pennine Way where it approaches from a rocky outcrop rejoicing in the name of Shitlington Crags. Evidently, it was once known as Shotlyngton, a name to be preferred, I would have thought. Perhaps there is good reason for the change. Ahead, in a grey distance, lay Bellingham, the 'capital' of North Tynedale. The landscape was changing now: where behind were lush meadows, ahead lay wild, barren moors and the wide spaces of Northumberland's vast wilderness. It looked bleak, but I looked forward to the long, lonely trek to the border and beyond.

Bellingham is a town by Royal Charter, but with a population of around 1,000, is nothing more than a village really. It was once the centre of ironstone and coal mining, and a railway ran along the North Tyne valley. Now, industry and railway have gone, leaving the cattle and sheep of the surrounding moors to graze in peace. I arrived there to find it cold and uninviting. I was hungry and wanted a meal and a rest. My luck was in, for a little café was open. Lunch was corned beef hash and a mug of tea. Sheer luxury! Alas, the woman who served me was as cold as the street outside, an unfriendly soul with none of the expected northern warmth. She spoke not a word to me.

Actually, I don't go along with this 'northern warmth' thing. Sure, northern folk are warm, kind, friendly. But so are southern folk. And eastern and western folk. And highland and lowland folk. And folk everywhere, from Norway to Nigeria. Drop me by parachute in Siberia and ten to one someone will put the kettle on (unless the plumbing's frozen, I suppose). The odd bad apple aside, all folk are decent, that's my opinion. It's nasty people with power who cause the problems of this world – as in the old days, as I mentioned earlier, when selfish monarchs had their armies do their dirty work, and latterly monsters like Hitler and others like him who somehow motivated and commanded ordinary folk to kill each other. During the war perfectly decent Germans dropped bombs on perfectly decent English people, whilst perfectly decent English people killed perfectly decent Italian people, and so on. All at the behest of the few, those who had *power*. And I mention all this because the woman in a café in Bellingham didn't speak to me!

Anyway, getting back to Bellingham, which has never to the best of my knowledge had any connections with Hitler, St Cuthbert's church roof was burned at least twice by marauding Scots. Cuthbert is often referred to as 'Cuddy', hence Cuddy's Well, a spring at the foot of a hill below the church. It is said that Cuthbert discovered the well whose waters today spring from a stone pant – a sort of small fountain – sadly now in a dilapidated condition. The waters are reputed to have miraculous healing powers, because a girl named Eda Brown, who had a withered hand, was cured when she drank here and went to pray in the church.

Today, in the churchyard, a curiously-shaped tombstone relates to the legend of the *Lang Pack*. The story dates from 1723 when a pedlar called at a nearby mansion. He asked for a night's lodging, but the maid refused to allow him to stay in the house, though she did allow him to leave his heavy pack in the kitchen until the following morning. After he'd gone the pack moved and a ploughboy fired a gun into the bundle. Blood oozed out, and when they opened the pack they discovered the body of a man who had been armed with pistols. The servants realised a robbery had been planned and a horn, found beside the body, was blown – a signal to the waiting robbers who came in the mistaken belief they could carry out their wicked plans. Instead, they were driven off, and the unknown body in the pack was buried in the churchyard where today the grave is marked by a long stone.

The road climbs steeply out of Bellingham to wild moors of green and purple, naked except for an isolated tree, an occasional rooftop. Darkening skies heralded my approach. I was settling in for a long march when a car pulled up and its driver, a middle-aged woman, got out and spoke. It had to be to me, for there was no-one else within a mile.

'D'you know where I can buy some petrol?' she asked with a worried frown.

'Bellingham, I suppose,' I replied. I'd not noticed a filling station but it seemed reasonable to assume there must be one.

'Just I've been driving for *miles,*' she said.' I was walking on open moorland, wearing boots and carrying a rucksack – did she think I was one of the locals? I could do no more than repeat my suggestion. 'Just point the car down the hill,' I suggested. 'You'll freewheel all the way into town.'

She peered into the grey distance, possibly wondering if there really was a town in such a wild place. Marching on, I glanced back to see her standing by her car, still looking in the direction of the unseen Bellingham. For all I know she's still there. At least if she is, she ought to be safe. It's just that from the late 13th century until around the middle of the 16th this was a lawless place, where the natives fought their own countrymen as well as those across the border. This was the *Terra Incognita*, where *no King's messenger dared show himself*. People were murdered, their homes burned, their property stolen, their cattle rustled. The men of violence were the Border Reivers, men from all social classes. Today I felt perfectly safe, alone on that vast moor. Safer than I would feel in any of our modern-day inner cities. They are the *Terra Incognita* now. Sometimes the rustled cattle were driven over the border. But before the rustlers, English or Scot, could escape, they'd be cut off and the cattle driven back – only to be rustled and driven back yet again. Not surprisingly, the cows got fed up with it all, hence the lament of the border cow:

I've hiked in years o' reivin'
Each weary border track.
At night the Scots are drivin',
Then southmen heard us back.
When reivers' scabbards rattle
And roof-trees light the howes –
Think of the spoils of battle,
The footsore border cows.

To ensure against rustling, farmers were forced to pay a 'black rent' in cattle to powerful reivers, who would then 'protect' them. This 'black rent' became known as 'black mail', hence the term in use today. Protection rackets didn't start with the gangsters of Chicago.

The rain came, the sort which gives you about five seconds to open your sack and get something waterproof on before you're soaked. It swept across the moor, visibility falling to yards as the mist came down. I marched on to the border forest, where millions of pines stand in regimented, straight columns for mile after mile, planted close together so that they vie for light and grow quickly. But where the pine trees thrive daylight is obliterated, so that nothing grows on the forest floor, and the birds and animals, which would survive in deciduous woodland, cannot live where there is nothing to eat and nowhere to hide. It is a forest of silence, with just the sound of the wind and the crunch – or squelch – of one's footsteps on the lonely forest rides.

There are 'side roads' in the forest, any one of which, had I strayed, might have meant a life sentence, destined to wander in vain hope of release. In the unlikely event of my remains ever being discovered, they would be identified as that of *Paulus Heslopus*, and they'd calculate how long I'd lain in my forest grave by my Silva compass, a device used until the late 20th century, long before navigation by satellite.

'How does it work?' someone asks, looking at the compass.

'You hold it in your hand, like so...'

They look at the needle.

'It always points north,' someone explains, wondering as much as anyone how it possibly could.

'But how does it *know*?'

Heads shake. They look down at *Paulus Heslopus*, still clad in green Gore-tex.

'No wonder he got lost,' someone says, and they all burst out laughing.

At Blakehopeburnhaugh – reputedly the longest place-name in Britain – I left the forest road and followed the Rede, where the path degenerated into a muddy treadmill. I could scarcely stand upright let alone walk. There were long stinging nettles, so high they encroached over the path, with painful consequences. In the end I took to the road, for I could hardly see in the darkness which had come early on a day of leaden skies. I didn't want a sprained ankle or worse.

My sanctuary was the Byrness hotel, where I ate supper in the bar to the accompaniment of a loud, booming voice, the sort you have to listen to whether you want to or not. It belonged to an elderly gent of military bearing who was talking about the war. This wasn't surprising, as Byrness isn't far from Otterburn, where the armies of NATO hold military manoeuvres – tanks, Chinook helicopters, the lot. The good people at the receiving end of this bloke's monologue weren't really interested, but they were stuck with it.

'The Yanks,' our military friend was saying, 'say they won the war.' He knocked off his scotch. 'But they didn't.' He ordered a refill. '*I'll* tell you who won the war...'

We waited to see who won the war.

'The British soldier, *that's* who.'

What a surprise. But he wasn't finished.

'And I'll tell you something else...'

The suspense was killing.

'British tanks were nowhere near as good as German tanks.'

There was a pause, as though he expected a challenge. I did consider asking what he thought about Uncle Sam's tanks, but decided this might spark off world war three. Discretion being the better part of cowardice, I held my tongue. When he moved on to Lancaster bombers I called it a night and went up to my room.

A huge blister had appeared underneath my left foot. But the worst casualties were my toes. They were sore and some of my toenails had turned a shade of purple. I ran my fingers over the tops of my feet, stroking them, caressing them. It felt as good as an orgasm. Well, almost.

*

I'd a choice of route to take for Carter Bar, at the border of England and Scotland. I could follow the Pennine Way up onto Byrness Hill and plot a course along the Cheviot ridge, or take the road. This is good walking country. Yet I chose the road, probably because the day was wet and I suppose I just wanted to cover the ground more quickly. It was the wrong choice. Walking the roadside can never be as good as walking the hills.

I relaxed for half an hour or so. It's nice to 'get breakfast down', instead of starting off too early. I even watched the local news on t.v. The newscaster spoke with a Northumbrian accent, the last time I would hear it on my journey; at Hawick, the next town, it would be Scots. Then an attractive female presenter appeared on the screen and accents didn't matter any more. From the window of my cosy room, I could see low, dank mist clinging to the trees of the Border forest, and the headlights of traffic on the A68, like wolves' eyes peering through the gloom. This was disappointing, not least because I'd hoped to arrive at Carter Bar on a clear day, to look back over the country I had left, and forward to the Scottish lowlands.

Byrness is the last outpost before you reach the border. There's nothing much to the village: the garage, the hotel, and fifty or so houses, built in the 1950's for employees of the forestry commission. And St Francis' church.

The church was built in 1786 and lays claim to being the smallest in Northumberland. A stained glass window depicts workmen with barrows, picks and shovels, and a little girl who waits patiently to give her father his dinner, which she holds in a small, cloth sack; and there's a steam locomotive and some waggons. It's all done in little pieces of brightly coloured glass. Underneath, an inscription reads: *To the Glory of God & in Memory of those Men, Women and Children who have died during the construction of the reservoir at Catcleugh, this Window and Brass have been erected by their fellow workmen and friends 1903.* The names of 64 persons appear on a brass plate on a wall nearby. Byrness has paid proud homage.

From the churchyard outside, the pattern on the window is not apparent. Whether it was designed deliberately so I not know. It occurred to me that in modern-day Britain such artistic skill would probably be wantonly smashed by some passing hooligan – *if* he knew it was there. But he wouldn't know, for the picture is visible only to those inside the church, not a place normally frequented by hooligans, you might think.

Beyond Byrness lies Catcleugh reservoir. On a day of rain and low cloud it was difficult to imagine anywhere so bleak. The estimated cost of the dam was £55,000, actual cost £3,600,00. Got that wrong, didn't they! The reservoir provided the citizens of Newcastle with a plentiful supply of fresh water in Victorian times of bad sanitation. They might have done well to reflect on the words inscribed on the fountain in Hexham market place which (although written about the Tyne) seem fitting here:

> O you who drink my cooling waters clear,
> Forget not the far hills from which they flow,
> Where over fell and moor, and year by year,
> Spring, summer, autumn, winter come and go,
> With showering sun and rain and snow...

The road climbed steadily, the rounded, grassy Cheviots rising sharply on both sides where they disappeared into the mist. Wolves prowled hereabouts until as late as the Norman Conquest. Thankfully I wouldn't encounter any today. But mad motorists are just as dangerous. They sometimes appear in packs, too. At Carter Bar, the border, a 10 ft. stone monolith displays the name SCOTLAND to northbound travellers, whilst on the opposite side those southbound read ENGLAND. It may be a final attempt by the authorities to have any name at Carter Bar at all, for previous signs were forever being stolen.

Just up the hill a battle known as the Raid of the Redeswire took place in 1575. In those days the Wardens of the Marches of both sides of the border met to settle any disputes over cattle, and punish those who had broken the law. They must have been busy men. At one meeting, a dispute arose, resulting in the English firing off some arrows. The ensuing fight was won by the Scots who chased the English off, killing many and taking prisoners who were later released to prevent wholesale war between the two kingdoms. I'm talking England v. Scotland, not just a local tryst. This was the last ever battle between the English and the Scots – apart from the ones at Twickenham and Murrayfield, of course.

Today, the warring tribes are at peace – just – and here at the border there's a long lay-by where motorists can park, relax, take in the views without fear of attack. And here, on sunny days (it can happen) you may find a kilted Scot, the skirl o' the pipes welcoming the traveller to Bonnie Scotland – for a small donation, of course. The patriotism of the Scots may be compared with that of the English, for no Englishman greets those travelling south. You might have expected a Morris dancer or something.

Alas, no Scot, no tourists awaited my arrival. Where there might have been the vibrant, excited voices of children there was silence, broken only by the pitter-patter of the rain on the hood of my cag; and, every now and then, the sound of traffic roaring past where many, under sunny skies, might have pulled over. But wait! There *was* a 'kiltie', painted on the side of a hot-dog van, his presence no more than a representation of the real thing; and, truth to tell, having no less personality than the specimen of humanity that opened the shutter when I tapped lightly upon it. He didn't speak, just peered at me blankly from his cosy bolt-hole.

'One hot-dog, please,' I said, trying to look cheerful.

No sound at all emanated from this wretched soul, save to inform me of the cost of the hot-dog, which I wolfed down quickly to prevent it becoming soggier than it already was.

There was a solitary car parked in the lay-by. The driver's window was open about two inches, just enough for its occupant to utter something I didn't catch but after consideration thought whatever it was might allude to the state of my mentality. So, I'd walked from Cornwall to the England-Scotland border to find nothing but a hot-dog van and a car containing person or persons unknown and a view of nowhere. When I got going again I discovered Scotch mist to be every bit as clammy as the English.

This border was, until relatively recent times, as much a border as those shared by wholly independent countries. Then, in 1603, after the death of Queen Elizabeth, James I of Scotland became James VI of England and Scotland, an act known as the Union of Crowns. But if the crowns were united, the people were not. During England's endless wars with the French, the Scots harried the 'auld enemy' at her back door, over the border. 'He that will France win must with Scotland first begin' was a popular English saying.

In 1707, came political union, desired by the English if only to rid themselves of the constant menace from the north, and also out of convenience, having rid themselves of the Stuarts and installed a Protestant king, George, of Hanover. Lowland Scots, too, considered they would benefit from union with their prosperous neighbour, and when it was decreed they could keep their own laws the Scottish Parliament merged with Westminster. Note it was 'lowland' Scots. Highlanders and their countrymen in the far north wanted to retain independence and the restoration of Stuart rule, and the exiled Stuart king was in-waiting, in France. Today, of course, the Scots have had their 'Parliament' restored, with limited powers over the running of Scotland's affairs, and wide powers over the running of England's affairs. Lots of V.I.P.'s in gleaming limos, a beaurocratic nonsense costing a fortune, courtesy of President Tony. Seems to me if the Scots want *real* independence, and fair enough if they do, they should have it. So should the English, although whether they'd want it isn't known since no-one's asked them.

Just over the border, the A6088 turns off for Chesters, a name that proves the Romans were here before me. The road ran steadily downward, dropping out of the mist, rough moorland giving way gradually to fields and signs of habitation. I had checked the map for rights of way hereabouts, but of course there are none in Scotland, not in the English sense anyway. The road it was. As I marched to Bonchester Bridge, my toes began to throb. They'd been okay climbing up to the border, but now, on long downward stretches, my feet were thrust forward, every step turning into torture. To anyone

159

considering this journey might have been easier because I was obliged to do it in four goes, let me assure them this is not so, for every time I resumed the walk I had to 'break in' my feet anew.

Bonchester Bridge stands on the Rule Water, after which there's a long pull to higher ground again. If my feet were suffering, my legs weren't, for I went up without pause or discomfort. I followed the road, the only life form – apart from the ubiquitous sheep – for mile after mile. I wondered why there was a road; there were no motorists.

And so to Teviotdale and its 'capital', Hawick (pron. *Hoyk*), 'the auld grey toun', famous for rugby, a strange game played by men with oval-shaped balls. The town charter dates back to 1537, replacing an earlier one 'lost in times past through hostile invasion of Englishmen'. To celebrate an 'event' of 1514, when the Scots defeated the English somewhere, local young men, known as *callants*, 'ride the Marches' every June. The natives are known as 'Teris', a name evidently deriving from *Tyr-Ibus ye Tyr ye Odin*, which is a call for assistance to the Norse gods, Thor and Odin. Entering the town, a sign proclaims Hawick to be 'the home of knitting', and no wonder, for it owes its prosperity and growth to stockings, originally produced by its cottage industry in the 19th century, and latterly woollens produced by the knitwear mills. There's a poem by a fellow who was obviously proud of Hawick:

> I like auld Hawick the best,
> Each hill with heathery crest,
> That guards the grey auld toun below –
> I like auld Hawick the best.

It had been a long day. I wasted no time in locating accommodation and seeking food and drink, the latter in the form of Arbroath Bitter, as fine a pint as ever you'd get. Then I hobbled up Hawick's main street, which is dominated by the town hall, or rather its massive clock tower. It seems utterly disproportionate to the adjacent buildings, so much so that if someone built a scale model you'd surely consider the clock tower to be too big. But I wasn't looking at a scale model, I was looking at the real thing. And, truth to tell, once I'd got accustomed to it, it looked grand – as indeed it is. Better than some of today's monstrosities, but that goes without saying.

*

I'd not seen the sun since leaving Middleton in County Durham, and here I was deep into the Scottish Borders. With time to spare in the 'auld grey toun', I lingered in the cold of a grey morning. I liked Hawick. Its grey stone buildings give the town a solid, almost defiant appearance, a hint that nothing will change here. I was just about to resume my journey when to my amazement I saw something, which, in modern-day Britain, is as rare as hens' teeth – a uniformed copper on the beat. At first, I wondered if it might be some attempt at a tourist attraction, or maybe they were making a movie. But no, PC Forsyth was for real, and no sooner had we introduced ourselves than he provided the second shock of the day by informing me that the knitting industry still thrives in Hawick. And there was me thinking it was history. I just hope he and the natives keep it to themselves. If our political masters in Brussels hear of it they'll probably close it down.

A quiet lane led to higher ground, where a dotted line on the map indicated a footpath. I regarded it with suspicion, thinking the footpath, such as it is, might peter out – as it did. Strategically-placed signposts helped, but what didn't help were newly-planted conifers whose presence will make progress hereabouts impossible in the not-too-distant future. Here was naked soil, and all in all the next three miles or so turned out to be a tiring slog. Mercifully, it ended at a quiet backroad that led to a place called Woll, where Ashkirk parish church stands close to the road in a quiet setting. The churchyard was in good trim, with close-cropped lawns and fine trees. A plaque on the wall is dedicated to the memory of a soldier killed at Arnhem, a reminder that from every part of Britain there were people who gave their lives for freedom, so that today the likes of me can walk unhindered. I arrived at the church, my feet throbbing; I left it feeling proud, with no thoughts of my feet at all.

I climbed to Woll Rigg, with rolling countryside all around. What is it about the higher ground? I see beauty everywhere in Britain, be it by rivers, in woodland, by the sea. Yet the high ground somehow evokes grand feelings, of freedom, of accomplishment – after all, you have to climb up to it! Ahead lay the unseen Ettrick Water, and beyond, the Yarrow. I sang all along that ridge, a full three miles non-stop. As usual, there was no-one to hear. Just as well.

At Oakwood Mill I crossed the Ettrick Water by an ancient suspension bridge, and passed by a house with a strange-sounding name, Gillkeeket. I was in marching mode, not pausing to see the sights. Ahead, alongside a vast wood, a column of vehicles approached. It turned out to be the army, on manoeuvres, I supposed. As it turned out, the entire area was swarming with soldiers. Mercifully I wasn't taken for the enemy and shot. Further on I turned up a narrow lane for Newark Castle, a spectacular ruin atop a promontory above the Yarrow Water. Ruinous it is, yet still it is an imposing sight which must be given a wide berth; you get the feeling that at moment it might collapse. Further on I dropped down to the lovely Yarrow. From the bridge, the view upriver was splendid, the silver waters of the river backed by trees of deep green foliage.

A path led past the houses of Yarrowford, and cut through a wood, where late afternoon sunbeams shone brightly through the trees, and below a gushing burn provided the music to this lovely scene. I wanted it to go on, but suddenly I emerged with pin-point accuracy at Broadmeadows youth hostel and had to accept that the woodland walk was a brief but grand finale to the day. Well, not quite a finale; that would be provided by the lady warden at the youth hostel, and was not grand at all.

My stay at Broadmeadows was memorable for a number of reasons. First, the hostel is superbly situated in a clearing, overlooking the wooded hills above the Yarrow. Good so far. Second, it's of 'simple' grade, meaning it would probably be quiet, and occupied by walkers and cyclists, people who *do* something in the countryside. Good again – but now comes the down-side. Being a 'simple', it does not provide meals or, in this case, even a packet of biscuits. As I had arrived with a Yorkie bar and a packet of crisps, this would be my first food since breakfast, and my last until the following evening. Fair enough, if I died of hunger it would be my own fault. But then there was the warden.

I had arrived a few minutes early, and when she appeared she was obliged to walk right past me which she did without a hello or kiss my watsit. Her commanding voice boomed out on the stroke of five: 'Come and sign it *NOW*', notwithstanding, had I so chosen, I could have waited for another four or five hours. At reception – cold reception in this case – I enquired about a sheet sleeping bag, which you always get at a youth hostel. Except here. 'The clean laundry doesn't arrive until tomorrow,' I was told. OK, so I'd just crawl between the quilt and mattress, hoping no-one with scabies had slept there before me, and that I wouldn't contract galloping knobrot. No supper, no bed to make: what could I do? Go for a walk, of course. I strolled down to Yarrowford, saw more soldiers, and sauntered back to the hostel where, would you believe, I bumped into Mrs Warden again. 'I was wondering,' I said bravely, 'if you might be able to help me out with a bedsheet for tonight.' Meaning, of course, she might have one at home. 'The clean laundry doesn't arrive until tomorrow,' came the reply. She was obviously programmed to say the same things, like a Duracell-driven doll.

Indoors, three other guests had appeared – a bloke and his young daughter, and a young woman who rolled up in her car. Things got difficult when they started cooking supper; I pretended I had eaten earlier and did my best to ignore the aroma from the kitchen. To occupy myself, as the evening had turned cold, I gathered some wood and coal from the back and prepared a fire in the stove. At first, this seemed to irritate my fellow-guests, but they were pleased to enjoy the warmth of the living fire after they'd scoffed their food. I have to admit spilling one half of a thimbleful of dust on to the floor. Then Mrs Warden appeared. She was giving instructions about not using a tea towel to dry saucepans when she spotted the little pile of coal dust. We might have been in Colditz.

'What's happened here?' she demanded, looking at my blackened hands, clearly suspecting I'd been trying to tunnel my way out.

'It happened as I was lighting the fire,' I told her, not adding that in real life I was a serving detective inspector with many responsibilities, like investigating murder, rape, child abuse, burglary, robbery, assaults, car crime, dealing with the victims of same, looking after a squad of detectives and turning out to suspicious deaths, suicides, attending crown courts and other trivia. There followed a barrage of orders, everything from tidying up the mess to the certainty of being shot in the event of trying to escape. Her final command was to ensure the fire had died down before we turned in. I was glad when she buggered off.

Meanwhile, back in the world of social discourse, the young woman proved to be excellent company. She cycles hereabouts, usually alone. Good for her. The bloke turned out to be a quiet chap. He went out into the darkness wearing one of those torches you strap around your head. Come to think of it, I don't remember him coming back. In my disease-ridden bed, my journey to slumber was accompanied by the theme music from *The Great Escape*, some bloke waking me up by persistently roaring through my brain on a motorbike. Looked a bit like Steve McQueen, actually.

8

Central Scotland

I lingered long enough to devour a packet of smoky bacon flavoured crisps before fleeing Broadmeadows youth hostel. I did consider knocking on the warden's door and asking if she'd do me a cooked breakfast, but decided against it on the grounds that she would only have reminded me that the clean laundry was due today. I was bound for Peebles, and I didn't need to consult the map to know that the total number of places where I could find a meal without straying too far off route totalled precisely nil. Never mind. I'd survive, and I could always enjoy a slap-up dinner tonight.

It was a grim, grey morn, the ground sodden after heavy overnight rain. I was in fine spirits nevertheless as I climbed steeply for the Southern Upland Way, which traverses the high ridge just a mile off. Nearing the ridge, I became engulfed in dank mist, but when a stile in the fence at the top appeared eerily out of the gloom I knew I had hit the target.

The Southern Upland Way traverses southern Scotland from Portpatrick, near Stranraer, in the west, to Cockburnspath in the east, a distance of 212 miles. I had joined it near Broomy Law, from where I would head west across grand, rolling country, covering six miles of the route. I was on high ground, walking the sort of country I love: nice and soft underfoot, the path keeping faithfully to the ridge. The ridge does not maintain equal height, but is formed by a series of hills, with deep troughs in between. For an unfit, couch-potato it would be hard going; for a fit, determined walker, even a hungry one, it was a joy.

The mist lifted, revealing a greyness that would last the day. Other than setting the scene, there is little to report, except that at one point I came upon a strange wooden box mounted on a post, with a notice inviting anyone who happened along to write down any comments about the Way on a printed form, and kindly pop it into the box. They even provided a pencil, tied to the post. I dutifully completed the form and posted it, wondering if my opinions, whatever they were, could ever have any bearing on the Southern Upland Way. You can see the maps and guidebooks: 'Turn left at the stile, keeping the river on the right. It used to be on the left but Paul Heslop thinks otherwise...' Moving on I encountered three women, all gorgeous and smiling and calling hello as they passed me by. I smiled too. Shame they were walking in the opposite direction.

The path led to Traquair Forest, where the words 'Cheese Well' appear in blue on the map. It turned out to be a well marked by an ancient stone. A sign explains that in past times travellers would leave pieces of cheese for the fairies here, and so bring themselves good luck. If I'd seen any cheese it would have been quickly devoured, never mind the fairies. I carried on along a seemingly endless track that led out of the forest to a road, the B709. Thus I left behind the Southern Upland Way which, hereabouts at least, merits ten out of ten in anyone's book.

A quiet backroad, the B7062, would take me to Peebles, now seven miles away. With the best of the day's walking behind me I pressed on. Soon I was alongside the Tweed, and here the skies opened up and the rain came. I had just struggled into waterproofs when a Land Rover screeched to a halt and I found myself looking at two uniformed policemen.

Had I seen a red Vauxhall with its rear window smashed, asked one? I had not. There had been a burglary at Innerleithen, I was told, and such a car had been seen speeding off from the scene of the crime. Whereupon, naturally, I revealed to them the exciting details of my identity, which led inevitably to a chat. As the lads explained, this is such a remote and sparsely populated area it's easy for burglars to target remote houses. Then they sped off in search of their Vauxhall, leaving me to reflect on the chances of it coming my way along this country road, and if it did what I should do about it. Anyway, it didn't.

I pressed on in the rain, doing my utmost to put thoughts of food from my mind. Instead, I directed my thoughts to Peebles. I'd never been to the town, although I knew that it was once the county town of Peebles-shire, now swallowed up along with Selkirkshire and Berwickshire in the bland-sounding Borders Region. Head down in the rain I found myself on a sort of country estate, private property surely. I kept going anyway until I arrived unexpectedly at a sort of fancy-goods shop. I attempted to pass it by, but failed to locate a path, so went inside and, dripping wet and feeling sheepish, asked how I could get back to the road. The woman in the shop told me, whilst two people who looked like the landed gentry ignored me totally and left the premises. They could not have failed to see me, but to them the stranger was not to be acknowledged. Back on the road I motored at speed, my toes hurting again. Finally I came to a little walled flower-bed with a sign sticking out. Peebles, it said.

A tree-lined road led to town. On it I encountered an elderly gent who nodded and said something about the weather, as you do. What is it about the British and the weather? We see repeated weather forecasts on t.v., hear them on the radio, read them in our newspapers. And as if that isn't enough, we greet total strangers with some comment about the weather. Why can't we say something more meaningful for a change? Instead of 'hello, turned nasty hasn't it?' – which both parties know unless they are blind or stupid – why can't we say something informative, like 'hello, my Aunt Fanny lives in Ashby-de-la-Zouch,' or 'my haemorrhoids are giving me gyp today.' But no, it's the weather. Of *course* it's raining, can't you see I'm bloody soaking? Ah, but it was nice to exchange a civil greeting. The women on the Southern Upland Way, those coppers and now the old boy – they were all I'd seen all day. Apart from the woman in the shop and the landed gentry, that is.

When I started my hillwalking 'career' in the early eighties, in the Lake District, I was advised always to check the weather forecast. There was even a special number to call, displayed at youth hostels and Bed and Breakfasts. Dependent on the forecast, I would plan my day. A good forecast: go for the 'tops'. A bad one: best not to. Sounds obvious, except that for what use the forecast was, I might as well have stuck my head out of the window and judged the weather for myself (and licked my forefinger and held it up to see which way the wind was blowing while as I was about it). Time and again, following the advice of so-called 'experts' who predicted bad weather, I'd give the tops a miss only to find the sun would come out and beam happily away all afternoon. Or, having been told it would be a lovely clear day, the skies would darken and the heavens would open.

'It *might* be right,' people say, when criticism is offered of the forecast. Of course it might, as anyone *might* be right on anything. Or it's 'well it's usually right these days,' meaning they've got satellites and show computer graphics on t.v. – a map of Britain with a huge computer graphic cloud coming in from the west. If, one day, I glance up at the Sca Fells to see a computer graphic cloud hovering menacingly, I'll believe it.

Of course, if you're watching breakfast telly, you'll have to watch the weather forecast whether you want to or not. On the hour, every hour, and the half hour, along with the *regional* forecast, just in case the national one is wrong, presumably. 'It's a lovely morning,' the smiling weathergirl is saying from some rooftop in London, and never mind it's pissing down in Watford. Fortunately for the weathermen and women, theirs is not an industry that depends on success. They got the weather wrong in Godalming, but they were right about Arbroath, so there.

The imminent prospect of food spurred me on. I decided, though, not to eat a meal yet, but instead to have coffee and a snack, and devour a mountain later. But then, I was so hungry I wondered if I might fail to reach anywhere to eat at all, that I might expire just yards from the protein I desperately needed. I recalled a signpost I saw once, in the Lake District. It told of a man who had died in the snow, just yards from the safety of his home. In my case the plaque would tell of death through hunger, just ten yards from McDonalds, or whatever they have in Peebles. 'Here fell Paul Heslop, died from the need of a Big Mac with French fries'. I pressed on, and far from dying from hunger I was about to fall in love – with Peebles.

I crossed the Tweed by a Victorian suspension bridge and continued through a narrow passage leading to the broad main street. Here were handsome stone buildings, set far apart on the broad, main thoroughfare; and here were well-dressed people. Peebles is the sort of place to fall for at first sight. Somehow, I'd known it would be. But love came a poor second to hunger, and the need of a cup of coffee. At a bakery-cum-coffee parlour I bowled inside, water dripping everywhere, and plonked my sack down and consumed the second best cup of coffee ever, along with an enormous scone, the first food since the crisps at Colditz. (For an account of the best cup of coffee ever, read on, but it's ages yet). We drink coffee all the time. Or tea. And we say what a lovely cuppa. Believe me, it's not until you *really* need one it gets to taste like this. I was resisting the temptation to eat something else when a bloke I might aptly describe as the town drunk appeared.

Every town has one. A local guy who hits the bottle, slobbers and staggers and is utterly harmless. The staff knew him, of course. They humoured him, ushered him tactfully to the door. For a moment I thought he was going to cut up a bit, and turn nasty, a development which might have necessitated an English copper going into action on Scottish soil. But no, he teetered off and would be back again the next day, I shouldn't wonder. So I went off to a B and B where my host, a delightful, elderly lady, provided me with a hot bath and introduced me to her companion, a parrot called Ya-koo.

He was grand company, Ya-koo. He could listen, he could talk. Best of all, he didn't ask foolish questions, like how far had I walked today, and he never uttered a word about the weather. I particularly liked the way he tilted his head to one side, as though considering what was being said, before cackling out something which, admittedly, had nothing whatever to do with the conversation. He spent a great deal of the time perched on my host's shoulder, and that was cute. Ya-koo was intelligent, and had personality. I noticed my host left doors open as she moved about the house. She could see I was concerned. 'He'd never fly off,' she declared.

I duly devoured a mountainous supper, a T-bone steak, served up with everything imaginable. Peebles was awash with rain all evening. Tomorrow, I would see it in sunshine on what would turn out to be a memorable morning by that most beautiful of rivers, the Tweed.

*

I ate breakfast in company with a Yorkshire couple, late fifties, with Ya-koo a curious observer. He might be forgiven for believing, as far as the human race is concerned, that the female is the dominant species. Here was a parrot witnessing *homo sapiens* male being asked a question, while the female of the species answered. Host to male guest: 'Which cereal would you prefer?' Wife: 'He'll have the bran flakes.' Host to male guest: 'Would you like more toast?' Wife: 'He's had quite sufficient, thank you.' I don't know what Ya-koo made of it, but when the woman got to her feet he did no more than flap his brightly-coloured wings and land on her shoulder. In an instant she went from dominant bully to quaking jelly.

Head turned sideways, and eyes as far into the corners as they could go, she addressed Ya-koo in a shaky Yorkshire accent. 'Alright, alright,' she drawled, trying to keep calm, as one does when looking down the barrel of a cocked pistol held in the trembling hand of a madman. Ya-koo, unmoved, tilted his head. This was a new language. He would need to hear more before he was fluent. Meanwhile, our host, to whom this turn of events was nothing out of the ordinary, was talking about the weather (it *always* comes down to the weather in the end). Only the wretched woman's husband could save her now. Alas, where he might have stepped in, or at least reassured his missus that she was in no danger, he simply wandered out of the room. To this day I've wondered if, when the door closed behind him, he clenched his fists, raised his arms and mouthed a silent but meaningful 'Y-E-S!' Meanwhile, there being no further dialogue from this strange-sounding creature, Ya-koo returned to his perch.

'I often get couples like that staying with me,' my host remarked after the couple had gone. Like what, I wondered? My host was eager to explain. 'Councillors and politicians,' she said. 'They attend conferences at the Hydro (a plush hotel-cum-conference centre). They claim Hydro expenses, but book in with me and pocket the difference.' Ah, so they build a huge hotel and the little ol' B and B's get the trade. Well, it's only taxpayers' money. Nothing to worry about there.

After all, taxpayers' dosh pays for all manner of things, right? Like those jolly trips abroad by council officials. You know, 'town twinning', where they visit their oppos in Fontainebleau or some-where. You go to work, pay your taxes, and your local bureaucrats use the money for 'cultural visits'. You might wonder just what you're getting when you pay for unseen faces to fly off. I mean, do they come back and tell you the great benefits you've paid for? (apart from their smiling faces in the glossy brochure, which you also pay for). The only difference between today's gravy train riders and the fat cats I mentioned earlier, the bishops of Durham, is that where before, the latter prevented workers feeding starving families, today they just take workers' money.

You're paying taxes for police when there's no police on the streets (except in Hawick), for a health service where those who can afford it go to hospitals in foreign countries, for an education system that doesn't educate your kids. But don't worry about it. Really, don't, because there's nothing you can do about it. Instead, focus on Britain, a land of contrasts, a place worth walking through. As I was doing, except I didn't tell you I was carrying a soapbox in my rucksack.

Where was I? Ah, yes. Peebles. I stepped outside to a bright, fresh morning to find the town, having shown herself in the rain, now wished to display herself in all her finery. The name, says the brochure, derives from *Pebylls*, after tents pitched her by ancient settlers, the wandering Gadeni tribe. David II granted the town Royal Burgh status in 1367. During the border wars, Peebles suffered at the hands of the auld enemy, local feuds, the border reivers and retreating Scots armies who laid waste to the town to deprive English invaders. I wonder what David, or the wandering Gadeni tribe for that matter, would have made of officials fraudulently claiming money. 'Peebles for Pleasure' is the town motto, but who's paying?

Peebles was too good to leave on such a morning. It was after eleven when I headed west, by the Tweed. The path crossed open parkland, narrowing as it climbed, following the river. I encountered only a few people, locals, whose mornings would be spent just like today, strolling by the Tweed. Lucky me today. Lucky them always.

And so to Neidpath Castle. Ruinous now, it stands atop a high knoll. It was the seat of the Frasers, the last of whom, Sir Symon Fraser, in company with none other than William Wallace, shared a victory over Edward I, so-called 'Hammer of the Scots', at Roslin Moor in 1303. They also shared the same fateful end, being hanged, drawn and quartered in London. Wallace went on to achieve immortalisation, not least for a famous victory over the English at Stirling Bridge, and latterly in *Braveheart*, when he (a Scot) was played by an Australian actor in a Hollywood movie designed to make money, as opposed to the portrayal of an accurate account of history. The castle was famously visited by Mary, Queen of Scots, and bombarded by Cromwell. With walls over ten feet thick, it's hardly surprising it proved impenetrable. More romantic is the story of the Maid of Neidpath who, according to legend, had a *liaison* with the son of a laird. Her father objected, and her lover was dispatched abroad. This made her ill, so her father had the lad brought home. Unfortunately, the young suitor unwittingly rode past the castle, whereupon seeing this the poor maid died of a broken heart. Was he worth it? you ask, riding past like that.

P 2001   Neidpath Castle

Half a mile beyond the castle a magnificent stone bridge came into view. It carried the former railway, now 'dismantled', as the map says. This is the Queen's Bridge, constructed in 1864. It is truly a grand sight, in light grey stone, crossing the Tweed over eight arches. The line closed in 1954, so now the bridge is defunct, kaput, finito. The Victorians weren't only great builders, they were artists. That their work remains in situ is admirable; that it isn't needed any more is a pity. I pressed on, following the wide, sweeping curve of the Tweed. The river led south for a while, not the best direction for someone ultimately bound for the extreme north of the country, but with the Tweed as a companion I had no cause for complaint. I wouldn't have cared if I had gone full-circle. Finally, I ended up near a farm called

171

The Glack. You might wonder at such a name. Imagine it: they've just built a farm, so what should they call it?

'Let's call it Borders Farm.'

'Too bland.'

'Tweed View?'

'Don't like that either.'

'How about 'The Glack?'

'Brilliant!'

I found myself in an enormous field whose bovine occupants included a fierce-looking bull. To avoid being mauled to death I kept to the perimeter of the field, a long diversion necessitating a trudge across marshy ground, until I reached a wall over which I could confidently climb in the event of you-know-who spotting me. Better to be a live coward with wet feet than a dead hero with dry ones. Anyway, passing to safety through a gate, I blew the bull a raspberry.

High ground, as usual, brought grand feelings of freedom, and on the crest of the ridge, at the corner of a wood, I lay unashamedly on the ground and watched white, fluffy clouds drifting across a deep-blue sky. Here, the air was fresh, the birds were singing on a wonderful, wonderful day. Alas, I had to move on, and did so in good cheer, for now the way was downhill, with the Broughton Heights, hitherto unknown to me, now in full view ahead. They looked grand, Cheviot-like, rounded, grassy, uninhabited. They were just begging for someone to go forth and explore their secret delights, as though no-one had ever done so before today. First I traversed meadows of deep-green, occupied by cows of deep-brown, and came to Easter Dawick where I ended up in the farmyard. How bizarre! Perhaps they should erect a sign: 'Paul Heslop came this way'. Tourists might flock here. They could charge an entry fee, and later shops would spring up, selling tea and cakes and ice cream, after which a small town could grow. Disneyworld might even come to Easter Dawick.

I crossed the Tweed for the last time and headed for the hills by way of the Weston Burn. A narrow trod led through the heather, bound for a place called Hammer Head, after which care was needed to ensure I reached the Moffat road near Stirkfield. Atop the hill, at around 1,500 feet, I found myself in what may aptly be described as a sea of heather. It reached the horizon in every direction. I might have been in heaven. But now the weather was turning, with dark clouds looming menacingly. It was a long trek down to the Moffat road, where a firm path appeared, and I sang as I walked, safe in the knowledge that I was on the right course. At the road I glanced back to the hills I had just traversed; I had not seen a soul, not even a sheep on the lonely Broughton Heights.

Lingering in Peebles, daydreaming on that hillside and traversing the Heights had cost me time. I pressed on, arriving at Broughton-howe, a solitary house where, at last, I saw life in the form of children playing. Then I took a rutted lane north for Candy Mill. It was cold, it was getting dark and I was tiring when, at last, I knocked on the door of an isolated dwelling, my night's lodgings. The lady of the house cooked me supper, and I contented myself by watching t.v. It made a change.

*

The next three days, I knew, would not be so good. Not after the walk by the Tweed, or scaling the lonely Broughton Heights of yesterday. But that's what walking the length of the country is all about. I had gone to great lengths to ensure, as far as possible, that my journey would take in the best possible territory, but there was nothing I could do about the fact that I now had to cross lowland Scotland, before embarking on the West Highland Way. Not that I was complaining. Who could tell what lay ahead in uncharted territory, some of which might never have been 'walked' by anyone since the world began? We just don't know what life holds in store, do we?

On a grey Saturday I set off for Carnwath and, beyond, Carluke. There would be many miles of tarmacadam, although I did my best to take ancient byways across windswept fields whenever possible. After six miles, I came to Libberton, seeing not a soul on the way, nor indeed in the churchyard where I rested and answered the call of nature. I expressly asked the Lord for forgiveness, respectfully pointing out in mitigation that it was better than by the side of the road, where I might be spotted by a lady motorist in the unlikely event of one passing at the time. You know Murphy's Law: if it can happen, it will – or words to that effect.

And so to Carnwath, a large village strung out along the A721. On such a cold day, I needed a cuppa, and looked up and down the street in the hope of sighting a small café. Standing on a corner was a group of young blokes, not the sort who might be used to sight of a fellow wearing shorts, a silly hat and carrying a rucksack. In Peebles, yes; in Carnwath, no. I supposed there would be sarky remarks, coupled with hostile threats the moment I opened my mouth and they discovered I was a Sassenach. I told myself not to be so stupid/such a coward/so presumptive when they suddenly split and each went his own way. One headed straight for me, with a nod and an 'Aye, aye,' as he passed by. Far from being hostile he bid me 'good morning', Carnwath-style, proving you should never judge anyone on appearance.

And yet I was ill-at-ease in Carnwath. It's just that, walking up the main street I felt so out of place. I was the stranger, just arrived in town, like in those Spaghetti Westerns. All that was missing was the sagebrush blowing along the street, and the clatter of the batwing doors of the ol' saloon. I imagined I was Clint Eastwood, that at any moment four hombres would appear...

'S'ppose you think you're fast,' says one menacingly, six-gun dangling half-way down his leg, his twitching fingers ready to draw.

'Faster'n you'll ever live to be,' says Clint – that's me – before spitting out the stub of a cigar butt I've been chewing for six weeks.

Grave looks cloud their faces, and eyes peer around corners and out of the upstairs windows of the hotel. Clint – that's me, remember – stares at the men through cold, grey eyes. Then, lightening-quick, he lets 'em have it, blam, blam, blam, blam, and the men fall dead, mercilessly gunned down by the eight rounds Clint discharges from his six-shooter. Serves 'em right. They started it.

Back in the real world, I enter a newsagents. Faces turn on sight of the stranger. I'm ready for anything, thanks to Clint.

'A packet of crisps and a Mars Bar,' I drawl, tossing a coin on to the counter. I emerge on to the empty street unchallenged, and spy a small café opposite. Just a couple of customers and the waitress. She beckons me to a table and I'm head over heels before I reach it. She's attractive, but so are thousands of others. She's polite, welcoming, but so are thousands of others. I meet women every day, but it's never like this. She hasn't even spoken and I'm a lost cause. How can it be? 'Isn't it cold today?' Yes, it is. 'What will you have?' Coffee and a fruit scone. 'Are you going far?' I was, but now I've decided to stay here for the rest of my life, which has until this moment been utterly meaningless and devoid of purpose. She goes away. She returns with the coffee and the fruit scone. I, too, go away – into orbit. Now she's saying it isn't often we see hikers passing through Carnwath. Just minutes before I'd have said most people surely pass through, but now...

I watch as she goes about her chores – a tablecloth straightened here, a word to a customer there. I didn't *have* to go on to Carluke, I tell myself. I could stay here, in Carnwath. I'd ask her if she knew anywhere I could stay. There is nowhere, she'd reply, adding that, if I wanted, I could stay with her. Carnwath has gone from Dodge City to Mecca. I will never leave. I will transfer from Hertfordshire to Strathclyde, spend the rest of my life with my Scottish lover. Dream on.

It took ages to eat that scone, but it was no good, I had to go. What was the alternative? Get her name and phone number, of course. I would have, too, but she was wearing a gold ring. That's that, then. Out into the cold street I went, dragging myself away from the little café...

I did but see her passing by,
And yet I'll love her till I die.

It was written anonymously – with me in mind, obviously.

I headed out of town, taking a quiet road past a ghastly place rejoicing in the name of Ryeflat Moss, where peat was being hewn from the landscape – for garden centres, presumably. So this is where it comes from. I motored on, passing by a field gate, my presence prompting a herd of cattle to charge, as though they didn't like me for some reason. Even Clint would have been hard-pushed to do much if they got free, which they might have done – the gate did look a bit rickety. They glared as I passed by, which I considered strange, as cattle are usually docile creatures. Maybe they were related to the steak I had in Peebles. Further on I sat on a wall and rested, the sun having made a brief if pathetic appearance. Studying my boots – as you do – I realised I could discern the faint sound of creaking, like bedsprings. *Creak, creak, creak.* Surely no-one was at it, not here. I looked about, expecting to discover two lovers banging away on an old mattress, or having a tree-trembler maybe. But no, it was only an innocent cow scratching her ample rump on the fence. And a good old scratch she was having, too.

A leafy lane led ultimately to my lodgings in Carluke. The town was Kirkstyle in the 17th century, and grew with the cotton trade. Today, Mrs Carr took in a lovesick traveller, after which, cleansed and famished, I set off for town for food and drink, in reverse order. As I had suspected, Carluke proved the antithesis of Peebles. Where

Peebles was quiet, Carluke was boisterous; where Peebles was demure, Carluke was unreserved; where the pubs in Peebles were orderly, the pubs in Carluke were disorderly, loud Scots voices competing with noisy music. I enjoyed my solemn evening in Peebles. As far as Carluke was concerned, I wouldn't have had it any other way.

*

I'd been going for over week since Middleton, and it showed. Or, just as likely, reeked. Mrs Carr to the rescue! When I came down to breakfast the following morning my shirts, socks and underpants (both pairs) were hanging on her clothes line, having been freshly laundered. I didn't ask her to do it, she just did – possibly to avoid neighbours peering out through their curtains and seeing a hobo departing her abode, or more likely because she is a kindly woman who just wanted to help.

Hitherto on my journey I had passed through just two major cities: Plymouth and Bristol. I was aiming to miss a third by about 100 yards. Glasgow lay across my bows, and I would ensure my footsteps were aimed to the north of this great metropolis. But there would be no avoiding Airdrie.

I left Mrs Carr on a bright and cheery morn, an easy day in prospect, albeit a dreary one. I headed north, to Newmains, where Sunday motorists were faithfully carrying out the ritual of whizzing to the shops for their newspapers. I decided I would buy one myself at a newsagents situated near a huge roundabout, where I found time to sit on a bench an have a read. Moving on, I had difficulty in calculating which of the many roads leading from the roundabout I should take. Nor could I remember which one I had used to get here. Utterly disorientated, I actually had to take out the compass and get my act together. This was the man who traversed Dartmoor and the Pennines.

I was on the A73, at the side of a dual carriageway. Here were square-shaped blocks of flats, designed by a cretin (as opposed to an architect). Surely we can do better than to blot the proverbial landscape with such monstrosities – or did the person who designed these flats win an award, I wonder? I bet he isn't living in one. Unexpectedly, the old road – pre-dual carriageway – appeared, and I found myself transported into a quiet world, free of traffic, where people walked their dogs or walked themselves. After half a mile I passed through Bellside – and on to the 26th map of my journey, the one with Glasgow on it, and what a massive place it is. I walked alongside the perimeter of a huge council estate, where old bangers in various states of disrepair were abandoned by the roadside. The sun still shone, but the day had turned chilly, and heavy clouds were gathering. Just the same when I spied a bench by the roadside I decided to rest my feet awhile.

An old boy occupied a place on the bench. In such circumstances, you're bound to speak. You can hardly sit eighteen inches away from somebody and stay silent. Well, there's some as would, I suppose. He opened up with a comment on the weather. There was a change. Then he asked me where I had come from and where I was going – broad Scots, of course. I said Cornwall – as I regard that as the start of my journey – and Dunnet Head. Not John o'Groats this time; I calculated a Scot would know where Dunnet Head is. Cornwall and Dunnet Head – he'd heard of neither. I began to explain.

'Och, I dinna ken doon there,' he replied, perhaps meaning if Cornwall's in England who the hell cares? Dunnet Head? Near John o'Groats, I said. Ah, he'd heard of John o'Groats, so that was okay. I told him my mother was born near Banff, which made me half-Scots, so I was half-okay. All in all, I took to the fellow. He had gnarled hands and a gnarled face and I reckoned he'd had a gnarled life, with not a lot to show for it. He'd probably never been far, nor had the opportunity to be. Maybe he had heard of Cornwall, but being denied the opportunity to go he denied knowing of its existence. He wandered off at last, a forlorn figure on a cold day – probably to roast beef and Yorkshire pudding, which was a damn sight more than I was having for Sunday lunch.

I moved on along a quiet backroad, arriving at what might be aptly deemed a low point of my journey, at least as far as the environment and man's desecration of it is concerned. Where the road crossed a burn flowing from the direction of a smelly chemical works, or similar establishment, what might have been a pretty sight – the swift-flowing burn pushing its way without fuss between tall grasses – instead was a disgrace, as into it flowed a brightly-coloured, oily effluent, chemicals I supposed, polluting its waters and presumably killing any creatures therein. I paused, breathed in the stench of industry, looked with pity at the poor little brook – and thought of other waters: Dart, Exe, sylvan Wye, the Dove, Swale, a host of others encountered on my journey – and the exquisite Tweed, perhaps the finest of all, here, in Scotland. Now this. It's strange, don't you think, that the supposedly most intelligent species on the planet is responsible for the worst excesses of pollution of the planet? Are there not rules against this? If I, a passing stranger, could see pollution from the road, surely someone in authority must know about it.

This was dreary country, with all around unseen towns and villages, some I'd heard of, some not. Bonnie Scotland, they say, but I'd seen nought in England to match this – but only, I concede, because my journey hadn't passed where such places in England are. I marched onward, eyes front, and came to a disused road with water-filled potholes. It led to a dead end where a brightly coloured notice fastened to a telegraph pole said 'Pedestrians Beware – Fast Traffic Ahead'. I knew what it meant: I had to cross the M8, which carries the Glasgow-Edinburgh motorway. There was no footbridge here, and this was no Pennine Way. I had to cross the carriageways.

After reading a notice with a set of instructions stating the obvious about safety, I went down to the hard shoulder and waited long enough to ensure I could reach the central reservation without being squashed, hedgehog-fashion, then likewise crossed to the far side. Then I marched to Chapelhall, an urban sprawl of disused buildings, and places where buildings had once stood but is now wasteland. Those politicians who would seize yet more of our countryside, why don't you send the bulldozers in to the Chapelhalls of the world and build your new towns there? That way we could be rid of eyesores and spare our precious countryside at the same time. It's money, of course; it costs less to 'develop' so-called brown-field sites. Anyway, just to make my afternoon, it started raining. But I wasn't complaining, and that's the truth. No, it was all a part of the experience. I'd expected it and I wasn't disappointed. I probably became the only person ever to pass this way carrying a rucksack. I should be in the Guinness Book of Records.

At a crossroads I had a choice: straight on for Glenmavis, where I had pre-booked accommodation (you don't think I was going to leave it to chance around here, surely), or turn left and visit Airdrie, where I might buy a cup of coffee. I had discovered, incidentally, that going for cups of coffee was an ideal way to get the 'feel' of a place, and get close to the natives, hear them talking and so on (and once in a lifetime meet the woman of my dreams). I chose the latter, and presently I caught sight of the Airdrieonians football ground, behind which were rows of terraced houses, a scene belonging to the industrial, smoke-ridden Britain of the thirties, but owned by the Britain of today. When I was a kid if a town had a football team you knew where it was, or you had at least heard of it. This rule was slightly different in Scotland. I mean, when dad checked his football pools coupon to 'Sports Report' every Saturday afternoon, and you got to hear names like St Mirren and Queen of the South, where were they? And where – or what – was 'Airdrieonians'?

Nearing the town centre the air was filled with a familiar, if unexpected aroma. Curry! And there were lots of little shops; confectioners, newsagents, greengrocers, and smoke-filled cafes with steamed-up windows which prevented one seeing if there was room for a bloke with a rucksack, or sight of the waitress for that matter. In a concrete precinct, with time to kill, I sat on a bench. Thirty yards away, on another, sat two men, one so fat his legs wouldn't close together. They were drinking lager and talking avidly, about what I could not discern. It looked like one of those conversations where one side has strong views about the ways of the world and is keen to get them off his chest, whilst the other agrees, if only for a quiet life. Only in this case it didn't seem to be quiet, for fatty had a loud voice, which was carrying as far as me. I should explain: the reason I was unable to discern what was being said wasn't because I couldn't hear, rather I couldn't understand the fellow's broad, Scots accent.

In the 17th century an Act of Parliament made Airdrie a market town. It achieved burgh status in 1821, and in 1833 a motion was put down to establish a police force. A number of men were interviewed, and four selected as sergeants on eleven shillings a week. Things moved on: in 1889 Airdrie police acquired a telephone, in 1902 a typewriter, the latter kept under lock and key and used only with the authority of the superintendent, and then only to a 'favoured few', freemasons probably. Anyone else needed permission from the chief constable. In 1919 the CID was established, with one detective sergeant (and a detective constable from 1935), its primary function being to investigate housebreaking and embezzlement. In 1932 Airdrie was the first town in the west of Scotland to have traffic lights, and in 1941 Airdrie got its first women police. Whatever police Airdrie has today weren't around at any point of my journey through the town, nor in the vicinity of where I sat watching my two lager-swilling buddies. Apart from sporting the first traffic lights, Airdrie is no different to anywhere else.

Glenmavis was but a couple of miles away, and I reached it in good time. My lodgings turned out to be a farm, which was almost surrounded by caravans. Beyond, on a now dank and clammy afternoon, a shroud of grey mist covered the town of Coatbridge, where the taller of its buildings stood silhouetted against a gloomy skyline. My host cooked me a lovely dinner and once again I contented myself with the delights television had to offer.

*

I stepped from my lodgings to a rainy morning and a view of a scrapyard; piled-up old cars and tyres. You get the picture. I was going to Bearsden, sixteen miles away, and the morning would turn out to be the low-light of my journey. I took a narrow, twisting country lane that led to a place called Glenboig. Hereabouts the rain eased, although I was in a deep depression. This is an area of urban decay. Where once Scotland had a proud industrial heartland, here is proof, if proof were needed, of the decline of industry. Still, it was good to see the sign 'British Steel' on a not-too distant factory, so it's not all bad, I thought. The lane crossed the M73, where workmen were gathered by a road works, looking at one another (as they do). Maybe it was their tea break. Not one acknowledged the presence of the first man ever to pass this way carrying a rucksack. Then I found myself looking across the waters of Johnston Loch, where I encountered an elderly chap with a Dalmatian. I decided the fact that I had a Dalmatian once merited conversation.

'I had a Dalmatian once which merits conversation,' I said, adding that his name was Jason, and that I considered him disobedient and possibly mad. (Later I discovered, according to a programme I saw on television, that one in four Dalmatians are deaf, so maybe it's no wonder poor old Jason didn't take any notice). The old boy was going my way (as far as the newsagents) and it turned out he was an ex-police sergeant with the Glasgow City force. So we chatted about 'the job', and how it's 'gone to ratshit' – his words. Funny, I keep hearing the same thing from former colleagues, including those not yet halfway through their careers. 'Y'never see a pollis these days,' he said, as though this only applied to this area. He also spoke sadly of the decline of industry, and when I said at least good old British Steel is still going he shook his head. 'It's a paper reprocessing plant now,' he explained.

Muirhead was next. My ex-cop buddy said I might get a cuppa there, which spurred me on. But Muirhead stank of chemicals, so much so I felt I could almost reach out and touch it. It filled my lungs, so I skipped the tea and pressed on for hopefully fresher air to the north. There are many highlights on the journey, too many to mention, and too diverse to discuss. But Muirhead, specifically, was the worst. No region of heart's desire, this.

Kirkintilloch loomed up. What would it be like, I wondered? I found the town enveloped in the greyness of a now misly day. I got a cuppa in one of those new-style shopping precincts. It was almost deserted, for this was a Bank Holiday and I presumed the natives had gone off somewhere for the day, leaving Kirkintilloch to me. Outside again, it seemed colder, with a blustery wind blowing along the main street. I was in no mood to linger, so went down to the Forth and Clyde Canal which I intended to follow as far as Cadder.

The purpose of the canal was to enable ships to sail from east to west, or vice versa, across the narrowest part of Scotland, thus alleviating the need to go all the way around the Pentland Firth at the extreme north of Britain. The idea of a canal was first thought of during the reign of Charles II, and various surveys were held with no conclusive result. Finally, after sanction by Parliament, work began in 1768, although the canal was not completed until 1790. The canal is 35 miles long, and when it opened, the price of grain on each coast was 'equalised'. In 1839 a light railway ran alongside, the locomotive towing vessels (as opposed to horses towing). Typically, the construction of such a grand project brought entire families to the area. The earnings of a man and a horse were one shilling per day. Like all canals, the Forth and Clyde gradually fell into disuse, save for holidaymakers I suppose, of which I saw none.

Scots will tell you that their kinfolk may be justly regarded as being responsible for many important developments over the years: The telephone – Alexandra Graham Bell; Penicillin – Alexandra Fleming; TV – John Logie Baird; roads and bridges – Thomas Telford. There are many more. Here, at least, the English can notch up a breakthrough of their own, for, it is said, it wasn't until the construction of the Forth and Clyde that wheelbarrows first appeared north of the border. The Scots, particularly those with allotments, would do well to remember this. England be praised!

I headed west along the towpath, with few people about save the inevitable doggie-walkers. It was somewhat disconcerting to see a couple of young fellows on the opposite side discharging an air rifle at an unseen target on mine, but I managed to pass by without being shot. I was following the line of the Roman Antonine Wall, and passed by the site of a Roman fort, although I saw no sign of it. Unlike Northumberland, here the Romans built a *murus caespiticius*, meaning a turf wall, on a stone base. It was, generally, 10 feet high, and was built by Lollius Urbicus in the reign of Emperor Antoninus, hence its name, and abandoned in 196 AD. A military road linked a series of forts along its length of 36 miles. Its purpose was probably to keep out the Celtic tribes of the north (not that it could, but that's just my opinion) and was probably built by Roman soldiers with local help. None of it was visible to me, yet here I was aware of walking along what was the most northerly Roman frontier of all.

Near Cadder Church I turned away from the canal, and headed north across a golf course. I got this bit wrong at first, turning from the canal too soon and ending up in a wide amphitheatre, not Roman but slightly more modern – an enormous rubbish dump. One moment I was in marching mode, the next I was surrounded by garbage. I sorted myself out, and proceeded to Balmore, there taking the A807 westbound for Bearsden. Near the Roman Temple of Boclair, which isn't there now or I didn't see it anyway but then I wasn't looking, I took the B8049, now on the very outskirts of Glasgow, where I headed directly into Bearsden.

Like so many other places, I wondered what Bearsden would be like. Unlike so many other places, at least during the past day or so, I was pleasantly surprised. For some reason I had presumed Bearsden to be a sprawling, industrial town. But Bearsden pleased me, with its big houses and air of prosperity. It seems the origin of the name is in dispute. One theory follows the story that the sons of a laird brought a bear home and kept it in a cottage; another that it's after the Gaelic, meaning 'the entrenchments of a fort'; another says it goes back to the barley (bear?) that grew locally in a dene, hence 'bearsdene'; still another is that when they were building a branch line of the railway to nearby Milngavie in 1863, the person responsible for naming the station was unwilling to call it New Kilpatrick, the accepted name of the town, as this would confuse it with Old Kilpatrick, another township to the west, so he simply called the station 'Bearsden' after a nearby cottage of that name (and if he did who could blame him?). But my favourite, and the one I hope is correct, is that Bearsden is derived from none other than Rabbie Burns' poem, 'A man's a man, for a' that...'

> Then let us pray, that come it may
> As come it will for a'that
> That sense and work, o'er a' the earth
> May *bear the gree* and a' that.

Bear the gree meaning 'to take first place'. That night I stayed with Mr and Mrs McGregor, who kindly escorted me a mile up the road to Milngavie, and pointed out the start of the West Highland Way, Scotland's most famous long distance path. Then they took me to a hostelry where I knocked back half a gallon of 'Eighteen Shillings' which, for the uninitiated, is strong Scots ale. I had good cause for celebration (as well as inebriation), for I was set fair for Fort William. Compared to the urban landscape I had just traversed, the mountains of the Highlands *bear the gree* right enough.

9

The West Highland Way

'From the outskirts of Scotland's largest city, alongside the shore of her largest loch, across her grandest moor to the foot of her highest mountain'. Opened in 1980, the West Highland Way, Milngavie to Fort William, traverses 95 miles of Highland footpaths, drove roads, old military roads, old farm and coaching roads and disused railways. The next six days of my life would be spent walking it in its entirety, of which today would be to Drymen, twelve miles across the land of Lennox.

It was a cold morning with a hint of drizzle as I set of in newly-laundered clothes, courtesy of Mrs McGregor. On a short day, I kicked my heels awhile in Milngavie's modern shopping precinct, where I watched – and heard – the locals going about their business, oblivious to what, to a 'walker', is a significant place, the start of a long distance route. I must have looked lost, for an elderly lady made it her business to enquire if I knew where, 'in Mull-guy', the start of the walk was. Fortunately, I was aware of the local pronunciation of Milngavie, else I wouldn't have had a clue what she meant.

In fact, around 1600 the township was known as 'Millguy', later 'Mylngavie', and later still 'Milngavie'. Thus, you say it more or less how it was spelt, but spell it different to how you say it now. Peculiar, maybe, but not as much as the one-time custom of Milngavie Fair where, as well as selling sheep and cattle, the locals 'exchanged' their wives too. I regret being unable to quote the exchange rate. The missus for a gaggle of geese and a fatted calf, maybe. In 1830, a cholera epidemic struck Glasgow and that put paid to the fair. Today's world of 'political correctness' would have put paid to it anyway, since wives couldn't exchange their husbands for a rampant bull, whatever.

Milngavie was once a place of mills (hence the name) – a snuff mill, a paper mill – powered by the Allander Water, and the town prospered thanks to the cotton industry. Later, when mills and factories closed, it became a place of political and industrial unrest. There was a 'radical war' in 1820, when the Glasgow Herald reported 500-600 people drilling with a view to marching into the city. They had to send in the troops to sort it out.

The path led off into a sort of park. In moments I had left a built-up area for open country, Milngavie – or Mull-Guy if you will – lost to sight and sound. I climbed steadily through gorse into Mugdock Wood which, together with adjacent land, was kindly presented for development as a country park for the people of the Glasgow conurbation by its owner, Sir Hugh Fraser. Evidently the woods are famous for insects, but I didn't hang around to verify it. Instead, I trod a soft, springy path, reaching the extensive and stark-looking Craigallian Loch, the haunt of Victorian and Edwardian naturalists. Today it is available to all, yet there was no-one about, not a soul, as I reached a minor road where, beyond, the Campsie Fells appeared. I was a man in his element, rejoicing within after the traverse of Scotland's grimy industrial heartland – what's left of it, anyway.

Here and there the ground was boggy, churned up by walkers' boots. As I have said before, this is the result of a 'long distance' route, here compounded by locals just going for a walk. The erosion is bound to get worse as walkers strive to avoid the worst bits by taking a wide berth, so that the path becomes wider and unsightly. I cared nought about this as I motored on, especially as the sun decided to make an appearance, turning grey skies into a bright, autumn day. I traversed the steep-sided Dumgoyach Hill, an extinct volcano, and further on arrived at the route of the former Blane Valley railway, along which the path runs north, straight and true, with newly-fallen leaves of autumn providing a ready-made carpet especially for me.

The railway was opened in 1867. Its owners had great hopes that it would serve the needs of Glasgow's businessmen who would be encouraged to move out of town to this area. Things didn't work out that way, although the line remained open until 1959. I trod my leafy carpet to Dumgoyne, where the inn held promise of refreshment, and where the girl who served me was the first person I had seen since leaving Milngavie. Be it noted that I kept to the direct route of the Way, without succumbing to the temptation of a visit to nearby Glencoyne Highland Malt Whisky Distillery, with its offer of 'a welcoming dram'. This was no hardship; I never touch the stuff. Bottle of Newky, maybe...

The path picked up the course of the old railway again, then deteriorated into a muddy treadmill. The authorities really must do something about this problem. Ever the pragmatist, I did the best I could by trampling on long grass by the side of the path – thus contributing, along with everyone else, to the problem of erosion. Nearing Gartness, I was startled by what sounded like a bullet or similar missile striking a nearby tree, and crouched down belatedly to avoid being shot. (There's no point in ducking a bullet; by the time you've heard it it's already arrived at wherever it's going). It turned out the missile was a golf ball, whacked by a young bloke in a nearby field, notwithstanding the proximity of the West Highland Way. As I was still alive I decided to ignore the incident. After all, I can remember whacking golf balls too in my time, and not necessarily in open countryside either.

Gartness turned out to be a place of pretty sandstone cottages facing the Endrick Water. Here I sat on a low wall and rested, to kill time more than any physical need. And, perhaps, to reflect on the fact that John Napier reputedly stayed at nearby Gartness Castle (now gone). Who was John Napier? The bloke who invented logarithms, that's who. Thanks to him I had to endure being taught logarithms at school. Or rather, they tried to teach me. You remember logarithms...

'A mathematical function to facilitate multiplication and division. Based on a law that a^x x $a^y = a^{x+y}$, two numbers, p and q can be multiplied together by writing them in the form $p = a^x$ and $q = a^y$ and then adding together the values of x and y.' x is called the logarithm of p to the base a, i.e. $\log_a p$. Thus p x q is found by looking up their logarithms in books of tables, adding them together, and looking up the antilogarithm of the result'.

No wonder I never got to be a brain surgeon.

Sitting on the wall, I wondered if it was here that Napier had thought out the whole logarithms thing. Here, on this very spot, it came to him, crystal-clear, just like the waters of the burn. Evidently he also 'made valuable experiments in the use of manures', though where he was sitting when he thought that one out is anybody's guess.

A strategically-placed water trough provided an ideal opportunity to wash muddy boots before arrival at Gateside Lodge, where the luxurious bathroom included a massive iron bath and a bidet, the former into which I reclined and fell asleep and almost drowned, the latter which I did not put to use. Then it was down to Drymen (pron. *Drummen*) for supper at the Clachan, reputedly one of the oldest inns in Scotland. Tomorrow would find me alongside the biggest lake on mainland Britain. Loch Lomond's bonnie banks a-beckoned.

*

Another short day, just 13 miles to Rowardennan, where I would stay at the youth hostel, the last chance of accommodation for many a mile. Unfortunately, what should have been a delightful stroll turned out to be a day marred by heavy rain and mist. A stinker, in fact, but the air was fresh and so was I; what more could anyone ask (apart from sunshine)?

As it was tipping down, I decided to walk into Drymen for a coffee, my reasoning being that if I lingered long enough the rain would stop. I put the cag on, but not leggings; wet legs are no bother, unless you're at two thousand feet or more, which I wouldn't be today. To anyone observing my passing, it appeared I wasn't wearing any trousers, something worth bearing in mind if only to keep one amused. I dallied over the coffee, only to find when I emerged outside the shop-cum-café the rain was heavier than before. I got as far as a bus shelter, and was still there when an elderly chap joined me and passed a civil word in broad Scots.

'Good mornin',' he said, contradicting himself by adding 'wet day'.

'Good mornin',' I said, also contradicting myself. (When in Rome...).

'Are ye on the West Highland Way?' he asked grimly, in a voice like Fraser's, the dour Scot on Dad's Army. I nodded. He carried on in 'we're doomed' mode. 'There's only one in a hundred makes it.' Ah, he'd deducted I was walking the Way, had given up and now I was waiting for the bus. 'Most of them pack up at Drymen,' he was saying. 'This country's too tough for them, y'see.'

By 'them' he meant *English* people. The West Highland Way was too hard for me, that's what he thought, and here I was, waiting for the bus, only one day's march from the start. I wondered if I'd missed something on the map: a mountain range, or crocodile-infested waters, or some other unforeseen hazard so severe that only one percent of West Highland Wayfarers who departed Drymen arrive at Fort William. If only I had a lion, a scarecrow and a tin man for company. He said he thought the weather might clear. I glanced up at the blackened sky and driving rain, and decided he was either blind or the greatest optimist of all time. Anyway, to prove him wrong on his assessment of this particular Sassenach, I shouldered the sack and marched off. To this day he probably believes he was responsible for changing my decision to give up.

I took the trail into Garadhban Forest, knowing that ahead I would have to make a decision based on the weather: either to continue on the main route to Conic Hill, or go down to the road. I marched along the wide forest ride, seeing no-one except a group of women horseriders, and stood aside to let them pass as they approached from behind. Every one smiled and said 'good morning' (the women, not the horses), every one was clearly enjoying the experience (the women, not the horses), and I watched their huge backsides (the horses, not the women) as they passed me by. Their presence cheered me (the women and the horses), so I sang as I marched, Elvis Presley or somebody, at the same time wondering if the women were smiling at seeing what they thought was a bloke with no strides. I'll never know.

Further on I turned for the road. There would be no point in climbing Conic Hill for a view of nowhere. And so it was I arrived at Balmaha, on the shores of Loch Lomond. There were lots of little boats moored off-shore, but elsewhere nothing moved on the surface on this rain-sodden day, where in the distance the greyness of the loch blended in with the greyness of the sky. The West Highland Way follows the eastern shoreline of the loch for nearly twenty miles, many of them hard going. Still, unlike Loch Ness, no monster is reputed to dwell in Lomond's murky depths, so at least I wouldn't have to worry about being grabbed and eaten, or falling over nerds with cameras looking for that special photograph.

There was a café at Balmaha. Doubtless it's a busy place in the summer months; today there was only a handful of customers. Nothing like a cup of tea on a day like this, and dialogue with other wet souls made a welcome break. Resuming, the Way climbed steeply to a hill called Craigie Fort, a renowned 'viewpoint'. Sure enough, from the top you can see over the treetops to the little islands and expansive waters of the loch, here some 3-4 miles wide. Somehow the mist and rain contrived to make it look even wider. Loch Lomond is a jewel in Scotland's crown, to be sure.

Craigie Fort is but a brief sojourn from the lochside, after which again, here and there, were sticky bits – especially today, with the rain ensuring the ground had no chance of drying out. The last five miles were spent walking through woods and, in places, on the quiet road leading to Rowardennan. Low cloud prevented a sighting of the Munro, Ben Lomond, now towering above. Munros are Scotland's 'separate' mountains of 3,000 feet or more as listed, with amendments, by Sir Hugh Munro about a hundred years ago. At present there are 284. The number changes because the authorities keep reclassifying the more dubious ones, ostensibly to ensure accuracy, but just as likely to ensure 'Munroists' who endeavour to climb them all have to buy new guide books and maps, and return to bed and breakfasts at places they thought they'd never see again in order to climb a mountain which before they needn't have but now they must. Okay, so I'm a cynic.

I climbed Ben Lomond once, on a scorching-hot day in May, in conditions I could aptly describe as exactly the opposite to today's. On the summit the views were superb: of Loch Lomond, the Arrochar Hills and mountains galore. The occasion was memorable for another reason: it was my first encounter with the dreaded midge.

I have heard the Highland midge – *Culicoides impunctatus* – described as a vicious carnivore, and after experiencing the little blighters first hand I would not contradict this assessment. If you happen to be where midges happen to be you will be bitten. Period. At least by the females. (Males are vegetarian). Well, actually, the females don't bite either, they *drill* their way into your skin. Midges tend to hang around glades, where they have a penchant for emerging at twilight on balmy evenings to declare war on the human race. By the time you are aware of their presence and swot the appropriate place on your face, nose, ears, lips, neck, arms, hands, legs and anywhere else they can sneak into, they've gone! You don't get to kill a single one.

Life for next few days will be purgatory, as your white blood cells go into action to counter infection. Good for them – but there's a price: you will itch like hell afterwards, and then make matters worse by scratching. Your skin will turn all blotchy, you will go to hell and back and you will curse midges and even Scotland itself – which is why the authorities, I'm told, have spent millions on research in an effort to solve the problem of the midge. Then again, people like me come back. We keep away from those glades, but we come back.

Nearing Rowardennan I came upon a fellow who told me he'd been on the West Highland Way to the north – where I was going tomorrow – and that the path was in a dreadful state, with mud 'knee-deep' in places. Thus encouraged, I pressed on for the youth hostel, for though the rain had stopped the skies were leaden and darkness would be early. Tomorrow I was bound for Crianlarich, with tough going in the forest by the shores of Loch Lomond and beyond. An early start merited an early night. There were barely half a dozen others staying at Rowardennan, so a good night's sleep was assured.

*

I departed Rowardennan under bright skies. After yesterday's rain, I was pleased at the prospect of facing 21 miles over hard country without another soaking. Ahead, I dreaded what the conditions would be underfoot. 'Knee-deep in places,' the man said. But then, I've learned to take what people say with a pinch of the proverbial salt. We'd see.

Ahead were twelve-miles of forest ride and footpath, the former firm and allowing good progress, the latter the 'we'd see' bit. Below, on the left, the waters of Loch Lomond lapped the edge of the forest; on the right Ben Lomond towered, unseen above the forest canopy. I motored along easily to the 30-mile point of the Way, where the lower path from the lochside and the forest ride merge. This was the 'we'd see' bit, and although it was hardly knee-deep, it was very muddy, and what with the many ups and downs, ins and outs and tree roots growing across the path it was hard going. Much of the forest is natural oak woodland, so much better than the sitka spruce of manmade forests. Hereabouts is home to straggly-haired wild goats with long, curved horns – fortunately not liable to attack passing hikers. I wondered if I might see one, and as if on cue one appeared in font of me on the path. I had read about the goats' pungent smell, and sure enough, even from fifteen yards I could smell matey. He too walked the path, same direction as me, which meant I would continue to smell him until such time he decided to clear off. Anyway, as he had kindly chosen to be a sort of guide, I christened him Pongo. I just hoped he wasn't going all the way to Fort William.

The path crossed an endless number of burns, cascading down the steep hillside with some force. Every time I checked the map, it seemed ever more unlikely that I would reach Crianlarich by nightfall, as progress through the forest was pitifully slow. Or seemed to be. As a means of trying to speed up, I tried to narrow the gap on Pongo, but as I picked up speed, so did he. I anticipated arrival at a place called Inversnaid, but as it appeared to be merely a building or two, I wondered if I might have passed it by. In fact, I was no longer sure how far I had progressed. Suddenly, Pongo did a sharp right turn, and without so much as a sniff he was gone, taking his Goats No. 5 with him.

Emerging from the forest, I found myself in a huge car parking area, occupied by a few motor coaches and cars. To the right was the enormous Inversnaid hotel, quite out of keeping with what you might expect. I mean, there I was, fighting my way through the jungle in circumstances where a machete might be useful, and where I half expected to bump into Johnny Weissmuller (he played Tarzan if you're under forty), when suddenly, I'm standing outside the Ritz. I checked the map: five more miles of forest, fourteen to Crianlarich. I'd never make it.

Panic set in. The only thing I was confident about that if I wasn't going to reach Crianlarich I couldn't afford this hotel either. Then I noticed a passenger ferry here crosses Loch Lomond, and decided if I caught it I might secure accommodation at Ardlui or somewhere. A notice said enquire at the hotel for the ferry times. Notwithstanding my muddy boots and bedraggled appearance, I bowled up to Reception. What time is the next ferry? I asked the nice young lady, hoping none of Pongo's stench hung about my person. There's no more ferries today, she replied, giving me a have-you-done-something look. Thank you very much, I said, giving her a no-I-haven't look. I returned to the car park knowing there was nothing for it but to get cracking for Crianlarich, supposing I had to run the last bit.

I got going, back in the forest again. It was as though Inversnaid hadn't existed. But now I was angry with myself. At Inversnaid, enquiring about the ferry, I'd been prepared to give up. That's what it amounted to. Damn it, is that what I'm about when the chips are down? Like hell! I'd get to Crianlarich, of course I would.

The path led to the foot of Sroin Uaidh, a hill with massive cliffs where, reputedly, the famous Highland freebooter and protection racketeer, Robert MacGregor, better know as Rob Roy, had a cave (Roy deriving from the Gaelic *ruadh*, meaning 'red', owing to his red hair). Rob Roy is a legendary figure, around whom folklore has been written. Among other things, he borrowed money from the Duke of Montrose after which, being unable to pay, his lands were seized and his wife and children turned out of their home in winter. Rob Roy then made war on the Duke, and had lots of near escapes as his enemies, the redcoats, searched for him. He became a sort of Highland Robin Hood, giving to the poor at the expense of the rich. In 1727, he was caught and sentenced to transportation, but surprisingly pardoned. I never saw the cave, and no wonder, the speed I was going.

Through the trees I noticed a small island in the middle of the loch. It has the curious name of 'I Vow', a corruption of an old Gaelic name, apparently. Then I came to Doune bothy, an isolated building in a clearing above the loch. It's stone-built with a green door, one window and a view to die for. A bothy is a simple shelter, usually with stone-slab floor, a fireplace, a table and a chair or two, and possibly somewhere to put down a mattress. There are bothies dotted all about the Highlands, used mainly by Munro-baggers. Many of the mountains are miles from normal access points, and can only be reached by wild camping or dossing down in bothies. I considered Doune to be a romantic place, though to be honest, resting in the sun, I would have preferred company here, if only to share the wonderful view the length of Loch Lomond.

Beyond Doune the path went down to the loch again. Here I came upon a 'signal hoist', a simple but ingenious method of attracting the ferryman's attention – rather like the one at Helford on the second day of my journey, only here you hoist a bright red ball up a pole. Then the path climbed steeply for the col below Cnap Mor, another great viewpoint. I took a last look back at Loch Lomond, which here seems to stretch to infinity, with the forest through which I had come lining the shore. Across the loch are the so-called Arrochar Alps, whilst to the north coming into view was the Beinn Laoigh group – Munros all. I was now twenty miles from Balmaha, where I had first taken the loch-shore path, and now Britain's greatest lake was about to be left behind.

I moved on, downhill, to lonely Glen Falloch, where I rested my feet. The forest trail had taken its toll! I would have paid £5 for a cup of tea at this very moment. With seven miles still to Crianlarich I got going again along the glen, where I encountered a shepherd. He was trying to usher his flock through a gate I had to pass through, so I waited; there's nothing worse than hikers disturbing the natural course of events in the countryside. Three sheepdogs had the sheep into the field in no time. Shepherds work alone, and with great skill. No idling time, or chatting in corridors for them, nor going sick at the first sign of a sneeze, nor being paid a fortune in unearned – and undeserved – money for 'stress'. Work in all weathers, at all times of year. That's their itinerary.

I was crossing open pastures now, a far cry from the forest trail earlier. The river was my guide, all the way to Carmyle Cottage where the Way passes beneath the railway, then crosses the A82 to take the old military road, built by General Wade – the same General Wade who built the military road on top of Hadrian's Wall, in Northumberland, if you recall. The military roads were constructed to facilitate rapid troop movements to foil Jacobite uprisings. This one was built in 1752-73 by soldiers of the Royal Welch Fusiliers. From here on, the Way follows many of the old military roads of the Highlands, except instead of redcoats there's the likes of me on the march. As the path climbs steadily, there is a great view down to the glen, where the River Falloch, the railway and the main A82 trunk road run side by side, just yards apart.

According to the map, a huge forest lay across my path ahead. Sure enough, the treetops appeared. Ahead now lay the unmistakable, bulky shape of Ben More, Scotland's 16th highest mountain (3,843 feet). Whenever I look at the mountains I have climbed, I always recall events of the time, whatever they might be. So it is with Ben More, which I climbed wearing new boots that turned out to be a half size too small. This wasn't apparent – at first – but after reaching the top of the ben, and moving on to nearby Stob Binnein and completing the round, my feet were very swollen, and I recall the blissful moment I removed the boots. Needless to say, I never wore them again.

It was all but dark when I reached the forest fence, where a footpath leads through the forest to Crianlarich. It was vital I didn't lose my way, otherwise things could have turned very unpleasant. I all but raced the last mile to Crianlarich, where I went down to the 'T' junction – it's left for Fort William and the north-west, right for Central Scotland. Crianlarich is thus known as 'Gateway to the Highlands'. My fondest memory of the place dates back to an evening one May. I was walking through the village, killing time after a long drive from Hertfordshire. Three elderly fellows, locals probably, were having a natter as I passed by, when one of them let rip an almighty blast. You could have heard it on the top of Ben More. 'Did you say something, Willie?' asked one of his companions dryly. 'Och, take no notice,' said the other, 'he's always talking through his arse.'

Crianlarich was in pitch darkness as I sought out my lodgings, a guest-house just outside the village. As I walked the roadside, lorries and coaches sped past, lighting up the road ahead. I was warmly received by my host, before being shown upstairs to my room (it's always upstairs when you've walked over 20 miles). After a bath, I retraced steps to the village where I drank half a gallon and ate half a cow in the Rod and Reel. Back at my lodgings, I reflected on the state of play. I was tired, but I'd be OK in the morning; Loch Lomond had been splendid, but now lay behind; tomorrow I'd walk to Tyndrum and on to Bridge of Orchy, in the shadow of those big brothers, Beinn Odhar and Beinn Dorain. Wild country, but given a bit of sunshine it would be a doddle.

*

I sat over breakfast, looking out over the wild, rain-swept Strath Fillan. It was in for the day for certain. Still, with only fourteen miles to Bridge of Orchy, it wasn't so bad. I was just thankful I didn't have yesterday's arduous trek today.

Crianlarich isn't only a 'T' junction for the roads; here, the West Highland railway forks, for Oban along the western side of Glen Fillan, for Fort William along the eastern. The Way accompanies the latter, on and off, all the way to Bridge of Orchy. I treated myself to a newspaper, and retraced steps to the forest fence, thereafter following the forest trail for two miles which, needless to say, I had to myself.

The trail crossed a thousand burns and, twisting and turning, contoured the hillside a few hundred feet above the glen. Finally, in teeming rain, I scampered over the A82, and took the path to the bridge over the wide Fillan and the ruins of St Fillan's Chapel, whose ancient walls stand crumbling yet defiant in a clump of trees.

St Fillan was an Irish monk, who came here as a missionary in the 8th century. His chapel was raised to priory status by Robert the Bruce, in 1318. In 1798 St Fillan's bell was stolen by a tourist, and only retrieved in 1869 when it was found in possession of a man from Hertfordshire. The bell was supposed to help in the treatment of insanity. Anyone thought to be suffering from this unfortunate ailment was dipped into the River Fillan, carried to the chapel and tied to a tombstone for the night with the bell over their head. If they weren't crackers to begin with, they would be afterwards.

The rain swept unhindered across the glen as I re-crossed the A82 and followed the River Cononish to Dalrigh. It was memory lane time again, for here I had sight of Beinn Laoigh (pron. *Ben Lui*), one of the first Munros I climbed, and one of the best. Apart from the glories of this grand mountain, my lasting memory of my expedition that day was forgetting to take a packed lunch, and not realising my mistake until I had walked many miles up Glen Cononish. Loth to turn back, I climbed the mountain, then pressed on for another, Ben Oss, only to discover first hand what it's like to undertake strenuous effort on an empty stomach. I traversed the summit of Ben Oss without pause, the only hill where I have done so. Mountain-tops are made for lingering, eating one's grub and drinking one's tea. As the latter two were not an option, nor was the first. But Beinn Laoigh more than made up for a day of hunger – as did the double helping of the roast lamb dinner I devoured when I got back to base.

I pressed on for Tyndrum, taking the soggy trail through another forest where I encountered another pilgrim. He was foreign, German maybe, walking the Way north to south. He was carrying everything, including the kitchen sink. I have never seen so much on the shoulders of a human being. He'd camped out the previous night, he said, and asked if he would get to Rowardennan today. Considering the weather, the terrain, the size of his pack and the distance I said if he did to let me know and I'd fax the Guinness Book of Records. OK, he said, without knowing what that was. He looked soaked through, but clearly neither the rain nor his weighty pack daunted his enthusiasm. He made me feel a tad guilty – him carrying a full pack, me carrying the bare essentials; him in his tent tonight, wet and cold; me in a bunkhouse tonight, dry and cold. Ah, well, each to his own. I should mention he also sported a huge, friendly grin. He was a stout fellow.

The forest footpath wound its way to Tyndrum Lower station. There's an Upper station too. It's unusual for such a small place to have two railway stations. It's accounted for by the two railway lines I mentioned earlier. Tyndrum is frequented in summer by tourists and walkers, in winter by hardly anyone. The village grew, for want of a better word, thanks mainly to lead mining and cattle droving. In the 19th century there was a gold mine near Tyndrum, and alluvial gold was washed down in the burns. The locals could help themselves by placing sheepskins on to the riverbeds to collect the 'grains', and thus return home with a golden fleece. I headed directly into the village, and without passing 'Go' plonked myself at a table in Tyndrum's Little Chef, ordered coffee and looked out the window awhile at the rain, and read my newspaper. And now it's time to highlight the problem those who would go solo encounter – being treated *different*.

Accommodation. On your own, you seek a room. Sorry we don't do 'singles' – or, if we do, there's a 'supplement'. Restaurants (at busy periods). On your own, the waiter bars the way to a table, saying sorry, we only take couples and families. Restaurants (at non-busy periods). On your own, couples stare sympathetically at what they perceive to be a lonely soul and isn't it a shame he/she has no-one to talk to? Pubs. On your own, seated near the fire, you go to the bar for another pint, and return to find six people sitting at your table. Little Chef (for lunch). On your own, you leave your still half-full pot of coffee and spread-out newspaper to go to the loo, and return to find the table cleared and newspaper gone. No kid, I'm thinking of adding one of those inflatable dolls to my kit-list, so it can keep me company in restaurants, and keep my place when I disappear to the gents. Who knows, I might even find one or two other uses for it.

I made the waitress recover my newspaper from wherever she had put it and went out into the rain. With eight miles of open moorland ahead, the remainder of the day would be an invigorating march beneath two mountains, Beinn Odhar and Beinn Dorain. There would be no shelter, unless a narrow tunnel under the railway may be deemed such. It was me vs. the elements all the way to Bridge of Orchy. Although the rain swept mercilessly across the moors, the going would be easier than, say, that day out of Middleton, when three high ridges were traversed en route to Blanchland.

Just outside Tyndrum, the Way takes the old military road again, and keeps to it for much of the way to Fort William, still 42 miles away. This section also served as the old road between Tyndrum and Bridge of Orchy, before the construction of the modern A82 in the 1920's. With Beinn Odhar towering on the right and high, afforested hills rising on the left, the A82, railway and military road run close together, vying for the limited space afforded by the narrow valley. At one point the Way passes beneath the railway, through a narrow tunnel, more aptly described as a 'slit', and then I was alongside the Allt Coire Chailein which leads directly to the foot of Auch Gleann. Here the railway sweeps away up the valley, where the Allt Chonoghlais is bridged on firmer ground (*Allt: Gaelic for stream or burn*), whilst the old road carries on, rejoining the railway a little to the north.

Above towered Beinn Dorain. I had not climbed the Munro then, but I have since and, typically, another 'memory' comes to mind. It was a grey day, with low cloud clinging to the 'tops'. I knew from reading up in advance that it's easy to miss the summit cairn, especially when you can't see it. Having located it, I was making my way back to Coire an Dothaidh when I encountered a lone woman, forty-ish. She was clearly unsure of her bearings, as I had been fifteen minutes earlier. I called out a warning about the possibility of missing the summit. Her response was to give me a steely glare, and turn away. Alone and afraid she was, up there in the murk. In our modern world, the stranger cannot be trusted, even on top of a mountain. Perhaps especially on top of a mountain. I wonder if she knows how I felt about her response to my gesture of assistance. I hope she found the cairn anyway.

The rain was lashing down as I pounded the three miles to Bridge of Orchy. I was going like a train, speaking of which one appeared, rattling along just yards from where I walked. I could see the faces of the passengers, cosy beings who were staring vacantly in my direction, probably sympathising with the plight of the unfortunate walker, out in this terrible weather. But I didn't need sympathy; I needed them to understand that today I was free and having a great time. No doubt they would all be bound for Fort William, so I would not have the opportunity to tell them how grand it was, and that I would never forget the march along the old road.

Bridge of Orchy comprises a scattering of cottages and an hotel, the latter of which has a bunkhouse at the rear. Dripping wet, I checked in, and located my room. It had four beds, and it seemed I was the sole occupant. After the experience with the monster at Lothersdale, I was not disappointed. I was cold, even after a shower, but returned to the hotel and ordered a meal – good old neeps and tatties. It seemed a long, lonesome evening was in prospect, but far from it. Instead, I got on chatting to a few fellows from Glasgow, one of whom turned out to be a copper called Paul. Inevitably, we talked 'shop' for a while, after which we all drank and played cards for matchsticks (I had to borrow some) until they called out 'last orders'. I'm talking six hours of booze and gambling. Part-way through the evening a crowd of women appeared. We gave them the once-over (as you do), deciding they weren't worth the 'chat'. You've guessed it; by 'time please' they looked bloody lovely. Were they perchance staying in the bunkhouse, we wondered? Maybe they were, maybe they weren't. I never knew. By now, stuffed with turnips, potatoes and Eighty Shillings, it was all I could do to drag myself to my bunk, just yards away. Hoots mon!

*

Another twenty-miler, this time across one of the most desolate parts of Britain – Rannoch Moor. That said, the going is straightforward on the old road to Glencoe. Without the old road, that old boy at Drymen might have had good cause to tell me 'only one in a hundred make it' to Fort William. Once again I would have rain for company; once again an 'invigorating' day was in prospect. The Eighty Shillings must be a good beer, for I'd not a shred of a hangover. Just as well, I'd need to get moving pronto, given the distance and the weather.

I couldn't leave with saying goodbye to my mates. They looked downhearted when I saw them, not at the prospect of parting company with me; it was the rain and low cloud that threatened to spoil their day. They had intended to do some walking, but didn't fancy it. They were astonished when I told them I'd be going over Mam Carraigh and then Rannoch Moor, never mind there's a clear path and a rough road all the way. They lingered at the door of the bunkhouse, worry about my welfare lining their faces. It was no good, I told them. I had to go. Humphrey Bogart would have played the part to a 'T'. 'Here's looking at you, kid,' I said, bidding Paul and the others goodbye, and setting off in the downpour. I've often wondered what they did that day.

Every piece of waterproof gear I possessed covered my being as I crossed the old bridge over the River Orchy, and took to the trail. The Way enters a forest, and climbs steeply onto the flank of Mam Carraigh, where a curious pile of stones around a tree marked the highest point of the hill visited by the path, before dropping down the far side, where Loch Tulla lay cold and still and desolate in a misty shroud. I reached a quiet road and turned for the hotel at Inveroran. Hotel it is, but it's not the grand. It stands in the proverbial middle of nowhere, a snug little haven for weary travellers, ancient and modern. Like many in the area, it probably served the drovers of old. It has its place in history: in 1803, William and Dorothy Wordsworth ate breakfast here, and complained that the eggs were too hard-boiled. Don't blame 'em. I mean, fancy coming all the way up here to find you couldn't dip your soldiers. Later, Wordsworth's pal Robert Southey stopped by, and described the inn as a hovel.

I bowled on towards Victoria Bridge, where I noticed a car parked at the roadside. I could see it contained two men, who were looking at me through the steamed-up windscreen. I knew the score: they were here to climb Munros, Stob Ghabar and the others of Black Mount probably, but didn't fancy it. Couldn't blame them in this rain. Maybe they were hoping the weather would clear up, though I doubted it would. Climbers must be optimists, otherwise they would fail to climb anything. The rain never eased all day, so they probably gave up and went off to drink gallons of Eighty Shillings and play cards for matchsticks at the Bridge of Orchy Hotel.

I crossed Victoria Bridge and took the old road across Rannoch Moor, nine miles to Kingshouse. The road skirts the western flank of this bleak place. Without it anyone trying to cross the moor would probably get lost among the myriad of peat hags and lochans, not a wise thing to do as the moor is reputedly haunted by kelpies, strange horse-like creatures. Whether or not they are dangerous I do not know. William Wallace and Robert the Bruce waged guerrilla warfare on the English here, no doubt running them ragged in what for intruders would be bewildering terrain. It seems the moor was formed during the last ice age, and now the flat, ill-drained landscape is a vast bog. Curiously, it forms a watershed for both Atlantic and North Sea – Rivers Etive and Orchy drain into the former, the River Ba into the latter. Robert Louis Stevenson described Rannoch Moor as a 'country lying as waste as the sea' in *Kidnapped*. He'll do well, that chap.

Rannoch Moor was not always a bleak and open place. Once, the ancient Wood of Caledon stretched from Braemar to Glen Coe, from Glen Lyon to Glen Affric. Here were brown bears, wild boar, wolves and bandits. The extensive woodlands were progressively destroyed by – you've guessed it – man. Between the 9th and 12th centuries the clans set fire to the woods, to cover their retreat from Viking invaders, and to smoke out the bandits. From the 15th to 19th centuries Scots and English alike felled the trees for iron-smelting and to make ships, and Highlanders burned still more to kill wolves. And much of what was left, which wasn't much, was used in the two world wars of the 20th century. Here and there a few remnants remain; old roots, preserved in the peat, can be seen where exposed. I'm glad there are no wolves. I can cope with the weather and the occasional midge (just), and even threatening dogs (of which I'd not seen any for ages), but not your saliva-dripping gangs of starving predators. I read once of somebody's mad-brained idea to reintroduce wolves to the Highlands. If they do, I hope the plonker who thought of it is made to traverse Rannoch, then we'll see what he thinks.

I crossed the River Ba. To the west, two Munros rise steeply, Stob a Choire Odhair and Clach Leathad. Both were lost in cloud, a pity. All along this stretch of the old road across Rannoch, as it rises to around 1,500 feet, you begin to realise what a forbidden place the moor is. Further on, Blackrock Cottage is used by climbers, and photographers who like to see it portrayed on calendars. Behind is a towering mountain, Buachaille Etive Mor, the Great Shepherd of Etive, beloved of all Munroists. Seen from the Glencoe Road you'd never think it possible to climb the Buckle, as it is known, its sheer, rocky face barring all, surely, except the most experienced climbers. But the Buckle has a weakness, a narrow cleft that permits ascent. It was my 10th Munro. I had looked forward to renewing acquaintance with the Buckle, only to find it in cloud on this beast of a day. C'est la vie!

I crossed the A82 for Kingshouse, yet another drovers' inn of times past. Hereabouts the drovers were armed to fend off those bandits I mentioned, even after the 1745-6 Jacobite Rising, and that's saying something. It's said the inn is named after George III, whose troops were billeted here, and that it is the oldest licensed house in Scotland. Dorothy Wordsworth said she'd never seen such a wretched place. Okay, things will have improved 200 years on, but the truth is I was loth to enter in case I got too comfortable. There was much to do, not least climbing the so-called Devil's Staircase.

The next three miles were mainly along the old military road to Altnafeadh, a huge place consisting of about three buildings alongside the A82. The last bit of this section is a boggy footpath, cruelly churned up in places, leaving you with no option but to slither as best as possible in the hope that you won't fall over. Here I encountered a lone fellow who greeted me like a long lost friend and told me he was thinking of opening a little café at Inverarnan and did I think it was a good idea. I said I thought it would be a good idea if he opened a café anywhere on the West Highland Way, whereupon he filled in a little form, thanked me for my trouble and slithered off along the glue-pot that passes for a footpath. When I got to Altnafeadh my leggings had turned from green to black and my each of my boots weighed three stones.

Fifteen miles done, I turned for the Devil's Staircase, the old military road built by General Caulfield in 1750. The 'staircase' climbs over the ridge between the head of Glen Coe and the River Leven, so steeply that to counter the incline of about one-in-two the path zig-zags dramatically. I saw no sign of the Devil, nor anyone else until, at the summit I encountered a fellow who was standing beside a tall mast. He was in radio contact with people below somewhere, something to do with a race of some sort. We chatted awhile, during which I glanced yet again in the direction of the Buckle, of which there was still no sign. I had become oblivious to the rain, incidentally, but not for much longer, for as I set off for the long walk down to Kinlochleven, it started lashing down.

At 1,850 feet, the top of the Devil's Staircase is the highest point on the West Highland Way (though still lower, let it be said, than Swinhope Head in County Durham). In past times it was used by the inevitable cattle drovers, the workers who constructed the aluminium works at Kinlochleven and the navvies who built the massive dam of the Blackwater Reservoir. It was a hard road to get to one's work. Many died in savage winter storms, in some cases their bodies not discovered until the following spring. What for me today was rain falls as snow in winter. You only have to look about this bleak, dreary plateau to fully realise what it must be like up here in December. For some reason it occurred to me I had not seen a single sheep all day. So, just what use is this land put to, if anything?

I'd heard that the journey down to Kinlochleven from the top of the 'Staircase' seems endless, and having now undertaken it I can confirm this. I actually had an early sight of the town through a break in the cloud, and although it looked close, it never seemed to get any nearer as the afternoon was wearing on and I was wearing out. The huge Blackwater Reservoir came into sight, and if ever there was an inhospitable place on the face of the planet it must be here. Seven miles long, it was constructed in 1904-07, and at the time had the largest 'water storage' in Europe. Its purpose was to supply water to the generators of the aluminium works in Kinlochleven, which it does through six massive pipes that run for 1¼ miles around and down the hillside. The catchment area for this supply of water is 60 square miles in an area with an average rainfall of 100 inches, all of which fell on the day I happened along.

I knocked on apace down the hillside, to where the path runs alongside the six water pipes leading down from Blackwater. Darkness loomed early. It was beginning to look as if I'd have to negotiate the last couple of miles by torchlight. Further on I heard someone running, and turned to see a skinny youth in a yellow shirt, the first of the fellrunners in the race across the Devil's Staircase. He flew past me with a greeting I could not comprehend, either 'what a wet bloody day' or just as likely 'get out the bloody way'. Five minutes later another two appeared. 'Have ye seen a fellow in yellow?' panted one, poetically. I confirmed his worst fears. 'Shite!' was his response, in the knowledge that so close to the finishing line they could only end up second and third.

I came upon a notice, nailed to a tree, its message, clearly directed at West Highland Wayfarers. 'If there was a tearoom at the cottage behind this notice board would you stop for refreshments?' There were two bell-pushes, one each alongside the words YES and NO. What is it about quizzing folk about tearooms? I've just walked over the Devil's Staircase in the pissing rain, of course I'd stop for a cuppa if there's one going. I pressed NO. Serves 'em right.

And so to Kinlochleven. The town grew as a result of the aluminium plant. Before that, Kinlochleven consisted of two shooting lodges, a few cottages and a farm. There was no road; Loch Leven had to be crossed by ferry at Ballachulish to the west. But aluminium changed everything, and the workers came, from all over Scotland – many of whom were only Gaelic-speaking – and abroad. They were, by all accounts, a 'rough body of men' who fought each other (as well as getting on with building the factory), but ceased hostilities if a woman was present, which might not have been very often, you might think. In 1907, the factory produced its first aluminium. To commemorate the occasion, they struck a medal with the inscription *De Nach-dean ant-Uisge nuair a rinn a mise*, which translated, means 'What can water not do when it can take me.' The first bit makes more sense.

They were going to call the town Aluminiumville. Can you imagine it?

'Are you thinking of taking a holiday this year?'

'Aye. We're going to the Scottish Highlands.'

Visions of shimmering lochs, rugged mountains sweeping down to the sea, a mighty stag, a kiltie, the swirl o' the pipes.

'How lovely. Where to exactly?'

'Aluminiumville.'

I presume whoever thought that one up was either suffocated with a giant haggis or certified.

I was hobbling now. Sore toes again. What's more, having got down to Kinlochleven town centre, I had to climb a steep hill to the bunkhouse where I was staying. It was occupied by a horde of women, twenty and thirty-year olds. They all sang out cheery 'hi's', obviously pleased at the arrival of the macho-male. I went into town for supper. Where elsewhere in the Highlands, history and tourism go hand in hand, and mountains, lochs, old buildings, castles, and the odd monster are exploited, Kinlochleven has the aluminium works and workers' houses. I liked Kinlochleven, where all around high hills rise steeply, giving an Alpine feel to the town.

Talking of which, one imagines those pictures of Swiss chalets, rising mountains, fields of deep green and edelweiss. In Britain there are few, if indeed any, truly Alpine settings. Yet here, at Kinlochleven, where at least we have something at least slightly comparable, they build an aluminium factory, with six huge pipes scarring the hillside. The Sound of Music? I don't think so. Still, it provided work, and the nature of that work demands a highly-sited lake for the purpose of providing water to run generators. They had to build it somewhere. Fair do's, I suppose. Ironically, the aluminium works is closed now, but money is being poured into the place to provide better facilities for walkers and even a business park. I wonder what the ghosts of the workers who built it all make of that.

Supper eaten, feet wrecked, I climbed up the hill to the bunkhouse, where I looked forward to joining the ladies in a room that passed for a lounge. They were watching Dame Edna Everidge on t.v. I started the 'chat' – the merits of long distance walking, climbing Munros, the benefits of an ice axe in winter. Strangely, their attention remained fixed on Dame Edna. I must be losing my touch.

*

'We get all kinds here,' the main in the bunkhouse was saying, having been told – in answer to his question – that, yes, I was walking the West Highland Way. 'Walkers, cyclists, blokes on motor bikes, *lasses* on motor bikes', he added, as though the latter was unusual. Maybe it is in Kinlochleven. 'One guy turned up pushing a canoe on a trolley. He was crossing Scotland, west to east, on the roads and on lochs. He was off to the Blackwater Reservoir when he left here.' I tried to picture someone pushing a trolley up the steep slopes above Kinlochleven. It wasn't easy. But the man wasn't finished. 'We had a bloke doing the West Highland Way on horseback. Tied it up outside, he did.' I nearly said 'it's a one-horse town anyway', but thought he might take offence. Then it occurred to me a horse was the only thing missing from my 'Dodge City' cameo at Carnwath (where I had assumed the role of Clint Eastwood). Carnwath! How fared the woman of my dreams, I wondered? She haunted me still, on the trail, in my bed. Love at first sight. It can happen. You'd better believe it.

Wonder of wonders, the sun was shining as I climbed through the birchwoods above Kinlochleven. Just as Kinlochleven had seemed to take an age to reach yesterday, today it seemed to take an age to leave behind. It got smaller, yet refused to disappear. Then, at last, it was lost to sight, and when I reached yet another old military road flanking the hillside I changed into shorts on what was a lovely day.

The 'road' is firm and gritty, providing great walking territory. I came to a roofless ruin, Tigh na-sleubhaich, the chimneys at its gable ends pointing forlornly to the sky against the backdrop of Stob Ban. I had Lairigmor to myself, until I came to another ruin, also called Lairigmor. Here sat a few couples, out for the day, and they certainly had the weather for it. Yet every one wore cags, breeches and gaiters. Why do people dress as though they are off on a traverse of a polar icecap when the sun is shining and they are at only 1,000 feet? Have the gear, sure, but stick it in your sack till you need it. I wonder what they made of the passing hiker in the sleeveless shirt and shorts.

After four miles the Way left the old road and I was on the last lap of the West Highland Way, which here enters a forest. I suddenly felt tired. I suppose there was something of psychology about it now; I was nearing the end of this part of my journey, and maybe the past few days had taken more out of me than I cared to admit. Eight miles to go, I plodded on, catching sight of Ben Nevis, dead ahead. The mountain is unmistakable, its huge, flat top dominating the skyline. It was bathed in sunshine, as though welcoming me to one of Scotland's finest glens. I overtook a man, his wife and their two children and sped past, not surprisingly as I calculated their speed to be about 0.001 m.p.h., and no wonder, the size of the packs they carried. They must have camped out on the hill somewhere. I saw them in Fort William later, so they made it OK.

The trail led down to the road through lovely Glen Nevis. The glen is packed on summer days, when it loses none of its glory. Man and his little cars cannot detract from nature's work, not on this scale. Ben Nevis towered above now, at 4,406 feet the highest mountain in the British Isles. Yet it is surrounded by grander peaks, rocky summits rising steeply and dramatically – the Mamores, Grey Corries, The Aonachs. The fact is, Ben Nevis is nothing more than an enormous plug of lava, thrust a little higher than the volcanic peaks around it. Superior in height, inferior in quality.

Ben Nevis has many moods, from benign giant to venomous monster. It can be a lovely day in the glen, life-threatening on the summit. Yet I've seen folk wearing sandals climbing the ben, whilst others carry fridges, furniture and other paraphernalia to the top, sometimes wearing top hat and tails. Good luck to 'em. For the record, I've climbed Ben Nevis twice, the first time by the so-called tourist route from Glen Nevis, and later from the north over Carn Mor Dearg and the famous 'CMD Arete'. The second is by far the better expedition, though it is much more strenuous. As far as the 'tourist route' is concerned, it's actually an old pony track, laid down in the late 19th century as access to an observatory, situated at the very top of the mountain.

It all happened towards the end of the 19th century. To see if an observatory was 'feasible', one Clement Wragg climbed Ben Nevis *every day* one summer, where he kept observations from a shelter covered with a tarpaulin. Whilst his efforts were commendable, it was hardly practical, so the Scottish Meteorological Society appealed for funds to construct a permanent observatory on the summit. The response was staggering, with £5,000 donated, including £50 from Queen Victoria. A simple, barely adequate building was constructed, followed by an extension a year later. Visitors came by the thousand, and an hotel, in reality nothing more than a wooden shed, was built, providing refreshments and accommodation.

Ben Nevis ℘2001

It couldn't last, of course. Not in winter conditions where, on the summit, 'two men roped together, crawling across the snow were in danger of being blown to certain death over a precipice'. I forgot to mention that the north face of Ben Nevis is a sheer cliff, situated only yards from the summit trig, and the old observatory for that matter. Looking at it now, the whole idea seems crazy, but then, in the late 19th century I suppose people had a different perspective. Anyway, the observatory lasted 21 years, after which, due to lack of funds, it closed down in 1904, ironically the same year they started building the Blackwater Reservoir. The pony track remains, and as well as providing a clear and firm route for those who would climb the ben, since 1895 it has filled the role of race track up – and down – the mountain.

William Swan, a hairdresser, was first to be timed over the 'course' of approximately 14 miles – Fort William to the top of the ben and back in 2 hours 41 minutes. Subsequent times could not be compared to Swan's, because they kept moving the start/finishing point. The Ben Nevis Race as such started in 1937, with just three competitors, two of whom quit, leaving J.P. Wilson to complete the course in 2 hours 17 minutes. Evidently the route is optional – it doesn't matter how you reach the summit, as long as you do. Consequently, with local knowledge, local people might be considered to have an advantage, although you'd have thought the pony route the best option. In 1909 a woman, Elizabeth Wilson-Smith ran from Fort William to the top of the ben (one way) in 1 hour 51 minutes. It once took a superb physical specimen of English manhood 4 hours to climb to the top from Glen Nevis, and 3½ to get down again, but then I wasn't in a hurry.

And so to Fort William – *An Gearasdan*, the Garrison. The town stands on Loch Linnhe, in reality a long sea-inlet, favoured by the Vikings who sailed up the loch in their longboats. In 1689 the Dutch King, William, sent troops here to build the fort, naming it after himself, and the township of huts that sprang around it he called Maryburgh, after his wife. Fort William became strategically important, notably during the 18th century struggle against the Jacobites, who attacked the fort during the Risings of 1715 and 1745-46. Today the town is a bustling tourist resort, with lots of pubs and restaurants and shops. Fort William is a place to love or loath, although in my case I'm never sure which. It's also the end of the West Highland railway, and the beginning of the journey by rail to Glasgow and all points south.

In my case, Hertfordshire.

10

Western Scotland and Skye

The curtains across the bedroom window were heavy. It was impossible to tell what the weather would be like outside. Would it be fine? Would it be raining? Would it be something in between – grey, or cloudy? I pulled the curtains aside and found Fort William awash with colour under a cloudless sky; from the house on the hill the town was a veritable picture postcard. Hallelujah!

I had decided to complete the fourth and final part of my journey the following spring. Not autumn, as I had first planned. Autumn, with its deer-stalking season and proliferation of midges, is no time to be traversing Scotland's glens. Anyway, I had started this undertaking in spring; in spring I would finish it. And, as I had started it with tent and sleeping bag, once again I carried them on my shoulders, but not, on this occasion, with the attendant paraphernalia – cooking stove and tons of food. Instead, I would eat whatever I could, whenever I could. So, I'd be OK for accommodation, except I might starve to death. Water, incidentally, was not a problem. Scotland's abundant burns would provide more than enough of the best water money isn't needed to buy. As a final measure in getting rid of unnecessary weight, I threw a can of shaving cream into the wastebin, and presented my host with my towel. Only those who cart their homes on their backs will appreciate what I mean by what must appear as foolish gestures.

I breezed into town in the already-warm sunshine. My quest was to buy sandwiches and chocolate to last me all day, tonight and all day tomorrow, and two packets of Walker's crisps (how appropriate) in reserve. Also, a face-cloth to replace the towel. Already the first of the tourists and shoppers were abroad, along with a few native 'kilties'. Oh yes, they wear their national costume in Scotland, the only country in the British Isles to do so, so I have read. And yet the kilt is a relatively recent phenomenon. It's only been around since about the late 17th century. For Sassenachs who wonder, let me put them out of their misery. Traditionally, a Scotsman wears nothing under his kilt. Considering the midges, no wonder it's Scotland the brave.

Supplies purchased, I set off for Dunnet Head by way of the West Coast and Skye, the Outer Hebrides and the Far North. A couple of weeks it would take me, assuming I didn't sprain an ankle or get eaten by straying monsters (I was giving Loch Ness a wide berth). I passed by the road to Glen Nevis, the route of the West Highland Way, expecting at any moment to hear the voice of some well-meaning soul telling me I should have turned up the glen. I heard no voice, either because no-one noticed or, just as likely, no-one cared. Then came what's left of the old fort, which isn't much, just pieces of the walls. They knocked the fort for six when the built the railway. I give then out of ten to the Victorians for their fine buildings, none out of ten for preservation.

At Victoria Bridge I left the A82 and took the famous 'road to the isles' for a mile, to the Caledonian Canal, where eight locks set close together are collectively known as Neptune's Staircase. From here I would walk alongside the canal for six miles to Gairlochy on a path wide enough to drive a car along with room to spare. The morning was truly wonderful, and I was surprised to find I had the canal path to myself. With the River Lochy on my right, and the wide canal on my left, I was soon in marching mode.

The Caledonian Canal is 60 miles long, and three or four times wider than English canals. It takes advantage of the natural geological fault running north-east from the head of Loch Linnhe to Inverness, where a 'necklace' of lochs is linked by waterways, ensuring a continuous route for shipping. It seems the main reason for the canal's construction was to enable naval vessels to 'short cut' the north-west corner of Scotland, thereby making rapid progress during the wars against the French. Work began in 1803, and the canal opened to shipping in 1822 – by which time the wars against France were over, and in any case they were building bigger ships that couldn't use it. So it was used by fishing boats and pleasure steamers, and today's pleasure craft cruise leisurely between Fort William and Inverness. In the two hours it took me to reach Gairlochy, on a beautiful Saturday morning in springtime, just one motor launch passed me by, northbound, none southbound. Those vying for space on England's waterways are in the wrong place if they seek peace and solitude. Then again, maybe they enjoy queuing at those narrow lochs of the Grand Union, wherever.

Ahead, high hills formed a barrier across the skyline. I knew I would have to climb them, and that tonight I would have to camp at around 2,000 feet, between the Great Glen and Glen Garry. I kept looking out for somewhere to sit down awhile, but on the entire six miles to Gairlochy I cannot recall sight of a single bench. Instead, I perched on a mooring post opposite Glen Loy. Across the canal I saw a little girl riding a pony, under the supervision of dad. The mooring post wasn't the most comfortable of perches, and I didn't linger long.

Gairlochy turned out to be a house or two, one which, to my delight, was a tea-room. I sat at a table outside, where the only other customer was a young woman immersed in a book. She looked up, gave me the briefest of smiles and went back to her book. It was more interesting than me, obviously. I wonder what it was about. Moving on, I crossed the canal, and had taken to the quiet road that passes through the forest at the foot of Beinn Bhan when I was offered a lift by someone driving what might be accurately described as a mobile ash tray. As the driver pulled alongside my marching form, and wound the window down, I was suddenly enveloped in a cloud of smoke which, when it cleared, revealed a wizened little chap smoking a wizened little fag from which a huge section of fag ash was ready to fall at any moment – just as others had, and many times, onto his clothes, upholstery and the entire fascia panel.

Where was I bound? he enquired in a kindly, cancerous way. Kinloch Hourn, I replied. It was quickly apparent that he knew the local geography when he declared I wouldn't get there today. It was equally apparent that giving me a lift, even if I accepted, which I wouldn't, wouldn't get me there either, unless his car could negotiate the 2,000 foot ridge which lay ahead. Still, he was eager to help, and enquired of my route which, I said, included visiting a church a mile or so up the road. He shook his head. 'Don't go that way,' he declared, urging me to take an alternative route. 'It's far quicker.' I said okay, but I knew I would ignore his well-intentioned advice, for, as I have said, there would be no point in my venture if I was merely taking the shortest route without seeing anything. As my Scottish Good Samaritan drove off, it occurred to me that I had walked all the way from Cornwall to the Highlands and this was the first time anyone had offered me a lift.

I was now by the shores of Loch Lochy, of which I caught an odd glimpse or two through the trees. Here I turned up a rough lane to the church I mentioned. St Ciaran's, Achnacarry, stands in splendid isolation, surrounded by tall pines, the only sound the breeze and the waters of the nearby burn, and the singing of the birds this Maytime. I went inside where the silence was absolute and the air was cool, and went to the altar where a splendid window above depicts a soldier, or a knight, or possibly St Ciaran himself, with an inscription, relating to the Great War: 'To the memory of the unreturning brave...'.

I explored awhile, even climbed the church tower, before reluctantly going outside and taking a moment to savour this lovely place. St Ciaran's wins 'best church' award on my walk the length of the country. I have been back since. I will return again. There is peace here, and peace is always worth seeking. And to think I had been urged to by-pass this place. But now I had to move on, and when I did I almost died of shock when a stag crashed through the trees across my path, and disappeared just as quickly. He almost took me with him.

I arrived at Achnacarry (*Achadh na Caraidh* – 'the Field of the Weir'). This is the home of Lochiel, chief of the Clan Cameron. The Camerons were loyal supports of the Jacobite cause, and after Culloden (1746) Bonnie Prince Charlie himself hid around the grounds of Achnacarry for five months before he fled, taking Lochiel with him. The castle was then burned by government troops and the land confiscated, although it was restored in 1784, after which another castle was built. Achnacarry was also the training base for commandos during the Second World War, 25,000 in fact, from British and Allied forces. It became one of the toughest assault courses in the world, with *live* ammunition used in training. Even today, as I passed through, there were soldiers. They occupied some sort of camp, with lots of tents, upon which, on one, was written in huge letters 'DONER KEBAB'. I crossed the bridge over the River Arkaig, where I encountered more soldiers, all in green and khaki. They looked so young.

I turned for the foot of Gleann Cia-aig (pron. *Glen Kaig*). Here is a lovely dell, where two waterfalls, collectively known as Eas Chia-aig, crash into the 'Witches Pool', right by the road. You could drive right by and never know. It's said the practise of 'trial by water' was carried out here in olden times, when any hapless soul suspected of witchcraft was tied to a ducking stool and thrown into the pool. If you drowned you were innocent; if you lived you were burned at the stake. Either way, you were doomed. The road from here to Loch Lochy is known as the Dark Mile, along which it is said Bonnie Prince Charlie came, and as he will, inevitably, reappear in my story, perhaps a short history lesson wouldn't go amiss.

Charles Edward Louis Philip Casimir Stewart (or Stuart) – Bonnie Prince Charlie, the Young Pretender – was born in Rome on 31st December, 1720. The Stuarts had ruled Scotland from 1371, and Scotland and England (after unification) from 1707 until 1714. Historic events meant that the throne passed over to the Protestant Hanoverians, and the Roman Catholic *Claimants* were exiled abroad, where the Stuart cause continued. As the Claimants were called James, the term *Jacobite*, meaning James, became a political cause.

Charles decided to go to Scotland and seize the throne for his father. He was supported by the French, morally at least, as their promise to supply armies to aid him never materialised. It was a French ship, *Du Teillay*, which brought Bonnie Prince Charlie, as he would be known, to the island of Eriskay in July, 1745, from where he made his way to Glenfinnan to a welcome by clan chiefs (but not lowland Scots of the south, whose loyalties lay elsewhere). Until that time, Charles Stuart had never before set foot on Scottish soil.

On arrival in Edinburgh, he was described as '...a tall, slender young man, of ruddy complexion, rolling brown eyes, red haired... he wore a blue sash, wrought with gold that came over his shoulders, red velvet breeches, a green velvet bonnet with a white cockade... he had a silver-hilted broadsword and was shown great respect by his forces'. What fearsome, claymore-wielding chiefs in their tartans thought of an Italian wearing red velvet breeches and a green velvet bonnet isn't known, but their loyalty to the man they regarded as the rightful heir was unquestionable.

Charlie's army defeated a Hanoverian force near Edinburgh , and a price of £30,000 was put on Charles's head by George II. Charlie returned the compliment, the same sum on George's head! The Jacobites then marched for London, taking Carlisle and a number of other towns, reaching Derby on 4th December, 1745. Their approach certainly had George worried, for ships were made ready in the Thames to flee if they got any closer. But, at Derby, Charlie was persuaded to turn back, and his army retreated in disarray to Scotland where, on 16th April, 1746, it was routed at Culloden, near Inverness, by Hanoverian forces under the Duke of Cumberland. Charlie escaped, but his Highlanders, even those wounded in battle, were butchered, and those who fled mercilessly tracked down and executed. The government then banned Gaelic culture, including speaking the language, and even forbade wearing the tartan and playing the pipes.

Charlie was sheltered by loyal Highlanders, never betrayed and never captured. He lived rough, and fled to Lewis, then to Skye dressed as an Irish servant girl, Betty Burke, assisted by a Skye woman, Flora McDonald. Finally, he departed Scotland on another French ship, his mission to seize the throne a failure.

I lingered by the Witches Pool, but gazing at waterfalls wouldn't get me far. The thirteen miles from Fort William had been hot work, albeit 'on the flat'. Now I had to climb through the woods of Gleann Cai-aig, and get as far as possible into the hills. The contours on the map told their own story; it would be a stiff 3-mile climb. I toiled through the forest above the crashing waters of the Abhainn Cia-aig until I emerged onto an open grassy hillside, and carried on, upward, soaked in sweat. Unexpectedly, I encountered two people, the last humans I would see until the afternoon of the following day. Finally, I gave up the ghost and dropped the sack. Between the road and this spot I had not paused. It was six o'clock. Enough was enough.

I looked south now, where Ben Nevis towered majestically on the skyline. Earlier, I described the Ben, perhaps disparagingly, as 'a plug of lava'. Now he stood proud, lord of Scotland's mountains, a stunning sight in the heat-haze. I put the tent up on the slope, washed my socks in the burn and hung them out on the tent cord to dry, and tucked into supper – a ham sandwich and a packet of crisps. Water there was a-plenty in the burn. There was not a cloud in the sky as the sun sank slowly behind the hills, taking its friendly warmth with it.

Cold, I repaired to the tent and slid into my sleeping bag. Putting a tent up on a slope, incidentally, means you inevitably slide downward in your sleep. Still, as long as you aren't upside down, you shouldn't end up with a headache.

Daylight lingers in these northern climes and sleep would not come. Finally, I drifted off to the music of the burn, and the distant call of spring's first cuckoo. The world and its problems were a million miles away.

*

Sunday morning, 8 a.m. I emerged from my cosy nest to a morning so cold I had to wear gloves. But the sky was clear, and another hot day was in prospect. Any lingering sleepiness was soon washed away by the ice-cold water from the burn, which also served to replace the traditional cuppa, whilst another sandwich replaced the traditional fry-up. I filled my canteen and broke camp. A long, hard day lay ahead.

First, I had to get over the hills into Glen Garry. The best route seemed west, by the Allt Tarsuinn and over the Bealach Carn na h-Urchaire, a mountain pass. But this seemed rather circuitous, so instead I shouldered the sack, and with a last look back at Ben Nevis headed up the steep hillside. It was a tough way to start the day, but I was up for it. If I wasn't in good shape I'd be knackered in twenty minutes. I reached the top of the ridge without pause, and found myself gazing across a bewildering, pathless landscape. Four miles away there's a bridge across the river linking Lochs Poulary and Garry and I absolutely had to locate it. It was time to get out the compass.

Coarse, tufted grasses, tracts of heather and the many ups and downs of uneven ground meant tough going. You can't get into your stride in country like this, where each step must be carefully taken, a sprained ankle or worse a possibility. Gradually, the ground slanted downward, and I aimed for what on the map is shown as a footpath which crosses, laterally, two deep valleys and flanks two large hills, then leads into a forest and joins another path, and *then* goes down to the bridge. Unfortunately, the 'path' turned out to be no more than a narrow trod that simply petered out, so I fixed a bearing and followed my nose; no matter what the terrain, I would end up at the bridge. I was mightily glad to have clear weather. To be up here in mist would have been ghastly.

Just as I thought I was making headway down into the glen, the ridge levelled out again to a featureless, grassy wilderness, millions of huge clumps, or sods, the sort you seem to keep tripping over no matter how much care you take. 'You sod,' I kept saying, as I stumbled bravely on. Another half mile brought no end to this place of desolation. It's fit for nothing except planting trees, and that's just what they've done; a new forest barred my way, the reason, no doubt, the old footpath as fallen into disuse. I was obliged to turn half-right, cutting through a plantation of young trees, crossing deep irrigation channels and zig-zagging down the hillside to a high fence (they are high to keep out the deer which eat the bark) which I climbed, then continued on until, at last, I arrived at a path running parallel with the River Garry. I checked the map. I had only to follow it into the forest, cross a river and turn right for the bridge. Alas, this path, too, disappeared, and I crossed more rough ground where, further on and below, I sighted the bridge. Still more diversions followed, and yards from my goal I found myself straddling a shaky fence at the top of a high embankment and then, and only then, could I get down to the bridge. In triumph I crossed the river, having just broken the world record for the greatest number of expletives to come from the mouth of a human being before lunch – and I wouldn't even be having lunch. At the road I turned and looked back at the lonely hills I had traversed. It had taken five hours. It was 2 p.m. and I was still 16 miles from Kinloch Hourn.

Kinloch Hourn lies at the eastern extremity of Loch Hourn, a fjord-like sea-loch. A glance at the map shows it to be no more than a scattering of cottages, if that. The road to it is a long, narrow cul-de-sac, which threads a sinuous course through Glen Garry and Glen Quoich, with ever-improving views to the west, of Knoydart, Scotland's great western wilderness. I had looked forward to walking the road, but this was now tempered with the need to march apace, instead of taking things rather more slowly as I would have wished. I rested briefly by the roadside, applied lashings of sun cream and got going. Sixteen miles is 5-6 hours, that would be between 7 and 8 o'clock at Kinloch Hourn.

I was soon in rhythm. Left-right-left. After a couple of miles I came to a smattering of cottages where I encountered a woman, the first person seen since yesterday evening. I think she was just walking from one cottage to another. It was one of those afternoons when the sun keeps on beating down; there was no cover. I applied more sun cream – this was not the time nor the place to be suffering sunburn. A few more miles and the shimmering waters of Loch Quoich were laid out before me.

Loch Quoich is awesome. Nine miles long, it stretches snake-like along the glen beneath towering hills, backed by the mountains of Knoydart, a remote, uninhabited wilderness, inaccessible except to those who would walk, a place of rugged mountains – Sgurr na Ciche, Ladhar Bheinn, Luinne Bheinn to name a few. And here, above the road, right and left, were still more – Gairich, Sgurr Mor, Sgurr Mhaoraich, Gleouraich, Spidean Mialach. Wonderful mountains, wonderful Gaelic names, belying the fact they are in Britain. Thankfully, most of the names of Scotland's mountains, mountain passes and burns have survived 'Anglicisation'. Alone on the narrow road, I must have cut an insignificant figure below these giants. We are all insignificant against nature's grandest creations. Walk by the shoreline of Loch Quoich and you will see what I mean.

Years ago, Loch Quoich was much smaller, but in the 1950's they built a dam and flooded the glen, raising the surface by 100 feet. And that's not all they did to Glen Quoich and its environs, for in the 1970's they ran the overhead electricity wires of the National Grid this way, to Skye. They did consider a route to the north, via Glen Shiel, but the authorities decided unsightly pylons and electricity wires would not look pretty for the tourists in their cars and motor coaches, so they opted instead for a virtually uninhabited place, where they would only be seen by occasional motorists, Munro-baggers and madmen out for a walk. Not that I particularly noticed the pylons and wires; they, too, are insignificant beneath towering mountains.

The shoreline of the loch was laced with yellow, and graced with the distinctive smell of coconut, given off by gorse which flourishes in Glen Quoich, along with rhododendron. I marched on, unexpectedly encountering a grannie and a gorgeous little girl. They were standing near their car, gazing in awe at their surroundings. Smiles all round as I pounded by. Strange, that on earlier parts of my journey I had suffered from sore feet; today, under a hot sun and carrying more weight and having crossed difficult terrain, they were fine. After a few more miles, the road turned away from the loch, twisting and turning between low, rugged outcrops of granite, boggy ground and more of those sods. There was nowhere suitable to put a tent up. I came to Loch Coire Shubh, and on its northern extremity I could see a lovely plot of green, an ideal camp site. Indeed, a solitary tent was pitched

216

there. I could have gone over, pitched mine. Might have made a friend. But with one sandwich and two packets of crisps to my name I wanted a breakfast in the morning. I pressed on for Kinloch Hourn. The name pounded in my brain as I pounded the tarmacadam. Kinloch-hourn. Kin-loch-hourn.

And then the little road was going downhill, steeply, and ahead I could see the verdant landscape of the valley floor of Kinlochhourn. Loch Hourn itself was largely hidden from view, save for its eastern extremity, Loch Beag (confusing, I know). Here was rhododendron again, and beech trees by the roadside, and the crashing waters of the outflow waters of Loch Coire Shubh. The road twisted and turned steeply; I kept in low gear. I was nearing the end of my day's journey. It was just after 8 o'clock.

Would there be a welcoming cottage? An inn? In fact, I was going so fast I found myself ascending a path on a hillside, and realised I'd not only arrived at Kinloch Hourn, I'd walked right on through it. I checked, turned, and went down to a house at the road end. Did they do accommodation? I asked the man. Yes, but the electricity generator had conked out so they only had one room to let and it was taken. The electricity generator? With ten million volts passing by overhead? Indeed, yes. It would cost too much to hook one humble abode up to the National Grid. Was there anywhere I could pitch my tent? Yes, an ideal site, close by. It would cost me 60 pence. And could you do me a breakfast in the morning? He went off to ask his wife. Yes, she could. Just give a knock at 8.30.

A good camp site and a fry-up in the morning, and a lovely valley in which to while away the remainder of the evening. What more could I ask? Tent pitched, last sandwich eaten, I took stock. Kinloch Hourn is little more than a farm and a cottage or two and the lodge. They occupy the flat valley bottom, surrounded by high hills, in a sort of rocky amphitheatre. I watched as the setting sun cast long eerie shadows across fields, as it has for centuries past. Man has worked well here; long after retreating glaciers had done their work, this valley would have been a boggy wasteland, probably occupied by forests. As I climbed into my sleeping bag, all was silent in the fastness of the hills. Except, that is, for the distinctive call of a cuckoo. Not the same one, surely.

*

A 'full breakfast' as a treat is one thing; for someone subsisting on sandwiches it's a necessity. Consequently, breakfast went down extremely well. My stock of food to see me through to Glenelg consisted of a packet of roasted peanuts, discovered in the depths of my sack and anything up to five years old, and the two packets of crisps held in reserve. I could have asked my host to prepare a packed lunch; incredibly, the thought never crossed my mind, thus prompting the question: do we eat as much as we do out of habit or necessity?

Once again, it was cold first thing, with the prospect of another scorcher. I'd a fair trek to Glenelg, on the coast. But today I wouldn't need the compass, nor even the map, at least as far as Gleann Beag. Thanks to the National Grid, I merely had to follow the overhead wires all the way to and over the Bealach Aoidhdailean, a high pass. It's rough, uninhabited country; between Kinloch Hourn and Gleann Beag I wouldn't see a soul.

I set off, north-west, climbing the steep slope. Part-way I took a long look back as the flat valley bottom of Kinlochhourn was about to disappear from view. Just an hour before, the hills had cast dark shadows across the width of the valley; now the fields were swathed in sunshine, and so was I. It was time for the sun cream again. To the north were the mountains of Glenshiel, including a 'classic' The Saddle (they Anglicised that one), with the magnificent Forcan Ridge providing an exhilarating scramble – another great day, another great memory. And to the west, Loch Hourn, backed by Ladhar Bheinn and the peaks of Knoydart. What country this is!

Sometimes I'm asked: which is the best Munro? I do not think this is a question that can be answered satisfactorily by anyone. It's a strictly subjective test: the 'best Munro', indeed the 'best anything', depends on many factors, in this case the weather, the terrain, who you might have met, how you felt after boozing the night before (if you did). Hitherto, in my case, if I'm pushed to answer the question, I nominate my 'best Munro' as Ladhar Bheinn, the westernmost mountain on mainland Scotland. I climbed it on a scorching hot day from Glen Barrisdale (on a return visit to Kinloch Hourn). Everything was right that day. I will never forget standing on the summit, looking at what seemed to be a million rocky peaks, across Loch Hourn to Beinn Sgritheall, and westward to Skye, where the unmistakable, serrated Cuillin ridge shimmered in a blue haze. Although I had the entire climb to myself, I chanced upon a fellow who arrived upon the summit ridge by another route. There was no wind, no sound at all, as we stood in silence and soaked in the splendour around us. Such moments have to be earned, and when they come they command respect.

'Makes you wonder, doesn't it?' he said at last. I concurred.

'God will come to put an end to wickedness in this world, he declared, nodding his head in agreement with himself, as though his declaration that this would happen was final. I was going to say He was taking His time about it, but he was too quick. 'I have some leaflets,' he was saying, and before I could tell him I didn't want any today, thank you, he added, 'but I've left them at the camp site.' What a pity, I thought, thinking that was that, but I could see he was in 'sell' mode, so I reached for my sack. It was time to go. He was giving me the look of one of Jehovah's disciples. It's one thing closing the door in their face, but on a mountain peak it's not so straightforward. It was either give him a deft push, or scarper. I did not consider his misguided philosophy merited a premature end – or a beginning in the next life – so I shouldered my sack and bade him well. Wherever he is now, my advice is not to forget the leaflets next time. You'll never sell anything in this world without the paperwork.

Today, I reached the top of the ridge and headed across desolate moorland – coarse grasses with unexpected marshy bits. All around were rocky hillocks. This is confusing country, even in clear weather – except, of course, I had the National Grid helping me out. Maybe the real reason they ran power lines this way was to help walkers, people like me who had never been here before who, if they got lost, would be there still. Then again, maybe not. Further on the ground fell away to a lonely glen with a vast riverbed of huge stones and an isolated, roofless ruin, incredibly only three miles from the summit of The Saddle. Did someone *live* here once? A shepherd, maybe, though there were no sheep now. I came to a secret glade where I sat down to rest awhile and fill my canteen from the burn, which crashed noisily among the rocks. There was shade here and I was glad to linger, if only to get out of the merciless sun.

It was two miles to the top of the pass. The path, such as it was, was of little help; it kept disappearing, so that no 'rhythm' was possible. That's what you need when you're toiling uphill: rhythm. I followed the electricity wires, and tackled the final section, the steepest, in the knowledge that at the top it would be downhill all the way to the coast. Ahead, the cables, where they cross the summit, almost seemed to touch the ground. Had they got the measurements wrong on this bit, I wondered? Maybe they'd cut them a bit short, and as nobody's daft enough ever to come this way they just strung them up between the two highest pylons, and never mind they were only six feet above the ground. I climbed the final stage in the belief that my upright body (if it was upright still) might act as a conductor, in which case *woof*! My charred remains would be found by that Jehovah's Witness bloke who say it was my own fault, and if only he hadn't forgotten the leaflets that time. Happily, as I took the last steps to the top of the pass, I realised the cables were the correct height and that I wouldn't be electrocuted after all. Might have expired through the effort of getting there, but not by electrocution.

Over the pass, the ground fell away so steeply it was like coming off the summit of a Munro. Having drank the last of my water, I was glad to take advantage of the fast-flowing waters of a burn, just yards from its source. Cold, clear Scottish water. I drank at least three canteen-fulls before taking advantage of a huge boulder on which to park my grateful posterior. I looked back up to the top of the pass. Boy, that was a bugger! I checked the map to find the path, far from ascending to the top of the pass, in fact goes off west into Coire Chorsalain. No wonder I'd had a struggle.

A long valley lay below me, through which I followed the waters of the Allt Ghleann Aoidhdailean. I kept looking back to the top of the pass, which seemed to look higher the further I progressed. The, in the distance, I spied the woods at the head of Gleann Beag. On this glorious day they marked the beginning of the final stage of my march to the coast, still some miles off. I followed the burn – or the electricity wires if you will – the sun hotter than ever on this glorious day. I could not yet see the sea, which was obscured by another grand Munro, Beinn Sgritheall. Another Munro, another memory, this time of an unrelenting climb on scree above Loch Hourn.

Approaching the forest a path appeared. I followed it around the head of Strath a'Chomair into Gleann Beag (pron. *Glen Beg*). Then a wide forest 'road' enabled me to step up a couple of gears. Here, at last, I parted company with the electricity wires, which continue over the hills, northward, whilst I was westbound for Glenelg. The day was wonderful, the walking was easy now, the surroundings superb. Is it like this in heaven? I suppose it must be.

I had learned in advance of my coming that Gleann Beag is steeped in history – *ancient* history. The map tells its own story: Dun Grugaig, Dun Troddan, Dun Telve. A 'dun' is a small Scottish fort, or fortified dwelling, and here in Gleann Beag are the remains of the homes of people who lived 2,000 or more years ago. The first, Dun Grugaig, lay below me, unseen, near the river, and I passed it by without pause. A little further on, I saw two strange-looking creatures. They were bipods and wore clothing. Ah yes, *homo sapiens*, the first I'd seen since breakfast. I'd all but forgotten about them. The male of the species was standing beside a sort of motorised chariot; the female was seated inside. He was holding a strange device to his eyes, which, he claimed, by looking through, distant objects were brought closer. He also had an enormous glossy hardback book, with pictures of forts and things. They asked if I could direct them to Dun Grugaig. They were Dave, an American, and his Scots missus, Sandra. I would see them again, and soon.

Then I came to the broch, Dun Troddan.

Brochs are dotted about the west of Scotland, and the islands. They were built between 100BC and AD100. 'Their evolution, the circumstances which gave them origin, and the purpose they were designed to serve remain obscure, despite careful excavation, a great deal of thought and debate'. (W. Douglas Simpson). What seems certain was that their purpose was defensive, probably against hostile neighbours rather than invaders, although they may have still been occupied when the Vikings came. They are prehistoric; they are unique.

They are of drystone construction, with a round, tapered tower rising to about 45 feet. The walls, which account for over 50% of the total diameter of the tower, are up to sixteen feet thick at the base, above which they are hollow with roofed galleries. Here at Dun Troddan, a stone staircase climbs to a level passageway, which runs around the inside of the walls. As with other brochs, many stones have been plundered for use in the construction of nearby buildings. Considering its age, it is well preserved, without doubt one of the highlights of my journey. I explored the inside and the outside, climbed the staircase, then reclined on the close-cropped turf outside, drinking in the moment. Close by, a number of sleepy-eyed sheep reclined in the shade of a tree, oblivious to the moment. Two millenniums ago people lived here, in perpetual fear of their lives, I suppose, before the Romans, before Christ even. There'd be wolves then, and bears. Dun Troddan, on such a day, is a place to come to and stay awhile. I stayed as long as I could and moved on. Time waits for no man. Yet, in minutes, I could have explored and lingered again, for just one-third of a mile down the glen is another broch, Dun Telve. Alas, further exploration must wait for another time.

Just beyond a place called Eilanreach I came to the sea, which, on my journey, I last saw at Plymouth Hoe. There was land just a mile or so off the coast – the Isle of Skye. But that was for tomorrow. Today, I followed my nose to Glenelg, where I hoped to find accommodation. And not before time, for I had walked three days in the baking sun and there are limits. None of the cottages on my approach to the village appeared to do B and B and the Glenelg Inn I considered rather swish for a man of the road. A local fellow provided details of three guest-houses. At the first, the woman who answered my knock said 'Sorry, I'm full,' with obvious regret at being able to help someone who was clearly in need of help. At the second the same. At the third the same again, this time with the suggestion that there was a camp site near the sea with a mobile fish shop next to it. I made my way. Yes, I could pitch the tent. When are you open for fish and chips? I enquired. Next month, I was told. I decided to call at the inn and have a drink and a bar meal or something, considering the only food I'd eaten since breakfast were the ancient peanuts. My efforts to secure accommodation, and my enquiry about the camp site, added two extra miles to my day's journey.

At the inn I dropped the sack, removed my boots and strode purposefully to the bar. Standing there in stockinged feet, a shirt streaked with white perspiration and possibly, just possibly, after four days' walking in continuous sunshine, a hint of sweat (if only men perspired, like women), I wondered if I would be allowed to stay. I was, and more. After downing a glass of lemonade I was asked if I might require accommodation. Surprisingly, there was room to spare, even for me. I was even offered a family room at a low rate. That was that. I carted my worldly goods upstairs to an enormous room overlooking Glenelg Bay, and with the sun sinking behind the darkening hills of Skye cast my rags to the floor and my body into a hot bath before returning to the bar where I encountered the aforementioned David and Sandra.

David, evidently having located Dun Grugaig, was so excited he could barely get his words out.

'The lintel's still in place,' he was saying, almost frothing at the mouth. He raised his hands, as though grasping an unseen block of stone. '*It's actually still there*,' he drooled, pre-heart attack mode. Or possibly pre-orgasm mode by the look of him. In fact, it crossed my mind that this must be what he's like when he's actually having an orgasm. I told him I'd called at Dun Troddan, and isn't it fantastic? It was multiple orgasm time. The guy was so far gone I thought it best not mention Dun Telve in case he had a heart attack. When, finally, he composed himself, relatively speaking at least, he ordered two pints. I said I'd have the same. He and Sandra were great company all evening after which, skinful consumed, I negotiated the narrow staircase to my bed. At least, I think I did. That's where I woke up the next morning, anyway.

*

The first thing anyone who walks or climbs does every morning is look out of the window. The weather again, only instead of a forecast it's what you can actually see. And what I saw this day was yet another clear, blue sky, this time accompanied by an even bluer sea, the low hills of Skye already bathing in sunshine, unashamedly naked, save for a smattering of trees. Another glorious day was in prospect, an easy day, only thirteen miles to Broadford, after first crossing over to Kylerhea by ferry. I would start with a minor hangover. Serves me right, I hear you say.

When my historian friends appeared, I asked David how his head was, after all those Black and Tans. He was fine, bright as a button. Damn Yankee! Breakfast usually starts with a glass of fruit juice. I downed a jugful. This, along with a good old fryup, soon had me back to normal. I stepped outside to find Glenelg awash in warm sunshine, a scene worthy of any postcard. 'Lush' is the adjective I seek. Lush grass, lush foliage of the trees lining the road. I have made comment elsewhere in these pages of my 'why go abroad' theory. I do so again without reservation. Glenelg is for honeymooners, a wonderful place to be on a morn such as this. I could not turn my back on Glenelg, so I sat awhile and savoured another special moment on my journey – alas without a bride. In the unlikely event of anyone marrying me and reading this, now she knows: forget Tenerife, forget Jamaica. Conjugal rights will be taken at Glenelg, so there!

I retraced steps of the previous evening, more leisurely this time, and tarried at the ruins of Bernera, one of four barracks constructed after the Jacobite rebellion of 1715 to house Hanoverian troops. I wonder what English redcoats felt about being billeted in such hostile territory on behalf of a German king. Maybe they were there for the money, as opposed to duty to one's country. Maybe they were pressed into it. The ruins symbolise oppression, yet looking at them now the whole idea of soldiers stationed here seemed crazy. But then, isn't all conflict?

I passed by the camp site I never used and the fish and chip van I would have if I could and walked the two miles to the little ferry landing. Naturally, the ferry had just left for Kylerhea, so I'd have to await its return, a matter twenty minutes or so. On such a morn, missing the ferry was a bonus, for now I sat on the rocks and took in the views, north and south along the straits, the narrowest point between Skye and mainland Scotland. Drovers brought their cattle this way once. After assembly at Broadford, the cattle, bound for English markets, were driven to Kylerhea where they had to swim over the straits, about half a mile wide. Seeing is not believing. Surely here, where the sea is forced between the two narrowest points, the current is strong enough to sweep away even the strongest swimmers. But the drovers had a special technique.

They took 3-feet lengths of rope, each with a noose at one end, and secured it around the head of each cow, or tied it to its horn, and tied the other end to the tail of the cow in front, to a maximum of six or eight, the front one being held by a man in the stern of a boat. Then they rowed like hell to the mainland. It seems few animals perished by this ingenious method. Dr Samuel Johnson (1709-84), English 'writer, critic, lexicographer and conversationalist', evidently remarked that the cows left Skye 'very lean, and were not offered to a butcher until they had been fattened in English pastures'. Considering they had to walk from wherever they lived on Skye, swim these narrows, then walk to England, this is hardly surprising. Johnson himself visited Skye with James Boswell (1740-95), Scottish 'man of letters', who was his biographer. Between them they had much to say about this and that. Johnson, incidentally, is noted for being grossly overweight. Maybe he, too, should have swam the narrows and walked to England, and thus become as lean as the cattle.

As I awaited the return of the ferry, motorists arrived and waited their turn. In this beautiful spot, on this lovely morning, did they step from their cars and take in the views, and breathe in air as fresh as God ever made it? They did not. Instead, they sat in their cars, looking forlornly at the car in front, or at the solid rock by the roadside. What is it about cars and people? Why are they so inseparable? They won't get out, will they? They didn't get out their cars on the ferry either, and so missed the sea otters diving into the sea from the shore. Skye, it seems, has many meanings. In Gaelic it's *Eilean a'Cheo*, the Misty Isle, or *An t-Eilean Sgitheanach*, the Winged Isle; to the Norse it was *Skuyo*, Cloud Island. The aforesaid Dr Fatty Johnson described the native language, *Gaelic* (they say 'Gallic' in Scotland, as opposed to 'Gaelic' in Ireland), as 'the rude speech of a barbarous people with few thoughts to express'. I wonder if he said so to their face. A Scot, Martin Martin, who wrote *A Description of the Western Isles of Scotland*, aroused Dr Johnson's interest in Skye in the first place. Martin noted that 'women in Skye observed that breasts contract to a lesser bulk when the wind blows from the north, and yield less milk when it blows from any other quarter'. Silly bugger. Perhaps the way his mother was facing explains the reason for calling him Martin when his surname was Martin.

Ashore, I was off. The road climbed steeply for two miles to Bealach Udal, 700 feet above sea-level. Nearing the top it's so steep it's a bottom gear job. I, feeling fit and breathing pure air on a wonderful day, didn't need gears. The road traversed a vast landscape of heather, with the sea in retrospect, and the promise of grand country ahead. I was not disappointed, as Glen Arroch opened up before me, with views of distant hills almost lost in a heat-haze. The road levelled, affording the perfect opportunity for a sing-song, although I was cruelly interrupted in the middle of Elvis Presley or somebody by the sudden blast of a car horn, sounded by a well-meaning motorist, accompanied by a loud 'hi, great day!' as he sped by. The whole world was aglow, or so it seemed.

Four miles on I reached the Broadfod Road. Facing me was a road-sign, with the names of places in Gaelic as well as English. Broadford was *An t-Ath Leathann*. I followed the road for half a mile, then left where the map indicated a 'grave yard', near Skye aerodrome. It's near the sea, a lovely spot. With time to spare I wandered among the graves. In a corner a row of headstones marked the resting places of seamen of H.M.S. Curacoa, sunk on 2nd October, 1942. One of the stones was inscribed simply, 'Known to God', others carried the inscription 'A sailor of the 1939-45 War'. These young men had their lives terminated one October day so that I could stand here and look at the sea, free to do as I pleased. Whoever heard of the Curacoa? Not I. But these sailors died for us all. At the going down of the sun and in the morning, we will remember them.

I took a dead-straight by-road, westbound for Broadford, an easy afternoon stroll affording grand views along the rugged coastline, where modern bungalows with well-tended gardens occupy little plots of an otherwise barren landscape. One of the great values of the British landscape is its variety, changing shapes in a land of contrasts. My 'stroll' slowed down to a mere dawdle – any slower and I'd be standing still. At Broadford I slid into a café for coffee and to rest my feet before setting off to find accommodation, which proved easy. My host told me the hotel had laundry facilities, so I was able to clean my sweat-ridden clothes – four hot days of hiking had taken their toll. I watched shirts, underpants and socks spinning around in a huge cylinder, and when I became bored – after about 0.075 seconds – I wandered off in search of food, then to nowhere in particular, before returning to my B and B where I watched telly awhile. Television didn't come to Skye until 1963. Typically, what I saw on the box that evening was so memorable it might as well never have come at all.

Tomorrow I would head south for Elgol. Such a decision is not easy to come by when your ultimate goal is the north coast of Britain. But at Elgol I hoped to fulfil an ambition, namely to take a sea cruise to Loch Coruisk, a 'true' freshwater loch, and from there hike to Sligachan, passing below the jagged peaks of the Black Cuillin, the finest mountain range in the British Isles. As I have said, the merits of my journey lie not in taking the shortest route, but in taking the best route. It doesn't get any better than this.

*

Scotland is famous for its clan system, which came into being around the middle of the 13th century. Each clan member undertook to serve his chief as 'his master by land and sea'. The chief would then protect him as though he were his own family. *Clann* means 'children', although the next in line for chief would not necessarily be the eldest, more likely the strongest. The clans were made up of warriors, and lesser men who tended crops and cattle. The clan system ended with the Scots' defeat at Culloden, after which former chiefs became landlords, and their subjects became their tenants.

Skye was the domain of several clans, notably the MacKinnons, MacLeods, MacDonalds and Nicolsons. South of Broadford, the lonely valley of Strath is MacKinnon country. Evidently the MacKinnons were kind to the aforesaid Johnson and Boswell, so

Johnson was 'much pleased'. How nice. The valley is bordered by high hills, where once there was a forest, the home of wolves and wildcats. Now there is only the heather and the lonely road to Elgol. Strath had a patron saint, St Maelrubha, (*Maol Ruadh*), 'the red man of the bald forehead' who introduced Christianity to the west coast of Skye. But in the 8th century the Vikings came and the churches were abandoned. They were rebuilt when Christianity returned, and two miles further along the road I came to Christ's Church (*Cill Chriosd*), a ruin, where the last service was held around 1843. The church stands on a small hill, roofless and broken, surrounded by tilted gravestones and the family graves of the MacKinnons, one of whom was Neil, the first Protestant minister. A plaque by the gate bears the following testimony:

"Neil's meanness and greed were proverbial. He grudgingly provided two meals a day to his workmen, but he was not prepared to allow more than one meal on a Sunday, the day of rest. One Sunday two of his workmen were sitting near Cill Church while their master was preaching goodwill to all men. They determined not to starve, so took up a foot plough and set to work, to the embarrassment of Neil, who was at that moment coming out of church with friends.

From then onwards the workmen received two meals on Sundays".

The ruin is a simple rectangle, gable ends pointing to the sky, and windows like the sightless eyes of a long-dead monster. It doesn't take much imagination to cast one's mind back to the time when he people of Strath would arrive at their church on a Sunday morning, and later tend their sheep and cattle. Now they are gone, except that some lie in the churchyard. Are their spirits here still? Were they watching even now as I wandered among their graves? Strange, they would think, that someone carrying a pack should pass this way. They would never understand, not folk who spent their entire lives within the confines of their own valley, working on their crofts.

Crofting was introduced to Skye at the beginning of the 18th century. Tenant farmers were allocated different pieces of land every two or three years, so that each shared the good and the bad. They could work the land, graze cattle and sheep. But they never *owned* the land; they never had real security. When their landlords realised sheep would pay better than the rents their tenants could afford, rich farmers brought in their flocks, and the tenants were evicted, or *cleared*.

A typical place of enforced eviction took place at Lorgill, on the west of Skye, in 1830, when the Sheriff's officer read out loud the following document to the crofters:

"You are hereby warned to be ready to leave Lorgill with all your baggage but no stock and proceed to Loch Snizort, where you will board the ship, Midlothian, that will take you to Nova Scotia, where you are to receive a free grant of land from Her Majesty's government. Any crofter disobeying this order will be arrested and taken to prison. All persons over seventy years of age who have no relatives to look after them will be taken care of in the County Poorhouse. God Save the Queen".

The children of Lorgill sang the 23rd Psalm, and placed flowers on the graves of their dead kinfolk. The next day, the entire community boarded the ship, which sailed as soon as they stepped aboard. Thus Skye, along with many other areas of the Highlands, was 'cleared'.

I moved on, passing nearby Loch Cill Chriosd, which is reputedly haunted. First there was an evil spirit, so deadly that anyone diving into the loch for a swim or drinking its waters would face death. Then there was a black horse, which took the guise of a handsome young man who seduced young maidens, before turning back into a horse and galloping off with them into the loch. He made the mistake of picking on a priest who converted him to Christianity and the horse was never seen again. I never saw it anyway. Today, a herd of cattle lazed in the sun. Their indifference didn't surprise me in the slightest, as tales of haunted places have never revealed to me any evidence of ghosts, ghouls, apparitions or spirits of any shape or size.

At Torrin came a superb view of Bla Bheinn (*Blaven*), which I climbed one sunny day from the shores of Loch Slapin. The path led up by waterfalls and, further up the mountain, to loose scree where every three yards upward seemed to be followed by two down. I had looked forward to the view from the summit, where I anticipated the Cuillin peaks would be shown to splendid advantage. Instead, I found myself engulfed in thick cloud. Of the Cuillin I saw nothing that day. Hillwalking in Scotland can be very frustrating. I was frustrated today, too, at Torrin, where I'd hoped to buy a cold drink. Alas, there was nowhere, although there is, or was, a well here. It has associations with an outlaw called MacRaing who reputedly robbed a girl, and when his son found out he was so shocked he threatened to expose him, whereupon his dad murdered him, cut his head off and threw it into the well.

Bla Bheinn, Isle of Skye   P 2001

At Kilmarie I spied a bull, thankfully secured behind steel bars in a sort of prison. Being kept frustrated until it was time to unleash his sexual drive on an entire herd, if looks were anything to go by. He had long, blond hair, which partly covered his eyes. He glared menacingly as I passed by, giving me a sort of 'if I could just get out of here' look. I checked possible routes of escape should the need arise. Then, turning through a gateway, I came unexpectedly upon a cemetery, where ancient gravestones leaned at crazy angles, their inscriptions rendered unreadable by constant wearing by the elements. Here, at Kilmarie, is proof that not only are our pathetic bodies mortal, but our names are too. Even set in stone.

Moving on, I found myself on the high cliffs above Loch Slapin, with glorious views across the deep blue waters of the loch to distant mountains on the mainland. A young woman approached, on the path.

On a High Street in any town we'd have passed one another without greeting. Here, we seemed to be the first to say hello. She looked happy, and with every right, for if she lives here she is fortunate indeed. Then the path led into a deep, wooded gorge, where shafts of sunlight penetrated the canopy above and beamed down on a vast carpet of bluebells. I rested awhile, for such places should be savoured.

I carried on in the late afternoon sunshine, to a quiet road leading across the empty moors of the Strathaird peninsula. Just before Elgol, I spied a small square of grassy ground next to a burn, an ideal camp site, and then found myself gazing across Loch Scavaig at the jagged skyline of the Cuillin, backed by the bright-blue sky, a splendid way to get sight of Britain's finest mountain range. Elgol, incidentally, is reputedly named after a warrior called Aella who fought a battle against the Picts and Scots here: 'Aella-gol' = Elgol. Anyway, I was hungry, and remembered a little café at the top of the hill. On previous visits it had been closed, but surely on a day such as this tourists must be expected – though there were none to see. I thought about what I might have for supper. Steak, perhaps. I'd not eaten since breakfast, and now my stomach was barely able to wait. Alas, the café was closed. Supper would be two bread rolls purchased in Broadford.

I retraced steps to the little square of grass, and pitched camp. As ever, combined operation by the local rabbits and sheep – probably their way of getting back the human race – meant I would need to spend a few minutes playing football. I took stock. I had been fortunate indeed, having walked all the way from Fort William and not a single drop of rain. Thoughts of the following day's expedition cheered me; I'd long waited to see for the first time the waters of Loch Coruisk. Tomorrow I would have my reward, after a grand fry-up in the café, of course. But in the night I was awakened by a strange yet familiar sound.

Raining, it was. Heavy, bucketing rain, the sort you only seem to get in Scotland. It lashed fiercely against the walls of my tent, which shook in a raging wind. I pulled the sleeping bag over my head to try and drown out the noise, prayed the tent would stand up to the storm, that water wouldn't infiltrate my cosy nest. Somehow, my cares ebbed and I drifted into slumber. I was content. No-one on earth knew where I was, and that pleased me.

The Cuillin Hills ᒣ2001

Morning. I lay in my sleeping bag pleased – and relieved – that my tent had stood up to the storm. The wind had dropped, but the rain was falling still. I unzipped the tent flap a few inches and peeked outside. All was lost in a dank sea-mist. It was as if an invisible hand had drawn a thick curtain across the Cuillin. There would be no cruise across Loch Scavaig. I considered sitting tight. Maybe the little boats might operate later in the day. But I rejected the idea, partly because I had little food, and anyway I might find exactly the same conditions in twenty-four hours. There was nothing for it but to press on, whatever the weather. Crossing the now-gushing burn, I considered myself fortunate it hadn't broken its banks through the night, in which event I'd probably have woken up at sea. What remote hope I nurtured of bacon and eggs soon died; the café was closed. As I departed Elgol, I realised I'd seen not a soul there since my arrival the previous evening.

In pouring rain I sought the path for Camasunary, a place indicated on the map by bold lettering, but which, I knew, would be a few deserted buildings, nothing more. I headed north, contouring the grassy hillside, with the sea – Loch Scavaig – below on the left, the grassy, heather-clad hillside rising on the right. I've a framed picture of this scene at home, with contented cows grazing in the sun. I saw not one this morning. The farmer would have had more sense than to put animals out on a day like this.

The path led down to a deserted beach. It was strewn with debris: oil cans, Coca Cola cans, bits of polythene, bits of paper, bits of everything, all washed in from the sea. Until that point I had soaked – literally – in the glory of the morning: the rain, the mist. Man's legacy was a smack in the face, testimony to his selfish betrayal of the planet. They who sail the seven seas, do they just chuck their rubbish overboard? When at last I climbed from Skye's unofficial rubbish dump the buildings of Camasunary came into view, backed by the rising hills of Sgurr na Stri, the peak of the conflict. It's said to be named after a dispute between the MacLeods and the MacKinnons over its possession. The two chiefs agreed on a demarcation line, and a poor boy was thrashed to near death so that someone would remember.

The waters of the Abhainn nan Leac, not surprisingly, were in spate, crashing down with a great roar. There was no question of wading, so I turned upstream, looking for a way across – stepping stones maybe, or a possible narrowing of its banks, which might permit a spectacular leap. Instead, I found a bridge. My relief at its discovery could not be measured, and I gave silent thanks to the army, who built it. At Camasunary – the name means 'bay of the white or beautiful shieling' – I sheltered as best I could in the lee of a wall. Lunch was a soggy scone. Little food, but plenty of water, enough to open a bottling plant. Never mind that French stuff, what about Camasunary Nectar? Why do we import foreign water when, here on Skye, beautiful, fresh water falls by the gallon. Sorry, litre.

The path climbed steadily, with eight more miles to Sligachan. It was possible the route was flooded, impassable even. In driving rain I had sight of nought but the ground at my feet, and water cascading like ribbons down the hillsides. Every few yards I encountered newly-formed rivers which either crossed my path or even came along it. At first I tried jumping over them, but inevitably ended up to my knees in gushing torrents. Past caring, I simply waded through whatever water came my way. Was it only yesterday, in glorious spring sunshine, I had explored the cemeteries at Cill Chriosd and Kilmarie, and lingered in the woods among the bluebells listening to birdsong?

I continued thus, enjoying this experience, yet having walked all this way I had been robbed of the magnificent views of the Cuillin, now towering above, their pinnacles lost in cloud. They are, surely, the grandest hills in Britain – for sheer, dramatic, exhilarating scrambling, Europe even. Not as high as those on the continent, but high enough. How high do you want to be if you fall? Will 3,000 feet suffice? For those who venture on to the ridge, the hard, gabbro rock renders the compass useless; if you climb on the Cuillin you must use your sense of direction, maps if you will and most of all your skill. The range is ten miles long. Their Gaelic names – some after famous mountaineers – were only given in the 19th century. Sgurr Dearg's Inaccessible Pinnacle should be climbed – by mere mortals at least – with the use of ropes. Ordinary Munro-baggers need assistance to complete ascent of *all* Scotland's mountains.

One of the Cuillin is Sgurr nan Gillean, 'the peak of the young men'. It was considered 'impossible' once, and the first recorded ascent was not until 1836, by Professor J.D. Forbes, who did most of his climbing in Switzerland. I climbed it on a grey day in 1991, by what is now regarded as the tourists' route. All is rock, and nearing the top you have to scramble up rock faces and rock chimneys, with a final step across an airy gap, where you must 'spread your legs'. On the narrow summit I could not at first bring myself to stand upright. Then, realising there was nothing to fear but my own cowardice, I stood to find myself looking down on tine thread-like rivers far below. The view along the ridge and out to sea was breathtaking.

Today, Sgurr nan Gillean looked bleak and inhospitable. Walking below its towering spire, I felt a sense of pride, of achievement. Yet, compared with many other peaks, Sgurr nan Gillean is not particularly difficult, just something to be taken in stride, as it is by experienced scramblers, whilst true climbers wouldn't give it a second thought. Later, I discovered other peaks further along the ridge were much more difficult propositions.

Under clearing skies, I emerged from the swirling waters of the glen where I sat on a rock to wring out my socks. Looking up, I could see the Sligachan hotel in the distance. I could *see* the hotel; getting there was another matter. As much as I progressed along Glen Sligachan, it seemed to get no closer. But after negotiating a thousand streams, I reached the road and strode around to the front of the hotel where I encountered *people*, the first I'd seen since the girl at Kilmarie, 24 hours before. Who says Britain in overcrowded? What had these souls been doing all morning while I'd been wading out of Camasunary? Keeping out of the rain, that's what. When I'd crawled from my tent they'd stayed in their beds. Now they were off at last for some fresh air and exercise, but they'd missed the best part of the day.

There's a camp site at Sligachan, with toilets and showers. A few tents were dotted about, each with a car parked alongside. I selected a spot and pitched mine. After a couple of hours in the sleeping bag, I went to the hotel for my first meal since breakfast at Broadford the previous day. Irish folk music trilled from speakers, fitting the occasion perfectly – almost. Should've been Scots, I suppose.

Back at the camp site, a lone fellow bowled up and pitched his tent, full of chat about sleeping out, brewing up, etc. Unfortunately, his every sentence was punctuated by the sound of him farting. 'Skye's the best place in the world,' he declared, letting rip. I didn't argue. Then, after letting rip again, he told me he'd taken trains and buses from God-knows-where to Sligachan only to find he'd forgotten to bring enough tent pegs. Between us we got his tent up, sort of, but he would have to catch a bus to Portree in the morning to buy some more pegs. He said he hoped his tent would stay up all night. So did I. I didn't want him in mine.

I was concerned about other campers who might arrive late after a few bevvies and drive over my sleeping form. So, as a precaution, I rolled a few heavy boulders into a defensive circle around my tent. If they were going to run me over they'd be ripping their sumps off first. I felt entitled to dream in safety.

*

As I looked up, water was gushing towards me, an angry, raging torrent that would sweep me to my doom, destined forever to float in the waters of a deep, cold lake. And for the rest of their lives, all the women who would have wanted me to marry them would wonder whatever had become of me. In my dying moments, as I struggled to recall both of their names, fleeting scenes of my life flashed through my fuddled brain. Then I heard a deep, distinctive voice, barely audible above the sound of the angry waters.

'Hello there...'

Gurgle, gurgle, gurgle.

'...anyone at home?'

234

I woke to find myself dry and warm. I wanted to be left alone. But there was the voice again.

'You awake in there...?'

It was some bloke wanting the fee for the overnight camp. I found some money, crawled from my nest and paid up.

Today, I was walking to Uig, 25 miles away, there to catch the ferry for the Outer Isles, where I intended to go over to North Uist and island-hop to Harris. Lunch would be taken in Portree, and further on I would explore a ruined castle, *Caistael Uisdein*, on the cliffs above Loch Snizort. Mercifully, the rain had stopped, leaving a cold, grey morning. How typical that the one fine day I needed for the cruise to Loch Coruisk was the only one blighted by rain in an entire week of dry weather. Still, unlike the previous morning, I was able to wash and take breakfast. Life was good!

Heading north, I found myself constantly looking back to Glen Sligachan, with Marsco and Sgurr nan Gillean seemingly reluctant to disappear. Both had new caps of snow; where it rained on me yesterday, the tops were under a blizzard. I headed for Portree, through Glen Varragill, a 10-mile hike with views mainly obliterated by huge forests.

Portree (*Port-an-Righ*) is the 'capital' of Skye. It's name means 'Port of the King', after the visit of James V in 1540. Some of the local clan chiefs had been acting up and James, not unreasonably, decided to assert his authority to keep them in line. James met the chiefs in the town square. Portree was also on the itinerary of Bonnie Prince Charlie when he was on the run from redcoats after Culloden. He dined at MacNab's Inn, now the Royal Hotel, as did our friends, Johnson and Boswell. Lunch was a Scotch pie – for me, not Charlie. Afterwards I went and sat in the square, where James and his Highlanders thrashed out their problems. You can't forget you're in the land of the Gaels. On one side of a large building there's a sign, *Bank of Scotland*, on the other side, *Banca Na H Alba*.

It was time to tend to blisters. There were people about, but off came the boots and socks. Some elderly women on one of those coach tours watched as I applied sticking plasters. One of them (inevitably) mentioned the weather, another complained of being cold. A third was clearly curious.

'Where are you going?' she asked.

'Uig,' I replied.

Blank faces all round. I explained it was to take the ferry for the Isles. 'Then I'll be making my way to John o'Groats.'

She seemed impressed. 'He's goin' to John o'Groats,' she told her pals. They all nodded, save one, who gave me a long look before having her two penn'orth.

'If you're goin' to Uig,' she said slowly, 'you're goin' the wrong way for John o'Groats.'

She waited for my response, the sort of wait tinged with doubt that I was going anywhere. I was obliged to explain the whole thing, by which time I had finished tending to my feet and had the boots on. But Doubting Doris was unconvinced. I could feel her eyes drilling into the back of my head as I hurried on.

I headed north, still fifteen miles from my objective. A few miles further the skies darkened, rain certain on what had turned into a grim afternoon. In the middle of nowhere the rain came, sweeping across the empty moors, rivers forming at once by the roadside. Amazingly, I spied a bus shelter, one of those glass-sided ones you normally find in town centres (only this one still had the glass in), and I stood inside to watch the downpour. It was the sort that soaks you through no matter what you are wearing – including expensive Gore-tex. Now and again a car splashed by, headlights peering through the gloom as mist enveloped the moor. The wind got up, and the temperature dropped dramatically as hailstones rapped against the shelter and covered the road in a neat, white carpet. The, as suddenly as it started, it stopped and the mist lifted, and all glistened under brightening skies.

I took a diversion along a backroad through a place called Borve, a sort of long village. The map indicated *Standing Stones*, and there they were, two ancient monoliths standing forlornly at the roadside. They've been there since time immemorial: before castles were built, before Bonnie Prince Charlie, before everything. A dog barked on my approach to the first houses of the village. I thought nothing of it until, in a moment, there was another, then another.

As I passed by each house in Borve, each dog warned the one next door of my impending approach until, finally, the entire dog population was in full cry, everything from aggressive Scotties to your Heinz 57's. I guess I was the only thing to happen all year. They were guard dogs whose only reason for living was to warn of the approach of the stranger, and this was their big day. Every dog in Borve was aware of my presence. More to the point, their owners were. You wouldn't want to be a burglar in Borve. Just to be on the public road brings the house down. What they might do to an intruder one might only guess.

Ahead were the blue waters of Loch Snizort, really an inner reach of the sea. A few miles further I passed the road end at Kingsburgh, where Bonnie Prince Charlie stayed after landing with Flora MacDonald. It was after their night's stay at Kingsburgh they went on to Portree, proceeding in the opposite direction to the way I walked now. (I wonder if they had problems with dogs at Borve). Later, Flora was arrested and taken to the Tower of London. As anyone remotely connected with the Prince was almost certain to face to death, it was amazing that Flora, who risked her life for her Charlie as much as anyone, should be spared. Equal rights didn't prevail in those days, obviously – imagine the fate of a bloke if he'd helped Charlie to escape. Anyway, Flora got married, had seven children and died of old age.

Sunshine and clear skies were with me as I reached the farm road to *Caistael Uisdein*. At the farm there was no sign of life. As the ruin stands on private land, I considered knocking on the door to seek permission to proceed. But what if I was refused? Then I should have to abandon this part of my venture. No, I would continue, as casually as possible, hoping my presence would not be detected. Or, if it was, that no-one would mind. I almost tip-toed across the fields. Have you ever tried it? Tip-toeing across fields? You feel a right plonker! As for the castle, there was no sign of it. I checked the map; it must be here somewhere. You can hardly miss a castle. Then I saw it, silhouetted against the deep, blue backdrop of the loch.

Caistael Uisdein was built by Hugh MacDonald of Sleat in the 16th century – full name Huisden MacGillespie Chleirich, meaning 'Hugh, son of Gillespie, the writer'. A sort of hollow stone block, the castle stands at the very edge of high cliffs. There is no door, so entry must have been through the roof. Evidently, Hugh decided to celebrate the opening of his castle with a 'castle warming', his true intention being to invite his chief and have him murdered. Unfortunately, Hugh must have drank too much Scotch, for his invitation intended for the chief mistakenly went to his accomplice, a fellow called Martin, whilst the letter giving exact details of how the murder was do be done, and to whom, went to the chief – his intended victim. Not surprisingly, the chief wasn't to pleased, so he laid siege to the castle until Hugh was starved out and taken to his – the chief's – castle where he was thrown into a dungeon and given salty beef and a jug containing no water.

Later, hungry and thirsty, Hugh was walled in by a stonemason. The moral of the story, I suppose, is to always check your mail.

In the sunshine of a lovely afternoon it would have been so easy to lie down on the grass with my back against the castle wall and drift off into blissful slumber. Alas, there was not the time. I retraced steps past the farm without (so far as I know) being seen, and resumed my journey unchallenged.

Three more miles found me above lovely Uig Bay. I had decided to spend the night at Uig youth hostel. It was occupied by a load of Germans and a few elderly Brits. I exchanged pleasantries, but was eager to be off in search of food. After a shower, I went down to the Ferry Inn.

'Do you do bar meals?' I enquired.

'Yes, but not after 8.30.'

It was 8.35.

'What about the restaurant?' I asked.

'Not after 8.30.'

It was as well I'd eaten at Portree, but I was still damned hungry.

'I'll have a packet of peanuts, then,' I said, resigned to my fate.

'Haven't any,' said the man, 'but we do have crisps.' He indicated several cardboard boxes on the floor behind the bar.

They were all there: Cheese 'n Onion, Salt 'n Vinegar, Smokey Bacon, etc. As I still carried the same two packets purchased in Fort William, admittedly now little more than crushed fragments, I declined.

The night that followed proved to be one of those ghastly experiences you can find in youth hostel dormitories. On an adjacent bunk, a bloke of sixty-odd crept into his sleeping bag, then, after I had dozed off, it started: snoring, persistent, just loud enough to compel you to hear. Things got worse. From elsewhere in the darkness came a wheezy, whistling sound from another, unseen soul. They seemed to be in harmony, as though they had carefully rehearsed their routine just for me – the faint, steady rattle of the snorer, followed by a steady, monotonous whistle. Snore-whistle. Snore-whistle. They, enjoying undisturbed sleep, whilst I, unable to block out the sound, could only lie awake and listen. It took great willpower to resist the temptation to suffocate them. Looking back, I should have. I could always have blamed the Germans.

11

The Outer Hebrides

I decided to get out of the hostel as soon as possible, before breakfast even, but not before doing my hostel duty: 'sweep the entrance'. The warden provided me with some useful information (as well as a broom) – the ferry times, and that breakfast could be bought on board and it would be good. Then the snoring monster appeared. I had exchanged a civil word or two with him the previous evening, but all he got this morning was an angry glare.

The lady at MacBrayne's ticket office was a stunner. I ordered a ticket for Lochmaddy, on North Uist.

'The ferry doesn't go to Lochmaddy on Saturdays,' she said with a lovely Scots smile.

'Oh really,' I said, with a lovely English smile, 'then how shall I get there?'

'Och, no problem. The ferry goes to Lochmaddy *tomorrow*. The Saturday ferry goes to Tarbert.'

Tarbert. That's on Harris.

I enquired if it might be possible to go to Tarbert today, then take the 'little ferries' – which ply between the little islands of the Western Isles – tomorrow, and 'island hop' to North Uist. No, it wouldn't, because the little ferries didn't run on Sundays. So, I was up the creek without a ferry. I could either spend a rainy day in Uig or take the ferry to Tarbert. Tarbert it would be. I ordered my ticket and she obliged, still with her smile. Anyone but her would have been strangled.

I fell into conversation with a young fellow who told me he was from New Zealand. He had travelled up from London the previous day by coach especially to see his grandfather who lived in Tarbert. 'He's 101, so I had to take the opportunity.' Better late than never. We hung around together inside the booking hall, the rain pouring down outside. It was 'Skye' rain again. The sound of the wind blowing the rain against the window told its own story. You couldn't see the sea from the pier.

No-one saw the ferry arrive. One moment it wasn't there, then it was. It was the *Caledonian Princess*, a similar vessel to those cross-Channel ferries you see. It wasn't long before the few awaiting cars and passengers were aboard and we were off. I dumped my sack and made a beeline for the restaurant. The shutter was down but, I was assured, it would be raised at any moment. I'm not one who normally fights his way through queues, but I'd not eaten since that Scotch pie at Portree and I wasn't going to miss out on breakfast. A couple held first place, then me, then one or two others behind. Other passengers just milled about, without seeming to care about food. They would have had good breakfasts, I reasoned, in their hotels and guesthouses. Then the ship's tannoy crackled into life, and a Scots voice on a pre-recorded tape was explaining the emergency procedures: the location of escape points and assembly areas, what to do if such-and-such a sound was heard and so on. Some children ran across the floor, only to be checked by their mother.

'Listen,' she ordered in a loud, authoritative voice, 'it's important to know what to do in an emergency.'

The children listened, their mother listened, everyone listened. At the bit about life jackets an assistant threw up the grill, revealing bacon and eggs, and other goodies, and the message on the tannoy was drowned in the clamour for places in the queue as everyone rushed forward. No rule about women and children first or anything. I just hoped with this lot on board we wouldn't hit an iceberg.

Soon, I was diving in: fruit juice, cereal, bacon and eggs, mushrooms, fried slice, etc. I am happy to relate that MacBrayne's breakfast lived up to its reputation. Having scoffed the lot, I sat down to digest my feed in contentment. Unfortunately, as the ferry pitched rolled with every breaker on the stormy Minch, my stomach had other ideas – like throwing it all up whence it came. The only answer was fresh air so I went outside, where I held onto the rail, the rain driving into my face. All around was grey, the sea heaving and randomly breaking into massive waves. It occurred to me that I fell overboard not one person on planet Earth would ever know what happened to me, and that some ambitious sod would find him or herself unexpectedly with a detective inspector's post at Watford. The scene reminded me of those films about the North Atlantic during the war, how convoys fought to reach Britain under the threat of being torpedoed. To those who served on the seas during the war I paid silent tribute.

I returned to the lounge and sat alone at a table with my head resting on my arms, and even managed to sleep – much-needed after the wretched night at Uig. When I awoke the jagged coastline of Harris was gliding by. It looked like those newsreels of the Falklands war. All that was missing were the Argie jets. The Norsemen settled here in the 9th century. After a 400-year occupation, they bequeathed many of their place-names, yet left no sign of their presence when they left. Gaelic is spoken by 90% of the population of the Outer Hebrides, where it somehow survived invasion by the English language and the Norse.

A giant is supposed to have lived at Tarbert. He and his wife imprisoned a young maid and forced her to spin cloth to make outsize garments of nettle leaves for them to wear. After she'd finished they would have eaten her, but her handsome young lover (it's never an ugly lover or a bloke with halitosis) promised to give Mrs Giant a string of pearls if she would set the girl free. He then endured many adventures, including a journey to a sea-king's palace (if he went on the ferry it wasn't a Sunday) where collected the pearls – giant ones, of course – and so secured her release. Huge boulders lying around Tarbert are said to be part of the giant'' castle.

Rain swept across the quay as silent passengers filed off the ferry. My New Zealand friend met up with an elderly lady, presumably his granny. Everyone seemed to have someone to meet or somewhere to go except me, as I found myself alone on the deserted quay. What sort of place had I come to? Was it in Britain? You wouldn't have thought so, seeing a road sign reading *Steornabhagh*. Skye had signs in Gaelic too, but always with the English name written alongside. If I hadn't been up on my geography, I wouldn't have known it meant Stornoway.

I hurried into the village, seeking out a grocer's. I'd probably have to camp tonight, so I needed something to eat. The shop was full of folk recently embarked off the ferry: mums and dads buying bread, kids queuing for gobstoppers and Smarties. I considered myself fortunate to find a dubious-looking sandwich, which I just manage to snatch from the outstretched hand of an old lady whose attempt to be first was thwarted by the crowd. Then I spied a cosy café with a sign saying OPEN. Inside, the waitress asked me what I wanted. 'A cup of coffee and a bite to eat,' I said. 'Sorry,' came the reply, 'we're closed.' I might have known.

I hoped the rain would stop tipping down. Or even that it would just fall as *ordinary* rain. Instead, it seemed to be falling out of unseen barrels. I sought refuge in the bar of the Harris Hotel, and ordered fish and chips and a beer. Two men came in and played pool. One of them was prolific at swearing. F-ing this, f-ing that. No-one took the slightest notice. Used to it, I supposed. He was part of the Harris scene, a cultural commodity, as much a part of the island as its peat bog and rugged coastline. You could imagine going into the tourist information centre...

'Any suggestions what I might do on a rainy afternoon hereabouts?'

'Och, no problem. You're just in time for Swearing Man.'

'Swearing Man?'

'Aye, that's right. Ye'll find him in the hotel, just up the road.'

He was in full cry.

'Comin' out for a f-ing drink tonight?' asked the British, European and World Swearing Champion.

His buddy potted a ball.

'Ye have a' the f-ing luck,' came the unsporting response.

I looked at the ladies. Not so much as a flinch.

'Careful aboot comin' off the f-ing black.'

When, at last, I went outside, the f-ing rain was still f-ing-well tipping it down. Well, I'd just have to f-ing-well get on with it.

I decided to buy a morning newspaper. Handy to have when you're lying in your tent with no-one to talk to. I found a newsagents, and yes, it was open. Scarcely able to believe my luck I went inside to find a long queue at the counter. Almost all the passengers off the *Caledonian Princess* were in the grocers or the newsagents. 'The papers aren't in yet,' I was told. I thought they'd have come over on the ferry. No, they come by plane to Stornoway, then by road to Tarbert. I waited ten minutes or so, hoping the weather might change. It did. When I went outside the rain had turned to sleet and hail. The wind was raging, and all that fell from the sky was blowing into my face. I wondered if I should seek out lodgings, but I determined to go on. This was going to be an experience not to be missed.

I headed east, bound for Glen Laxadale, among jagged hills, and took to the road with increased misgiving. What if Glen Laxadale was flooded? What if it wasn't flooded, but became flooded with me somewhere in the middle? What if I got lost? What if I didn't get lost but ended up sinking in bog, my fingers vainly grasping at thin air as I sank without trace? What if it snowed? Then the sleet and hail gave way to rain again. Concerned about my well-being, I splashed my way out of Tarbert, subconsciously changing the name from Glen Laxadale to Glen Laxative, and telling myself to write off to the ordnance survey people to get them to amend the name on their maps – if I ever got home.

The map suggests there is a good path, four miles through the glen, to the main Stornoway road. So it proved. It was just as well, for the weather was worsening. Water ran along and across the path; my feet were soaked in minutes. But the scene unfolding before me I will never forget: here was true wilderness, a landscape of barren rock and mist. And water, water everywhere: on my face, in my eyes, in my boots, in my everything. I reached the shore of Laxadale Lochs (one loch, though plural), a scene grim and foreboding, the rain, unrelenting, sweeping across its grey waters. Ahead, there was a high ridge. Soon, I was in cloud, climbing through bog to the top where, in triumph, I came to a backroad which, I knew, would lead to the main road ahead. I was tackling the considerable incline when, for just the second time on my journey, I was offered a lift. Where he came from I will never know, but he was an elderly chap driving a small van. With the rain lashing against us, he wound the window down about seven-eighths of an inch.

'I'm goin' t'Stornoway if ye want a lift,' he said.

'No thanks,' I replied, my words all but blown away in the wind.

He looked at me in disbelief. Either that or he misunderstood what I had said.

'I'm goin' t'Stornoway,' he repeated.'

I told him I could not accept his kind offer.

'It's thirty miles,' he reasoned, 'ye can be there in half an hour.'

'I can't accept lifts,' I shouted.

He looked at me, seemed to realise something of what I was about.

'No-one will know,' he said, tipping me a wink.

'You're wrong,' I said. '*I'll* know.'

He drove on, slowly at first, as though to allow me time to change my mind. But, of course, I would not. On that bleak hillside, on this dog's dinner of a day, I watched the little van drive off. But there had been no choice. If I had accepted I would never have forgiven myself, and the entire venture would have been ruined. Later, recounting the story to friends, they said I must have been tempted. But I wasn't, not even for a millisecond.

Further up the hill, the rain got heavier. At the main road, an old sign (in English) said Stornoway 28½. I'd not make the capital of the Outer Hebrides today. The road climbed high above the sea. The wind raged, and the higher I climbed the stronger it became. Then, totally, exposed to its venom, it hit me fair and square from the north. It was impossible to walk in a straight line, such was its awesome power. New streams were born, both on the hillsides and on my face, turning into rivers that crept inside my clothing. I was in for a soaking.

The road climbed to around five hundred feet. Here, I might have expected grand views of this magnificent coast. Instead, I could only peer through water-filled eyes at the rain as it swept across the road and, beyond, an undefined wasteland of bog and water. Atop the hill, the storm hit me head on, force mach-one, as it roared unhindered across Ardvourlie Bay. Eyes down, I battled on, a drunken soul whose only guide was the roadside. Looking ahead wasn't an option. At times the wind was so powerful it was as though I was held by an invisible hand that clutched me from behind, then it would drop suddenly, and I'd lurch forward into an unexpected vacuum. Time became an irrelevance; it was all a matter of moving forward until, finally, I staggered down a private driveway that suddenly appeared at my feet. I had not had the slightest idea of its existence. It led to an isolated cottage. I've banged on a few doors in my time, but never as loud as my knock on the door of that cottage, where desperation drove me to the point of almost knocking it from its hinges. Suddenly, it opened, and I found myself looking at an elderly woman. She was smiling calmly for the stranger.

'Turned nasty, hasn't it?' she said, without realising she had just uttered the greatest understatement in the history of the world. I didn't argue.

'Do you do accommodation?' I enquired, desperately hoping she did or, if not, she would take me in anyway. There was a kindly, understanding smile.

'No, but that house does.'

She was pointing to a house a mile off, just visible through the stair rods, thirty minutes' walk against this wind. I could live with that. Even if it was full I might be allowed to put the tent up. It would have to be put up on private land; there was not a square yard of grass anywhere, only bog.

The bed and breakfast sign looked old. I knocked and waited. There was no reply. I knocked again, louder. Just when it seemed there must be no-one at home an old man opened the door. He looked astonished at the sight of someone carrying a rucksack on his doorstep in such weather. I enquired about accommodation. He hesitated, his hand holding the latch. 'The wife's no' in,' he said, meaning his good lady was in charge of admitting guests. I realised that most – nay, all – visitors must arrive by car. I was a one-off apparition in glistening green. He was looking still, expecting me to go I suppose. But I wasn't going. I tried to look as forlorn as possible. It wasn't difficult.

'I could do with a bed.'

Still he held the latch, with me outside in the rain. 'I have a tent,' I said, 'if you can't put me up.'

The grass between the house and the loch-shore was level and trim, an ideal camp-site *if* the tent could be put up without being torn to shreds in the process. But I really wanted to be indoors, for beneath my cag my clothes were wet and I was cold. I told him I'd walked over from Tarbert, knowing he would know I would have taken a battering. Then he stepped aside, though still without total conviction. I took off my sack and swept past him into the hallway. Only a firm refusal accompanied by a loaded shotgun would have stopped me.

He led the way upstairs to a large bedroom, promising 'a cup of coffee and a digestive biscuit' at six. My window looked out along the length of Loch Seaforth, a grand view. I strung my clothing up all over the room and went directly for a bath, then put on dry gear. Right on time came the call for the coffee and digestives. It was clear Mr

Morrison had been uncertain about me at first, arriving at his door out of the blue. Or the grey, I should say.

This place, he said, is called Bogha Glas, meaning Grey Cow. Years before, he explained, he used to fish in Loch Seaforth, catching cod, mackerel, conger eel, whiting. But there's little nowadays. The fish have gone, taken by huge factory ships from abroad. In fact, the trouble started at the turn of the century, when the introduction of steam trawlers, trawling the sea bed, destroyed the breeding grounds. In the old days, Britain had a 3-mile limit around her shores; she was able to look after her own stocks. But this no longer applies: vessels from so-called EC countries, under so-called flags of convenience, plunder stocks once the sole preserve of the islanders. Then he turned to politics. There is little doubt that the majority, if not all, the islanders, feel left out and neglected by a government in far-off London, that the Outer Isles should be independent of England, of mainland Scotland even. What they think about being ruled by the bureaucrats of Brussels God knows.

Mr Morrison then declared he was off to visit relatives. This would leave me, a total stranger, alone in the house. But people here still believe in old-fashioned honesty, they still trust others. I repaired to my room where I spent the evening in isolation, looking out of the window. Still, the storm raged. I had no supper, but contented myself with the food purchased in Tarbert, and considered myself fortunate to be safe and dry. As darkness came, I watched as the rain swept across the surface of the loch, and lashed against the window, driven remorselessly by the force of the gale. It was a magnificent sight, nature in the raw – wild, untamed, a reminder that she can do as she pleases.

A better Saturday evening I never spent.

*

Sunday morning brought bright skies. No wind, no rain. Instead, Harris was at peace, left as nature had left her though the night: damp and fresh, with barely a whisper of a breeze. I went down to meet the still-unseen wife of my Good Samaritan. From the stairs I heard them talking. About what I could not tell, for they spoke in Gaelic. I was warmly received in English. After a grand breakfast they bade me a warm farewell, but not until I had declared politely but firmly several times over their kind offer of a lift. They are good people, with no airs and graces.

Today I'd head for Stornoway, 25 miles to the north. It's a long road, across a landscape of rock and peat and a million lochans. Within minutes I crossed the invisible border into Lewis. The name means 'a marshy place'. Never was there a more apt title. The map says 'Isle of Harris' and 'Isle of Lewis', yet they are not islands, for they are joined near Bogha Glas. But then, they natives will argue, an island doesn't have to be a piece of land surrounded by water; it can be an independent community. Who could argue?

Harris gives its name to the famous tweed, woven by hand by the crofters in their own homes – though, strangely, nowadays, mainly on Lewis. It all started in the early 19th century, when Harris was owned by the Earl of Dunmore. In those days crofters wove cloth for their own use, but the Earl's wife sent some girls to the mainland for training also, and when they returned their tweed – Harris Tweed – fell into demand, especially by the rich who wore it to go shooting on their private estates. In time, demand outstripped supply, and by the 20th century washing, carding and dyeing the cloth had to be done by machines. But *weaving* the cloth continues to be done by hand, and Harris Tweed's distinctive trademark, an orb, protects it from imitations.

A last look back over the Harris landscape, yesterday lost in cloud, revealed white-topped hills, including Clisham, at 2,000-odd feet, the highest. Hard to believe they were as high as the Himalayas before rain and ice wore them down. I took to the road, hills rising sharply on my left, Loch Seaforth below on my right; there was no traffic. My thoughts drifted back to the previous day. Thank goodness for the Morrisons, for without the shelter of their home I don't know how I would have fared. Drowned, probably, or sunk without trace into glutinous peat.

It was 'marching' time again, so to relieve the monotony I'll recount the story of John of Lewis who went to sea and was cast adrift in a raft for some reason. Then he found himself washed up on an island where he was attacked by robbers. They were going to kill him, but they considered him so courageous they spared his life, asking if he would like to join their band. Instead, he robbed them of their gold and seized a beautiful Spanish princess they happened to be holding captive. Naturally, John and the princess fell in love (it was probably her he was after all along) and ran off together. One day, seeking shelter in a derelict cottage, they found it occupied by three men who were holding their heads in their hands. They turned out to be a father and his two sons who had been murdered, and could not find rest until someone kindly put their heads back on. John obliged, whereupon the three men disappeared.

John and the princess married, but later, he once again found himself cast adrift at sea. There must have been something about the guy; maybe he came out of the closet in the days when you just couldn't do that among a load of sailors. But then, maybe not, for the three apparitions rescued him, whereupon he was more than happy to be reunited with his princess.

Three miles on I came to a long, straggling village called Arivruaich, where houses stretch for over a mile alongside the road. Hereabouts, the old road runs parallel with the new, the former an ideal walkers' route. There were huge signs, proclaiming that the new road had been paid for by funds provided by the European Community 'specially designed for the Highlands and Islands'. In other words, a tiny portion of British taxpayers' money was allocated to build a new road on Lewis, and isn't the EU wonderful! We could have built it ourselves, and still had billions left over for other British projects. Further on, at Balallan there was a small garage and a shop. Chocolates? Fruit juice? No such luck; both were closed. In the case of the garage, even for petrol. They don't charge around for the Sunday papers on Lewis. My hopes in this regard would never have flourished in the first place had I known what I was later to discover – that I was in the Outer Hebrides and it was a Sunday. I was in for a learning experience when I got to Stornoway.

The road wound its way between lochans and rocky outcrops. At every turn I looked ahead in the hope of seeing a roadside café, a shop. But there was nowhere. By Laxay – still nothing in the way of amenities – I had covered ten miles, and the further I marched the more I felt the need for some refreshment. Then, in the distance, I spied what looked like a large hotel by the road. It was busy, judging by the car park, which was full. I looked forward to a long, cold, sharp drink, a welcome sandwich maybe. Might even see the Swearing Man in action again. Sadly, my 'hotel' turned out to be a church. This was a surprise; living in England, I'd never seen a church with a full car park.

Just before six I found myself entering Stornoway, where I spied a fellow walking by the harbour. He was fat with a bald head, looked like Uncle Fester of the Addams Family. I was about to discover he had Uncle Fester's voice, too, and judging by his reply to my enquiry, Uncle Fester's mentality.

' 'Scuse me,' I said, 'could you tell me where I can find accommodation?'

'Y'know,' he replied, 'I was out on my bike yesterday and I can't find it now.'

'Really,' I said, keenly interested in what he had told me.

'Yes,' he wheezed. 'Rain was so heavy I couldn't see. Had to abandon the damn thing somewhere.'

'Hope you find it,' I said, 'but could you tell me where I can find accommodation?'

He looked thoughtful.

'You could try...' He named a few streets, in such a manner I was expected to know where they were. 'But you know what these places are like. Here today, gone tomorrow...'

'Thanks for your help,' I said, wondering whether I should leave him to find his bike or push him into the harbour. I expected something like 'that's okay,' or 'any time,' but he caught me out again – and this is true, I swear.

'Don't suppose you might have seen it,' he said, looking at me forlornly. He meant his bike, of course. Sadly, I had to admit I hadn't. Damn shame, but there it was.

I found a guest house in a tree-lined avenue. I mention the trees because trees are not a common sight on Lewis. Indeed, I could not recall seeing a single one the twenty-five miles since Bogha Glas. But trees thrive in Stornoway thanks to Sir James Matheson, who bought Lewis in 1844 with the fortune he made from the opium trade in the Far East. Matheson built Lews Castle (not *Lewis*, as might be expected), a 'mock-Tudor folly', complete with castellated ramparts. His wife wanted a garden, not feasible on such infertile soil, so Matheson imported thousands of tons of good quality soil from the mainland. Today, magnificent woodlands surround the castle, where rhododendron, palms and other exotic plants survive, aided by the warming effects of the Gulf Stream. Later, in 1918, Lord Leverhulme bought Lewis, intending to turn the island into a major fishing industry. He poured a fortune into his scheme, only to find returning from the wars didn't want it, so the venture failed. Leverhulme, to his credit, didn't take umbrage; instead, he gave the castle and its grounds to the people of the town. The castle's a college now. You can go there to learn Gaelic.

My plans to leave the island for Ullapool in the morning had to be scrapped when I learned there wasn't a ferry on Mondays. My timing, as far as ferries were concerned, was proving to be consistent in terms of failure. Still, I reasoned, it wouldn't do any harm to have a day off. And visit a laundry, for that matter.

Stornoway is the only town on the Outer Hebrides, with a population of around 6,000. It's name derives from the Norse, meaning *Steering Bay*. As far as food and drink is concerned, I would surely be spoilt for choice. Might have an Indian. Definitely have a pint somewhere first. Well, there were certainly lots of places of refreshment: hotels, pubs, bars, restaurants. But, this Sunday evening in Stornoway, they all had one thing in common: they were closed. What I didn't know but which, rest assured, I know now, is that in Lewis *nothing* is open on Sundays. I wondered if an ambulance would turn up if I had an accident. I was forced to accept defeat and accept another period of hunger after a long day's march. Yet there were lots of people about. Jumping into taxis, jumping out of taxis. Where could they be going if everywhere was closed?

To church, that's where. They were hurrying to or from their places of worship. The only people staying still were small groups of youngsters hanging around street corners, bored, with nowhere to go and nothing to do. The one thing no-one was doing was going for a drink or a meal, including the bloke who'd just walked 25 miles. At least at Uig I could have bought a packet of crisps.

As well as the ubiquitous taxis, there were cars flying about, driven by youngsters who could at least let their hair down by roaring around the streets. To them, Stornoway was Monaco. Yet it wasn't the speed of their cars that impressed me, but the endless sounding of their car horns. Car drivers in Stornoway can't resist sounding off. It's probably their way of greeting friends. 'Oh look, there's so-and-so.' Beep-beep. 'And there's old whatsisname.' Honk-honk.

I wandered the streets in the vain hope of finding somewhere to eat. Even the Chinese takeaway was closed, the first and only time I have witnessed such a thing. I passed the time by the harbour where I located an Indian restaurant – closed, of course. But I knew where I'd be eating tomorrow.

*

It's all down to religion. Sundays are strictly observed: women don't do their washing on Sundays; some don't cook Sunday lunch (they cook it on Saturdays and eat it cold Sundays); on Sundays, they even tie the kids' swings back in the playgrounds. There are no services at all on Sundays – except, of course, in church. 'It's only recently the ferry started running on Sundays,' said my lady host, 'so they changed it to Mondays instead.' *It* being the day the ferry doesn't operate. She didn't actually add 'because they knew *you'd* be wanting to leave on a Monday.'

As a kid, Sunday was a day of religion for me too. Sunday afternoon meant going to Sunday School, the only kid in our street who did. I had to be nice and smart whilst I was about it, so my parents bought me a blue suit, not the sort of thing to be seen in by my mates who'd be bound to start calling me 'Little Boy Blue' if I was seen. The only safe route was a detour along quiet streets. At Sunday School I learned all about the Second World War from our teacher, a lovely bloke called Ernie Bell, who was easily distracted from the holy scriptures by mention of the war which, if he was to be believed, he won almost single-handedly. You name it, he was there, from the D-Day landings, all through France and Belgium, right into Germany. Hitler would never have surrendered, except when he heard Ernie was almost knocking on the door of his bunker he understandably threw in the towel. Come to think of it, the only place I don't remember Ernie mentioning was Dunkirk. Strange, that. I also learned the words of popular hymns which, in later years, I sang at the Salvation Army, where once I was asked in front of lots of people to name a hymn the congregation could sing. I wanted to say 'Onward Christian Soldiers', but I was so shy the words stuck in my throat. Everyone looked at the mute kid in the blue suit and the red face, but I just couldn't get the words out. They gave up and sang 'Shall We Gather at the River' instead.

Despite Sunday School and the Sally-Ann and many visits to churches, I have to confess to having no religious beliefs. I visit churches because I enjoy visiting places I regard as historically important and interesting and where there is peace. I respect the views of those who do 'believe', although I cannot comprehend how they can. Much good comes from religious instruction nonetheless – such as the time I was given a small piece of paper bearing the words I have never forgotten: *Be strong and of a good courage*. They stuck in my mind, served me well over the years. I sought them out in the Bible once, finding them in Joshua, Chapter One, verse 6.

My day off in Stornoway at least enabled me to treat my clothes to another laundering. I spend the morning wandering the town's windswept streets, and the afternoon in its library. Afterwards, I hit the town, and enjoyed my visit to the Indian restaurant, where it occurred to me that folk of Indian origin might not like living in a land with such a bleak climate, where a cold wind blows in off the sea, bringing rain and sleet, where everywhere is a desert of black peat and rock, where you can't do anything on Sundays.

'What's it like living in a land with such a bleak climate, where a cold wind blows in off the sea, bringing rain and sleet, where everywhere is a desert of black peat and rock, where you can't do anything on Sundays?' I asked the waiter.

'It's just fine here,' he replied, adding that he didn't mind the climate at all, and that having Sundays off was a bonus. I asked him where he came from, expecting him to say Delhi or Madras.

'Luton,' came the reply.

No wonder he liked living in the Outer Hebrides.

*

Tuesday (I think). Breakfast was taken in the company of two Sassenach tourists: he was lordly, his wife was tall and ultra-thin. I christened him Lord Snooty, but couldn't decide whether she was Swanky Lanky Liz or Long Tall Sally. They persisted in enquiring of my mission Where did I start? Which route had I taken so far? Which route would I take from here? Never mind my mouth was stuffed with my morning fryup. They wanted to know what I did for water when crossing the glens. I drink from the burns, I said. You shouldn't, they said. Why not? I asked. Because there might be a dead sheep upstream, they said. I've been walking for years, I said, and I've never seen a dead sheep upstream. There must be sometimes, they said. Well, if there had been, it never did me any harm, I said. There followed a brief pause. That's that I thought, but Snooty wasn't one to be beaten. You might get one defecating in the water, he said. How nice, I said, devouring the last of my sausage. Having cleared my plate I enquired of the purpose of their visit to Stornoway. We're just driving around, they said. Yeah, driving me up the wall, I said (not really).

A battering wind removed my hat the moment I left my lodgings. We were back to the weather of the day before the last, only without the rain. In the distance, huge breakers – white horses – streaked cross the entrance to the harbour. The crossing to Ullapool should be interesting. None of your boring old cruise stuff.

I had to kill time before boarding the ferry, which was due to leave early that afternoon, so I sat on a bench in the centre of town to watch the world go by. That meant watching traffic going by which, unlike many towns in England these days, meant moving traffic. Around 60 m.p.h. in Stornoway. The horns blared away. Then, when it was time, I took a casual walk – more of a stagger in the teeth of a gale sweeping the length of the harbour – to the ferry terminal.

The ferry wasn't in yet. A woman was making enquiries.

'Will it sail in this wind?' she asked.

The man's patronising smile meant she'd asked a stupid question, and what else would you expect from a woman?

'Course it will,' he said. 'It's sailing in, it'll sail out again. It's just a bit late, that's all.'

Reassured, the stupid woman took a seat in the waiting room. I did the same. I had taken to Stornoway, but didn't wish to spend a third night here.

Other passengers arrived. We all waited. Now and again someone would go outside, only to return with the news that there was still no sign of the ferry. I did so myself, and after picking up my hat again looked out to sea where the white horses were at full gallop. No-one saw *Suilven* moor alongside the jetty. Like the *Caledonian Princess*, one moment she wasn't there, then she was. Ferries hereabouts seem to have a way of sneaking into harbour without anyone noticing. People and cars piled aboard. I felt uneasy, not least because my host had mentioned the ferry was an old ship. 'She's flat-bottomed,' she said, adding that she was built for the fjords of Norway, not for the open sea. 'She could sink, you never know,' she said, pointing out the 'unsinkable' *Titanic* failed to cross the Atlantic just once. But then, the ferry's been running between Ullapool and Stornoway for years. The stupid woman was staring anxiously at the white horses. I wonder how she and everyone else about to embark across the stormy Minch would have felt if they had known of the fate of *Iolaire*, which sank in a storm off Stornoway harbour in 1918. Her passengers were

Lewismen returning home from the war, soldiers who had been through hell in France and Belgium, seamen who had survived the perils of enemy warships. After all that they were to drown at the very entrance to the harbour which was home. Two hundred died, either with the ship or in futile efforts to swim ashore in heavy seas.

Suddenly, *Suilven's* tannoy cackled into life. 'Due to the prevailing conditions at sea the ferry will not sail until five o'clock'.

With time to kill we wandered about ship, looked at the white horses. People who would not have communicated now spoke to each other: about the weather, about storms at sea, about ferries. We were a mixed bunch: well-to-do tourists, economy class tourists, business people, residents making the trip to the mainland, Sassenachs asking stupid questions about dead sheep upstream, the inevitable Germans, a bloke walking to Dunnet Head. Until the announcement about the delay, each class had kept to itself; now passengers mingled, and new friendships were born. We were a contented bunch, all waiting patiently for five o'clock. But there were still those white horses. And the unspoken worries of many became reality when the tannoy crackled again.

'Caledonian MacBrayne regret to announce that due to conditions at sea, the ferry will not sail until five-thirty *tomorrow morning*.'

So, the stupid woman wasn't stupid at all.

Passengers milled about, uncertain of what to do. The voice on the tannoy again. 'You may wish to leave *Suilven* to have a look around Stornoway.' What the hell did they think everyone had been doing for days on end before boarding the ferry? I had said my goodbyes, thought I'd heard my last car horn. Just as was wondering what to do with the next few hours of my life, I found myself in conversation with a woman called Valerie, and the evening was transformed from one of resigned boredom to one of pleasure. Valerie has abandoned London for a little house at Barvas, on West Lewis; she's left the rat-race and the teeming hordes for peace and the simple life. But she has retained ownership of property in London, so every now and again she drives down to make sure everything's in order. Drives to London from Stornoway! That's what she was doing now, or would be at 5.30 tomorrow. Anyway, Valerie took me for a walk.

With the wind now no more than a balmy breeze, Valerie led me past Lews Castle into the famous gardens. After thirty-odd miles of wilderness, I found myself transported to a verdant paradise befitting a Caribbean isle. On a lovely, long Hebridean evening, with the sun beaming from a cloudless sky and the sea a deep, shimmering blue, we explored an arcadia of exotic trees and plants, all here thanks to the hand of man. It was hard to believe we were here because the ferry couldn't sail. It just a couple of hours Lewis had changed its cloak of anger for a shroud of tranquility. Fate had dealt a kind hand, for I had not intended to visit this place. That evening will remain in my memory forever.

My night's lodgings, of course, was the ferry. I mean, you wouldn't expect to sleep on a ferry, would you? As far as the different 'classes' of people was concerned, sleeping arrangements on board *Suilven* proved a great leveller. No matter what your status, you were on the floor or across the seats.

12

The Far North

5 a.m. Daylight. I awaken to the musty smell of the carpet on the ferry floor, and the faint sound of seagulls going about their morning routine of scavenging. There are bodies everywhere, including a young lass fast asleep on her back, one leg raised high in the air, the other draped over the side of the seat on which she lay. Weird!

People are stirring, subconsciously aware that it's almost time for departure. 5.30 the man on the tannoy had said. I look out of the window to see bright Hebridean skies. No wind, no storm. Right on time we're off, and Stornoway falls behind. A few of the passengers, me included – especially me, in fact – are not convinced we couldn't have sailed the night before, that the storm was an excuse to remain in harbour and so avoid making two trips with only a handful of passengers on board. I understand *Suilven* plies her trade in New Zealand now. If she can cross the Pacific, surely she could have made it to Ullapool.

Stornoway gets smaller and smaller. It was now Wednesday morning, and I'd been here since Sunday. It was almost like leaving home. Now a flat sea was waiting, and so was breakfast. I relaxed, knowing a walk of anything up to around thirty miles awaited. I chatted to one or two of the other passengers – we were old friends by now – and Valerie, then went outside where I was accosted by a bloke of eighty. I know he was eighty cos he said so.

'Don't look it, do I?'

I had to admit he didn't, and once he was satisfied I was suitably impressed he turned to someone else and broke the news to them too. I saw him again, from time to time, at different points on deck, breaking the amazing news that he was eighty and didn't look it. People nodded in wonderment. Fair enough, he's an octogenarian, but I quietly resolved if he came my way again he'd be unlikely to make eighty-one.

The ferry was due at Ullapool about nine – a journey across the Minch. The sea was as flat as the proverbial glass, such a contrast to yesterday. *Suilven* glided effortlessly across the surface. You could have stood a coin on end, it wouldn't have toppled. I found myself with Valerie again, on the port side of the boat, with the wonderful Coigach landscape now coming into view, a moonscape of jagged peaks, backed by Suilven (same name as the ferry), its unmistakable rounded hump a startling backdrop to this unique place. Suilven is beloved of many walkers, although to be honest I think it's an ugly brute. But Coigach isn't ugly, and Coigach isn't beautiful either. This morning, in the still, clear air, Coigach was a haunting temptress. You could almost hear the voices of sirens, luring you to her mystical depths. *Suilven* glided on, in silence and without fuss. Valerie and I just stared.

Finally I dragged myself away and sought out a place to change into boots and shorts. It was hardly done in private, but nobody cared. Back on deck, Valerie had disappeared, gone below for her car. I never saw her again. When my feet touched terra firma I was ready to roll, but first I paused to observe a uniformed police sergeant directing vehicles as they drove off the ferry, all twenty or so of them. He marched to the centre of the road, waved them off and marched off again, probably for his early-turn fry-up, I shouldn't wonder. Me, I had sandwiches and chocolate to buy before seeking out a cup of coffee, served by a bonny young lass who, notwithstanding the splendour of this Highland morn, went about her business zombie-like. Life's a routine when you live and work somewhere.

Ullapool is a relatively new town. It was chosen as a planned 'fishing village' by the British Fisheries Society, and work began in 1788 on building a town on a 'grid' system of straight roads. The site was carefully chosen, with ample land for building houses and a good anchorage. Herring was fished in Loch Broom, although today Ullapool serves as a port for the transport of refrigeration lorries and the Stornoway ferry. I like Ullapool, but I could linger no longer. I left town for the A835, the long road north, and set about the task of knocking off the miles.

The road climbed uphill, reaching high ground with fine views seaward. Traffic was virtually non-existent. Unexpectedly, I encountered a couple, fifty-odd, walking in the opposite direction. They were wearing boots and carrying sacks, so naturally we spoke. Lo and behold, it turned out they too were walking the length of the country, only north to south – John o'Groats to Lands End. They had skirted the coast of Coigach, which made me feel a trifle guilty as I had considered doing the same. But then, as they explained, they had ample time, whilst I, on annual leave, had to press on for the far north. Their names were Ken and Norma, and I've often wondered if they made it.

Presently, I came to Ardmair, with its long, shingly beach and views seaward to the Summer Isles. Landward, all is desolation; rocky outcrops and low, craggy hills. A huge, four-engined aeroplane roared over so low I though it was going to crash into the sea. I was climbing again, after which followed a long downhill section to Strath Kanaird, with the old road running conveniently alongside the new, the latter with freshly-painted white lines along its centre and at each side. It seemed to stretch to infinity. Then I climbed again, reaching more high ground, with Ben More Coigach rising to the west, followed by an old favourite, Stac Pollaidh (Stac Polly), a hill of contrasts. Seen from the east it appears castle-like, but from the south the ridge takes on a spectacular appearance, with jagged towers of rock pointing skyward.

Further on I rested, after which the road climbed steeply yet again, with another old friend, Cul Mor, now in view on the skyline. I climbed Cul Mor once (and, later the same day, Stac Pollaidh!). It was a lonely expedition, during which I saw no-one. On the summit, low cloud robbed me of views that day. And there was Cul Mor again. My visit to its rocky top had been no more than a blip in the mountain's long history. Mere mortals come and go, but the mountains are forever. Only those who climb mountains understand the feeling one gets when acquaintance is renewed, even at a distance – moreso, I daresay, when walking the length of the country.

Now the road was twisting and turning, leading steadily downhill to Elphin. Ahead, north-west, lay that unmistakable lump, Suilven, seen much earlier in the day from the ferry which bears its name. Elphin turned out to be a place of scattered houses, a village without a heart. The name means 'white stone', no doubt after the light-coloured craggy rocks all around. Elphin was once a 'crofting township', although now it seems to depend on crafts and the inevitable incursion of tourism. I spied a posh-looking guesthouse, and considering I'd been up since 5 a.m. I was tempted; but there was time yet to cover more ground and I pressed on, although it seemed unlikely there'd be anything in the way of accommodation ahead. As though to wish me a good day, a peacock in courtship mode preened his feathers as I passed him by. I felt sad at not having anything to preen in return. Even if I had it wouldn't have done any good.

It had been a lovely day, but now the sky was darkening, with a chill in the air and rain imminent. I reached a significant road junction at Ledmore, and after checking out a notice by the telephone kiosk turned left for Inchnadamph. The notice referred to accommodation at the Altnacealgach Hotel, two miles in the wrong direction. Other 'bed and breakfast' cards were clearly directed at motorists, they were so far away. As I headed north, the rain came.

It was around five, and it was going to be a cold and wet evening. I was tired and hungry – not having eaten a proper meal since breakfast on the ferry – and I needed a place to stay or to camp. I checked the map; an isolated house called Ledbeg was situated just off the road, and a mile further I turned down the farm road and knocked on the door. If they couldn't put me up, they might allow me to camp. Alas, there was no-one at home. Nearby was a perfect little camp-site, a piece of flat ground by the river. I was tempted, but without permission I didn't feel I could stay. I returned to the road. The map again. Another mile, another house, this time called Lyne. I turned up the road and knocked again, again getting no reply, and again a tempting camp-site beckoned. I thought I should leave, but this time I realised there was a difference: where before, at Ledbeg, no-one had been at home, here, at Lyne, no-one was likely to be, for the house was clearly abandoned.

I took stock. The rain had stopped, leaving a still-troubled sky. It was cold. Time was getting on, too. There was no other building indicated on the map for three miles, and that a solitary house. Here, at Lyne, I should be undisturbed. The fast-flowing river would provide fresh water, and the prospect of a wash in the morning. It was a grand little camp-site. Without further ado I got the tent up, in the lee of a stone barn.

I wrapped up warm and set off to explore. The now-deserted house was so prim you could have moved in at a minute's notice. I have to admit to a desire for some company, for the day and the journey from Stornoway had been long, and I'd seen no-one on the road, save the couple heading south. But the evening was superb, with clearing skies affording views to the west, where Cul Mor stood proud against the sky, cloud clinging tenuously to his rugged crest.

*

It rained in the night, but the sun was waiting when I crawled from my nest to what would be a sizzling hot day. I had looked forward to a wash in the cold river, but found my way to it unexpectedly blocked by a high fence. It was, I supposed, a 'deer fence'. They build them to keep the deer away from trees because they eat the bark. Once upon a day, when the Highlands were covered with forests, the deer had plenty to chew on, but since man saw fit to lay the landscape bare, what trees there are left must be protected, and now they have to build the fences. Nevertheless the deer thrive, their numbers too great to survive on a treeless terrain. They were once the prey of wolves and lynxes, but man put paid to them too, so there's nothing for it but to cull the deer every August and September to prevent them starving to death. Nature's way was best.

I packed my sack, ate what pickings of food I had and walked back down the farm track to the main road. I had no water, but considered I would last as far as Inchnadamph, five miles to the north. I prayed that the hotel there would be open, for beyond there was nothing for many a mile. I took a last, lingering look back at the little house of Lyne, with its clean, white walls and attic windows. It reminded me of my uncles' farms near Banff, where I holidayed as a boy. Now they are gone. And where now are the past occupants of Lyne?

At the road I encountered a lone cyclist, who called out a 'good morning' as he sped by. I had not expected to speak to someone so early, if at all, for I was bound for Assynt, a wild and lonely country of Lewisian gneiss, where rocky outcrops and secret valleys are scattered about the landscape. This is a vast wilderness of over 200 freshwater lochans, left in situ by successive ice ages. More modern was the sun cream I now liberally applied to my face, arms and legs. Further up the road I chanced a wee drink from a burn, but refrained from swallowing a gobful in case there was a dead sheep lying upstream.

A few miles to the east were two Munros, Conival and Ben More Assynt. I climbed them on a cold, blustery day by way of the splendid Gleann Dubh. Today I tried to catch sight of them, as one would old friends, but could not. I marched on, arriving at Inchnadamph – the name means 'pasture of the ox or stag' – and bowled up to the hotel, which, thankfully, was open. I went through to the bar at the rear. It was empty, and would remain so for the forty-five minutes or so I was in occupation. The pineapple and lemonade was nectar, after which I gorged myself on beefburger and chips. Then came the lifetime's best coffee I mentioned earlier. It was in a huge pot and I drank the lot. Believe me, when you've camped out all night, had no breakfast and no water to speak of and you've spent best part of two hours marching under the blazing sun, coffee is a godsend.

I emerged to find the sun blazing away, and made my way directly to a nearby, grassy hill, topped by a monument. A plaque, set in a recess, carries a dedication to Ben N. Peach and John Horne 'who played the foremost part in unravelling the geological structure of the North-West Highlands 1883-1897'. We must be grateful to these two men for being able to learn so much about Assynt, a truly magical place. There is a wonderful view, from the monument, of Loch Assynt, and a hill known as Quinag. The name means 'milk churn' due to its shape, when seen from this spot. Atop the little hill, on this wonderful day, I was tempted to lie down and rest, but there was not the time and in any case I was eager to reach the loch-side to explore the ruined Ardvreck Castle.

First, there were two miles' walking on the road, along which I came upon a group of workmen laying a new tarmac surface. You know the scene: a lorry or two, a road roller, lots of fumes, the unmistakable smell of hot tar and a couple of blokes, naked from the waist up, drinking tea. I passed by this site of activity, arriving at the ruins of Calda House. Never have I seen a building in such a ruinous state, for Calda House, whatever it was, is no more than two gable ends and part of a central section of stones, somehow standing but surely not for much longer. In fact, I wouldn't have been surprised if it had fallen as I passed it by. It was fenced off, and no wonder.

Ardvreck Castle   ℘2001

I'd seen it on calendars, now I would see it close up and for real. Ardvrek Castle, set close to the shore of lovely Loch Assynt, stood before me now as I crossed the close-cropped grass in glorious sunshine. A hundred yards from the ruin, I dropped my sack and set about exploring, as close as I dared, its crumbling walls. And crumbling they are, yet one can venture right up to them and see cellars and vaults, and imagine those who once lived in this tiny fortress. Here, by the loch shore, with Quinag for company, Ardvrek

Castle was a stronghold for the MacLeods, but you wouldn't have to sneeze if you stood by its crumbling walls today.

The castle was built in 1597. In 1691 the Mackenzies laid siege and forced out the MacLeods over the non-payment of a debt. In 1736, the Mackenzie laird was forced to sell the land to pay of his debts, and Ardvrek was bought by Lady Strathnaver who presented it to her grandson, the Earl of Sutherland. Alas, the castle cannot last much longer; its walls are beyond repair, beyond hope. It will fall to pieces, immortal as all things man-made are immortal – but Loch Assynt and Quinag will be there forever. Do visit, if ever you are in the area – especially if it's a glorious day in May. But don't take too long about it if you want to see the castle.

I took a farm road that climbs up the steep hillside. It led to a locked gate within sight of the farm. Was my way barred? I shall never know, for I climbed the gate, a trespasser perhaps, but not for turning certainly. There are times when going for a walk makes one feel like a criminal, but I wasn't seen, or if I was I went unchallenged. I was now crossing heather-clad moorland, with Quinag rising spectacularly across the deep valley on the left. Still I climbed, pausing to look at Loch Assynt and, in retrospect, Suilven, on the southern skyline. Suilven, with his ugly hump, refusing to be left behind. But left behind he would be as, with the path keeping good shape – it might be an old drove road – I strode out in high spirits on the high ground.

It was grand, crossing that moor. And when the path levelled, and I was able to step up apace, I sang my heart out, at the same time savouring the views opening up to the north, knowing that soon I would reach Kylesku and, hopefully, accommodation and food. Finally the path – and the singing – ended at the road again, which I followed for three miles to Unapool – not to be confused with Ullapool – where I chanced upon a cottage with B and B sign. It was like coming home.

Kylesku means 'narrow channel' and it is well named, for it occupies the narrows separating Loch a' Chairn Bhain to the west, and Lochs Glendhu and Glencoul to the east. Until recent times a ferry crossed the narrows, and you had no option but to use it if you were driving north. Now there's a bridge, and the ferry is no longer needed. Some feel this is a pity, that somehow tourists benefited from the delay in queuing for the ferry, being more likely thus to look about them at the glorious surroundings. Maybe, but if that was their choice the ferry would still be running, and it ain't. If travellers want to stop, they'll stop. If they don't, they won't. There's enough queuing on the M6 without waiting for ferries in the far north.

Suitably cleansed and refreshed, I wandered down to the Kylesku Hotel, where I hit the McEwan's Export and devoured a pile of fresh prawns, served on a long spike – 'fresh out of the loch', the man said. I sat in company with a bloke from Ealing who was 'just driving around' on his motor bike, and another from Edinburgh who hated Maggie Thatcher for some reason. Neither knew, I bet, about 'Tordeas's Revenge'.

The story goes that after a ship was wrecked in Loch a' Chairn Bhain, a keg of whisky was washed ashore and taken to the Ferryboat Inn, now the hotel, by a fisherman who kindly invited his friends to help him drink its contents. A 'seer' prophesied a calamity would befall them, but was ridiculed. Hardly surprising, really. Can you imagine a bunch of fisherman foregoing the opportunity to get ratted on the say-so of a nutter? Anyway, a drunken argument followed, in which Tordeas was thrown downstairs by his son, breaking his neck. In his dying words Tordeas uttered, 'My son I shall return to have my revenge', and would you believe soon afterwards his son was found drowned in Loch Glencoul, and every year on the anniversary of Tordeas's death, his ghost appears in the hotel snuggery at midnight. Scary, eh?

*

At Kylesku I was well on course for Cape Wrath, situated at the north-western tip of Britain – the secondmost northerly point of the mainland. But this was a most southerly to most northerly venture, and Dunnet Head, which is about 3 yards further north than Cape Wrath, was therefore my objective. As Dunnet Head lies near the most north-easterly tip of Britain, I had to traverse the width of northern Scotland, an overall easterly, northerly, easterly, then northerly direction. If this doesn't make sense, I can only suggest you look at a map. I did, and no matter how many times I did the answer was always the same, that to Dunnet Head I had to go.

From Kylesku, the next reasonable place of habitation was Tongue, on the extreme northern coast, a full two days' march, the first over high ground and through lonely glens, the second by way of Strath More and the dreaded Moine Path. I say 'dreaded' because I'd heard tell the Moine Path is a watery, boggy hell, traversing, as it does, a watery, boggy wilderness. So, I'd be camping out tonight, with not so much as a corner shop along the way. The packed rolls, etc, prepared for me by my kindly host, would have to serve for lunch and supper today, then breakfast and lunch tomorrow. Needless to say, the powdered crisps I had carried for many a mile had long since been disposed of, or maybe I scoffed them somewhere. I can't remember.

Grey skies had replaced the glorious sunshine of yesterday. I felt very fit as I made my way to Kylestrome by way of the new bridge. Unlike many of today's monstrosities, the bridge is pleasing to the eye, as it curves aesthetically over the narrows. I read that it won an award, and this is not surprising. Beyond, I toiled up the steep incline, and my journey might have come to premature end then and there when I was almost gassed by the exhaust fumes from a slow-moving lorry which overtook me (just) as it toiled up the hill. I was pleased to leave the road.

The morning had a 'damp' feeling to it, and the air was fresh. Then again, so would anywhere have been after an experience with carbon dioxide. Kylestrome is a place of greenness, with pretty houses. A woman passed me by on my approach. She wore a summer frock and a lovely smile, which I found pleasing, not least because I knew she might be the last person I would see today. I located the path that runs along the northern shore of Glendhu, and at the same time the sun located me.

Oh, what a walk that was, along the shoreline of the loch. A mile and half, that's all, in beauty unsurpassed. It all came together: the sun, the grey, flat waters of the loch, reaching to distant hills; behind, the pleasing features of the bridge. This is a place for lovers, honeymooners perhaps; a place to stroll on Sunday mornings. Bridge or ferry: all who come here should explore this path, savour its delights. It ended at the Maldie Burn, the outflow of Loch an Leathiad Bhuain, set high in the hills to the north. There are a series of spectacular waterfalls here; I had noticed them from my lodgings on the opposite side of the loch the previous evening, and considered exploring them this morning. Alas, this proved difficult, as the burn crashes down a narrow cleft, a dangerous place to venture into and in any case too time-consuming for the man with a mission. Here and there I took a peek, but concentrated mainly on climbing the steep hillside. It was hot work in the sunshine.

And so to Loch an Leathiad Bhuain. As I arrived at its stark shore-line, the sun took its leave and would not reappear this day. This is a lonely place, and I might have been the only person ever to venture here, except that a fair track in the heather led upward to Bealach nam Fiann, a high pass. It was hidden in cloud. Correct navigation was vital, but not difficult, for the track held good as, in silence, I plodded upward. A 'shieling' (shelter) was marked on the map, and I aimed for it; there is nothing like a positive point for taking an accurate bearing. It appeared, spectral-like in the gloom, a ruinous pile of stones at around 1,500 feet. I rested awhile, before being driven on by the cold and damp.

It was downhill now, through Achfary Forest. When I reached the grounds of Lochmore Lodge, I ended up in a muddle, thankfully reaching the shores of Loch More, on the A838, meaning, you might think, a major carriageway, where motorists (if there were any) might speed apace to their destinations. Not here. As a lorry approached, its wheels touched the grass verges on each side of the road, along the centre of which ran a long, grassy strip. Along the road, I passed by Achfary, a place of horses and manicured fields and exquisite houses. Then I took a farm track for Airdachuillinn, where, beyond, I would climb through Strath Luib na Seilich to the next mountain pass, Bealach na Feithe.

Hereabouts I spied a deer in a field. She stood statue-like on my approach, the next best thing to running away, escape being barred by a fence. As I passed by she did not move a muscle, and no matter how often I glanced behind still she stood rigid, except that her head turned progressively to enable her to observe the progress of her natural, feared enemy. But she was crafty, for she turned her head only when I wasn't looking. When I took one last look back, she nodded slightly, as though to acknowledge my passing her without harming her. Or maybe she just had a twitch.

I crossed a wooden footbridge to Lone, an aptly-named stone building by the shore of Loch Stack. Here I took stock. Westward, Ben Stack towered above the waters of the loch that bears its name, the rugged side of the mountain disappearing grimly into heavy cloud. Northward, unseen, were Arkle, and beyond, Foinavon, two famous racers! Eastward, the lonely glen rose steadily into the cloud, three long miles to the top of the pass. For what possible reason would anyone venture into this remote wilderness? Who, but a lonely pilgrim, a purist whose ultimate objective, Dunnet Head, lay but a short distance further to the north than a feasible alternative, Cape Wrath? It had to be done, and it would be, for this pilgrim was enjoying true, unadulterated bliss.

I rested briefly at Lone, savoured its grandeur as one might when visiting somewhere for the one and only time. Then I was off apace for the bealach, and then came the rain, steady at first, turning heavy. It was going to be with me all the way, I knew. Is it my imagination, or does Scottish raid fall in bigger drops than, say, English rain? And does it fall at a greater speed? Whatever, it was falling hard and fast, faster than I could get the waterproofs on. Half a mile on I came to a rocky outcrop. I scrambled steeply up and followed the path, clear in the grass and heather, here running alongside a fast-flowing burn that provided an accurate means of navigation all the way to the top of the pass. The higher the climb, the worse the visibility, until finally all save my immediate surroundings was lost in the gloom. Here and there I paused, as one does when climbing, but always I looked to the front, seeking out the way; to go astray here didn't bear thinking about. I'd be there yet. In triumph I made the top, and kept on, downhill now, the rain finding its way inside my cag. I passed through a forest, emerging again to reach the Abhainn Srath Coir an Easaidh, a gushing river, by which time the track widened, and the way was clear to Gobernuisgach Lodge. It was still pouring down.

Here, by the river, I sought out a camp-site. The ground was flat enough, and God knows there was plenty of water. But in all directions were course grasses and boggy ground, no place for a tent. What's more, I had the feeling the river might burst its banks before long, spilling onto the flat landscape. The track developed into a rough road, where suddenly I saw some people. There were three of them, and two dogs – golden retrievers. I noticed, too, meadowland ahead, where horses grazed, oblivious to the rain. Surely here would be a suitable camp-site – if I could get permission. I enquired of the group, telling them that I had walked all the way over from Kylesku. An elderly woman, who spoke with some authority, told me to enquire at the gamekeeper's cottage, and to say she had sent me. In other words I could camp, it was just a matter of finding out where.

I duly found myself putting the tent up on the grass by the side of the private road to the lodge. Under clearing skies I stripped off my wet clothes – we are talking naked in broad daylight but what the hell – and put on dry. My wallet, which of necessity bulged with twenties and tens – there are no cash dispensing machines in the glens – was sodden, and when I checked its contents my money was even soddener. So wet, in fact, that I had to carefully (and lovingly) pull apart each note from the next, and spread it out along the floor of the tent for it to dry. This was a particularly delicate operation – some of the notes hadn't seen daylight for years. After that I ate a crust and, pleased with the day's work, wondered how I might now put in the evening.

First, I spent some time looking at Ben Hope, Scotland's most northerly Munro, just a few miles away to the north. I had been unable to catch sight of the mountain earlier due to the mist and rain. Looking at it now from below, it appeared huge. Tomorrow I would pass by the foot of the mountain, then take the Moine Path I mentioned. Anyway, looking at Ben Hope put in ten minutes, so what was there to do now? Walk up to the cottage and back. Another ten minutes accounted for. I looked at Ben Hope again, after which thinking of something to do became difficult. When idle, I tend to start reflecting on life's mistakes. I checked my watch. Only five hours of daylight left. There wasn't time to fit them in.

*

It's one of backpacking's golden rules: you must always ensure that one set of clothes remains dry – hence I was able to wear dry clothing the previous evening after my soaking. But there's another golden rule: they have to go on being dry. So back on to my back went damp shirt, pants and socks, whilst on to my feet went the still-sodden boots. All part of the fun, eh? As for the money, the notes had dried reasonably well. Even so, I had to be mighty careful about how I put it all away. The tent, wet from overnight rain, had to be packed wet, not a good idea but there was no option. Wet tents, according to my scoutmaster, lose their waterproof qualities. Whether that applies to modern-day nylon, as opposed to 1950's canvas, is unknown to me.

Tongue, on the far north coast of Britain, was twenty miles away. It was a dull morn, with Ben Hope once again lost in cloud. I went down to the cottage where a young lass of sixteen or so kindly filled my canteen; there would be no drinking from streams today, not by the Moine Path anyway, where there is water aplenty, admittedly, but not *running* water. 'Have a safe journey,' she said with a beaming smile. She fair made my day, just falling short of attaining royalty status by not offering to cook me a whopping great fryup. But the water was more important, and I mean that.

I packed the sack, wet tent and all, and set off without eating anything. This wasn't a particularly difficult decision, as the only food I had left consisted of a soggy sandwich and an equally soggy cream cracker with cheese falling out. A 2-mile hike along the rough road would take me to Strath More, after which I would head north. It was a Saturday, not that it makes the slightest difference. I passed through a forest, after which the road climbed steeply for a full mile to the main road where, at last, I could partake my salubrious breakfast, which I enjoyed seated on a convenient flat rock. Never has a cream cracker tasted so good.

I'd only gone two miles yet I felt weary. I don't know why, I always find walking a stimulating experience. I can spend a day on the Lakeland 'tops', or climb Scotland's mountains, or trek through Chilterns beechwoods, I always feel alive. Sit around the house and I doze off in front of the telly (who wouldn't?). I would have expected an 'alive' mood today: walking wild, remote country, traversing unknown territory, the Moine Path, and beyond. Yet I was jiggered. But I wasn't fed up, and that's important. Like all things in life, if you have the will, you will find the energy. I was going to Tongue. So I got up and set off for Tongue.

Typically, the road was almost devoid of traffic, human or vehicular. It passed below Ben Hope, with the wide Strath More and the Strathmore River below. I bowled along, machine-like, finally arriving at a broch, Dun Dornaigil, also known as Dun Dornadilla. It's in good nick, considering its age, one wall still high, although grass grows inside where once people saw fit to hide from their enemies, human or otherwise. There were two others present, Dutch I believe. They were clearly fascinated by this ancient piece of history (the broch). In silence we surveyed the ruin, walked around it, looked up at it and into it. Then they got back into their car and I got back into my stride.

I pressed on, passing Alltnacaillich, famously the birthplace of Rob Donn, a Gaelic poet who was illiterate and who couldn't stop poaching deer, less famously the starting point for the climb of Ben Hope. The sun blazed away. Three scorching miles further I came to the Moine Path. It traverses open, heatherclad moors for fully eight miles, wild terrain, the domain of the curlew – and frogs and toads, I suppose. It's an ancient byway, always obvious underfoot, but wet everywhere where water running off the slopes of Ben Hope gathers before soaking away to the waters of Strath More and Tongue Bay, and anywhere else it might find its way into, including hikers' boots. But it wasn't impassable, and it presented no problems other than a need to tread carefully around deep pools and soggy bits. Even so, it's a tasking journey, beginning with a long pull to the flat plateau, then around Ben Hope until it reaches Kinloch Lodge. The weariness I mentioned evaporated with the challenge of the Moine Path, replaced by soaring spirits as once again true freedom was joined.

Atop the plateau, the vast open landscape seems to stretch to infinity. To the north, in the distance, the sea; eastward, Ben Loyal, a grand mountain; to the south, nearer, the towering Ben Hope. All around is heather, nothing else (except water). I called this place the 'Badlands'. Hot countries have their deserts, where epic journeys are made, and Scotland has the Moine Path, where this epic journey was made. In each case the crossing is made under a burning sun, in each case there's no water (except deserts have 'poisoned water', and the Moine Path has 'undrinkable water'), in each case, at some point, there will be a mirage – I distinctly saw Kate Winslet standing in the heather, holding a glass of cold lager. It was a slog, but in the end, when heather gave way to a vast area of gorse and the now-familiar smell of coconut, I knew I'd cracked it.

I was still feeling tired, due, I suppose, to (a) not having eaten a proper meal since breakfast the day before, (b) the taxing journey from Unapool to Gobernuisgach Lodge the day before and (c) the effects of the sun today. But with Tongue just four miles away – a little over an hour's march – I girded up my loins, and turned north. It's a grand experience that, girding up your loins and turning north. I recommend it.

The road to Tongue is narrow and quiet. After crossing the Kinloch River, it climbs steeply, passing between two lochs. I came to a granite monument, a fenced-off pillar bearing an inscription, which reads: "Dedicated to Ewen Robertson, 1842-1895, Bard of the Clearances. Died at this place". He perished in the snow, as it happens. Beyond, I climbed steeply to the village, being greeted en route by an attractive woman on a bike who flashed me a dazzling smile. This may not seem much, but after the past few days' exertions in a world devoid of humanity even a bloke's smile would have been welcome. Not as welcome as hers, admittedly.

And so, thirsty, and with knees and ankles throbbing, I came to Tongue, which was just as deserted as everywhere else, and where my sweat-ridden being was accepted by an elderly couple who had a room and a bath to go with it. And, just as important, a washing line on which to hang my still-wet tent. On a wonderful northern evening, I wandered through the deserted village to the Ben Loyal Hotel where I mingled with the other customer in the bar and ate and drank my fill. Tomorrow, I was eastbound, along the 'top' of Britain. To where exactly God only knew.

*

Whenever I had a better view at breakfast I do not know. But the now-distant Ben Hope and the wild green landscape of Sutherland, already aglow in early morning sunshine, were fit for an artist's brush. When I stepped outside at 8.30 to wax my boots the heat from the sun was unbelievable. Actually, stepping outside so early wasn't such a good idea, for I realised my host, hovering just inside the doorway, was concerned about me doing a runner. Making off without payment, as they say. How far did she think I'd get, on foot, carrying a backpack? Which reminded me: my tent was still hanging on her washing line.

My next main objective, Thurso, was 44 miles away. Too far for one day. I decided to get as far as I could anyway, given the splendid morning and the promise of settled weather. I headed north, the wide, blue waters of Kyle of Tongue below. The Kyle is bordered on one side by fields of lush-green, on the other by scrub and heather. A mile on I turned up a rutted road, passing a cottage where a teeny-weeny dog yapped a warning. Compared with its English counterparts it was pathetic. The track became a path in the heather, flanking Ben Tongue. Ahead was the open sea, the Atlantic no less. Somehow, I got in a muddle, ending up off-route, all hot and bothered as I stumbled through the heather. Heather loosens bootlaces as you stride through it, and having fastened them for the umpteenth time, I reached the road again and headed east without pause by Lochan Dubh.

I was in route-march mode, as I set about traversing the width of Scotland's far north. To Sassenachs who think it's always cold up here, let me enlighten them: it isn't. Nor are winters hereabouts as severe as southerners might suppose, thanks to the sea, which carries the Gulf Stream all around Britain's shores. It is said that Scotland's north-west has a 'variable' climate: 'if you don't like the weather, wait five minutes'. Today, the sun beamed down relentlessly as I walked the road, a road devoid, almost, of traffic, a long, snake-like artery running up and down and in and out, disappearing into the far distance as each hilltop was reached. I had to take the road, as to the south lies a vast, uninhabited and trackless wilderness.

I reached Strathnaver, where the road turns up the valley. Further on it crosses the Naver and climbs steeply to Bettyhill. The village is named after Elizabeth, Countess of Sutherland. She married George Granville Leverson Gower, who in 1833, was created Duke of Sutherland, so Elizabeth – Betty if you will – became Duchess-Countess. I forgot to mention: this was once the county of Sutherland, but, elsewhere, under the grand scheme of things, 'Sutherland' was scrapped and, together with its neighbour, Caithness, became Highland Region.

By the time I'd climbed up to the village I had run out of water. I checked the map. Hotel! It was a Sunday, would it be open? To my relief it was, and I went inside to drink two pints of lemonade and pineapple and rest my feet – not my legs, they were fine – and cool off inside the bar.

Strathnaver is synonymous with the Clearances, perhaps more than anywhere. Until the late 18th century, cattle and goat farming flourished hereabouts, along with potato production. Housing was primitive, each dwelling consisting of a low stone wall supporting higher turf walls and a roof, where farmers and their families shared the one room with livestock. Smoke from the fire rose up through a hole in the ceiling. You were warm, but you got wet; you had shelter from the wind, but you near choked to death on smoke. And no-one would rustle your cattle. You worked hard, made the most of things, but you didn't own the land. And those who did would bring in sheep.

It was, supposedly, an 'experiment'. The sheep, hardy Cheviots mainly, could graze on the high ground in summer, and be sheltered in the Naver valley in winter. This excuse for 'improvement' also 'happened' to increase the value of the land, as well as 'supporting the nation's needs' in time of war by the production of wool and mutton. The problem was, tenants' homes and livestock, and potatoes were in the way, so the landowner cleared them out of the way. Some were encouraged to try their hand at fishing, others were provided with new, uncultivated land on bare headlands, still more were offered alternative employment, as gamekeepers for example, whilst many simply emigrated. Whatever, the very many gave way to the very few. In all, 15,000 people were 'cleared' from land they and their ancestors had farmed and lived upon for generations.

I was eastbound again, following the Atlantic coast, just two or three miles off. Now and again I'd get a glimpse of the ocean, but mainly it was eyes forward on the long and winding road that leads to someone's door (hopefully). There were many long, uphill sections, always followed by downhill bits to river valleys. At the top of one steep section I was offered a lift by an elderly couple, which of course I refused. This road, incidentally, like so many others in the far north, is single carriageway, with passing places marked by diamond-shaped signs. The conduct of motorists hereabouts, British and foreign, always intrigues me. Without exception, drivers on vacation almost race to be first to pull in at a passing place and thus give way to someone coming in the opposite direction, an unwritten code of conduct exclusive to the far north. After you. No, after *you*. This ritual is invariably followed by a courteous wave, or a nod, a smile even (yes, motorists smiling), knights in shining armour, one and all. Put 'em on a road anywhere else and they'll risk life and limb before giving an inch.

At six o'clock I reached Strathy. There was an inn with a sign proclaiming 'accommodation'. Eight hours' walking merited a stop, but the shorter the day today, the longer tomorrow. I decided to take advantage of the sunshine and press on. I didn't even blink at Strathy. The road out of the village was long and steep, and somewhere hereabouts I must have passed the 30-mile mark for the day. I encountered an old boy who gave me a long look, must've wondered why I was walking here. I was wondering the same thing. On an absolutely wonderful evening, with the sun at my back, I pressed on, Melvich my clear goal. A place I'd never heard of that morning was now the only thought occupying my mind. Legs a-pumping, toes a-throbbing, I came to this straggling community and almost passed straight through before I spied the Tigh-na-Clash guest house. With great relief I knocked on the door. There was no reply.

Great detective work located the owner in the nearby Croft Inn. Thankfully, she had room for a sweaty male and two self-propelling walking boots. As I ate and drank my fill, my legs kept trying to walk off. No longer could they comprehend the notion that there are times when they are permitted to remain still. In my bedroom, when I gratefully removed my boots, they marched four times around the room on their own. My socks would have done the same, but they never got the chance. They smelled so bad I threw them out of the window.

*

Today, Thurso, last town on my journey, seventeen miles away. The morning dawned dank, cold even. I took to the road, which here crosses wild moors, inhospitable country over which it climbs steadily to the former Sutherland-Caithness county boundary. As though to defy the loss of identification, an enormous sign advertised 'Caithness Glass'. Not Highland Region glass, be it noted. The former boundary ran over the higher ground, and just beyond the sign it was downhill, all the way to what turned out to be a pastoral landscape. I could've been in Hertfordshire. The road even got wider. Busier too. I was now on map 39, the last of my journey.

Hereabouts, a sign said: 'Reay Golf Club, founded 1893'. The Royal Scottish Game, according to *Old Scottish Customes*, (published more recently, in 1895), was prohibited by James II because it interfered with 'weapon showing', whatever that means (actually, it was the 'assembly of the populace in military array and properly armed', as organised by the sheriff twice a year), but James VI played golf, so it must have got back into favour at some point. Golf was played on 'links', and there were rules about clubs and balls and holes.

There were five clubs (play club, scraper, spoon, iron and putter). The balls were 'extra hard', the size of a tennis ball. Holes were made in the ground (where else?) one quarter of a mile apart. Needless to say, the person with the fewest strokes was the winner. What is didn't say was that competitors were expected to walk around the course, unlike on one golf course in Hertfordshire I could name, where – and this is the truth – having teed off, they get around *by buggy*. You'd think they'd be in it for the exercise, but as they say in Yorkshire (where they also play golf nowadays, presumably), 'there's nowt as queer as folk'. The down side to golf by buggy, of course, is that you still have to walk about three yards to the ball and back, before proceeding to the next shot. Necessity being the mother of invention, it can only be a matter of time before someone, probably from the Land of the Rising Sun, comes up with a device that lifts a golfer from his or her buggy, places them over the ball for their stroke, and returns them to the buggy again. It could be adapted to take them to the clubhouse for a drink, as well as to the toilet, or even get a round in. It goes without saying that it will take them home afterwards, put them to bed and tuck them in.

I pounded on, the only interesting feature to report being the Thurso-Reay bus.

It was a single decker, and like all buses these days it was empty. Unlike everywhere else, this might have been down to the low population hereabouts (as opposed to highly populated areas where buses run empty because everyone has cars). It passed me by on its journey from Thurso to Reay. Further on, it passed me again, on its journey from Reay to Thurso. Then, further on again, it passed me heading back to Reay. Again, Reay to Thurso. Always empty. My astute detective's brain calculated it was the same bus by its number plate, and anyway I began to recognise the driver. I wondered if I should smile next time it came along, or wink even. I thought it would be nice for him to know someone cared. Then again, maybe not. Anyway, glancing over a stone wall protected by yellow gorse, I got sight of Dounreay nuclear power plant.

It was opened in 1955, its present-day functions being the decommissioning of its prototype fast reactor and materials reactor, and reprocessing nuclear fuel. The good news is Dounreay employs 1,200 people and forms one-fifth of the gross domestic product of the former county area of Caithness; the bad is it's a nuclear power plant. Once, I didn't think such places were dangerous. After all, Britain paved the way in atomic science (so my schoolteacher said when Calder Hall became the world's first atomic power station, afterwards known as Windscale, afterwards known as Sellafield – evidently they change the name every time something ghastly occurs). But when you read about 'missing' uranium being discovered in the floor at Dounreay, and remember the Chernobyl disaster of 1986, you have to wonder. Never mind Dounreay's location, out of sight, out of mind at this remote outpost. Nuclear fall-out knows no boundaries. It might as well be smack in the centre of London or Edinburgh if it goes bang. The problem is: once you have nuclear waste, you're stuck with it. You can't just chuck it in the bin. Then again, if they did, who'd know? Or, to put it another way, who'd tell us? Management? I don't think so. Politicians, their focus on secrecy before security? Don't make me laugh.

I read an interesting analogy: 'if the Romans had nuclear power we would still be looking after their waste'. Radiation kills, gives people cancer. Dounreay? *Doom*reay, more like. Anyway, there it was, its unmistakable white sphere, just a few fields away from where I now walked and the Thurso-Reay bus drove. There were sheep in the fields, innocents who could know nothing of the horrors they'd face if Dounreay became a Chernobyl. Remember Murphy's Law: 'if something can go wrong, it will'. Every nuclear plant is something waiting to go wrong. Never mind you're in the next field; you'll cop it wherever you are.

Further on my feet began to hurt, and no wonder: I had been walking on road surfaces for over two days, apart from that brief excursion in the heather on Ben Tongue. I longed for somewhere to sit down, but there was only the grass verge. In desperation, I plonked myself down on a raised drain cover by the roadside, and further on found respite on the parapet of a bridge. The sun had appeared, and on another lovely afternoon I reached the first houses of Britain's northernmost town.

By now I was well into the habit of subconsciously trying to imagine what unknown places would be like when I got there. Like everywhere else I had tried to judge Thurso. Unlike everywhere else, I had been unable to conjure up a picture of any sort. In the event, I found myself tramping past smart-looking houses with well-kept gardens, with the Atlantic providing a blue backdrop on one side, my left. There's a feeling of cleanliness, of well-being, about Thurso. The town centre is pleasing, with fine stone buildings lining fine old streets, due in no small part to Sir John Sinclair, 'Agricultural John' as he was known, thanks to his interest in improving farming methods. His 'vision' of broad, evenly-spaced streets and squares has happily been maintained by Thurso's developers over the years.

Considering its position – on the extreme north coast of Scotland – it's not surprising that Thurso dates back to the days of the Vikings. Its name derives from *Torsa*, meaning 'River of the God Thor', and the town served as a major Viking 'gateway' to mainland Britain. Unlike most coastal towns, Thurso did not develop through fishing. Instead, it served as a port for the exportation of grain, grown in Caithness (told you it's like Hertfordshire), to Scandinavia. So important became this trade that King David II decreed its measure, the *pondus Caithaniae* ('weight of Caithness') should become universal throughout Scotland. Thurso's later decline was checked by the advent of the aforesaid Dounreay as a major employer, a situation that must end, either by Dounreay's closure, or the day when the whole caboodle goes bang.

I quickly found accommodation, an upstairs room overlooking a walled garden. After the usual bath, etc, I stepped outside to find the town aglow in late evening sun, and wandered to Thurso Bay where, for a change (for most people living in Britain anyway) I found myself looking *northward* out to sea. Then, in the town centre, I chanced upon a small park where a prominent sign gave rise to concern.

'Attention Dog Owners' it said, and in small print below proclaimed that 'it is an offence for a person in charge of a dog to let it foul in this park'. OK so far, but then it added that 'an exception is made for blind owners of guide dogs'. Fortunately, I'd happened along when no blind owners were taking the opportunity to defecate on the grass. Damned embarrassing if they did, what?

Finally, I took the opportunity to feed my face at Britain's most northerly Chinese restaurant before steering a course for my bed.

Thirteen miles to go.

*

My host was a man who did not know the meaning of punctuation. As he directed me to a table for the inevitable bacon and eggs, he was stringing words together in such a way that had they been in written form they would have appeared without commas, full stops or even any spaces in between. Nor could he remain still. As I ate he perambulated about the room, first looking out of the window, then standing by the sink in the corner, crossing over to the radiator, appearing by my side at the table. He should have done it to music, Strauss perhaps. It would have gone down well to *The Blue Danube*. I christened him Mr Fidget. As he glided past the door I said I might wish to take the room again that night. He kindly said he'd keep it until six o'clock, by which time he was at the window again, ready for another circuit.

It was a cold, dry morn. Once again, I'd be on the road. No rights of way in Scotland, y'see. But never mind, three of the eight miles along the main A836 would be on a stretch of dead-straight road, the longest, straightest stretch of my entire journey in fact. And, since the shortest distance between two points is a straight line, this meant the shortest possible time on the road. As I left town I was offered the fourth and final lift of my journey. A bus – empty, of course, and driven by a different driver to yesterday – pulled up. Did I want a lift? Bus drivers are so desperate around here they stop and offer lifts for free to pedestrians. I declined, of course, reflecting on the fact that although I'd only been offered four lifts, all were in Scotland. Soon I was at that long, straight bit of road, and to relieve you of the monotony I'll recount the tale of the Caithness mermaid.

It concerns a fisherman who allegedly saw a beautiful girl sitting on a rock. Naturally, she was singing and combing her long, yellow hair and had a tail like a fish. (Not a dorsal fin, thankfully). She was *maighdean mhara* (a mermaid). She brought the fisherman gold and silver from ships that had been wrecked offshore, which he naturally presented to the local girls, presumably for favours returned, but that's just my opinion. Anyway, he starting forgetting to turn up to see the mermaid (you know how it is), who understandably became jealous, so she invited him to a secret cavern to see vast treasures and he, succumbing to temptation, followed her and hasn't been seen since.

Along the road, I fancied I could see my goal, Dunnet Head, in the distance. My heart sank on sight of what I believed to be the 'distance to go', before, belatedly, I realised I was looking *beyond* to the Orkneys, across the Pentland Firth. I arrived at Castletown, which I found cold and uninviting, but this might be down to my desire to reach journey's end. Just beyond the village the road runs right alongside the sea, where a long sandy bay curves around Dunnet Bay for two miles. If it was on the south coast of England there'd be amusement parks, ice cream and candy floss and thousands of people, including topless beauties, last seen in Cornwall, an eternity ago. Here, zilch of anything and anyone, except a woman and a small child sitting in a car, facing the sea. She was giving me the once-over, the 'suspicious male' look, but I quickly put her out of her misery by moving on, not along the beach – two miles on soft sand being too much like hard work – but on the road, as far as Dunnet village. Just five miles to go.

The Dunnet peninsula is generally flat and barren, with just a small hill or two to relieve the monotony. After Brough (pronounced *Broch)*, the most northerly village on mainland Britain, I came to the Tea Room, Britain's most northerly place of refreshment. I had been walking three hours without respite, so went inside to take it easy over a cup of tea and rest before the final leg of my journey. It was deserted, save for an elderly couple. The proprietor told me the RAF had had flown target practice manoeuvres over Dunnet Head during the war. This didn't surprise me, for a more remote spot is difficult to imagine. There were photographs of smart women in their RAF uniforms. They looked so young. Now they are old or dead.

Although Dunnet Head is Britain's northernmost point, it's Lands End to John o' Groats for people who choose to walk the length of the country. I don't know why. Land's End is not the westernmost point of Britain (that honour falls to Ardnamurchan Point, Scotland), whilst John o'Groats is no more than a scattering of buildings to the east – and south – of Dunnet Head. But there's a hotel and accommodation at John o' Groats, nothing but a lighthouse at Dunnet Head, so maybe that's the reason. This, of course, was why the Tea Room was almost deserted. Shame, but there it is. Anyway, as everyone's heard of John o' Groats, I'll provide some information about it, even though I wasn't going there.

It seems there are two conflicting reasons for the name. The first, according to tradition, is that it stems from one John de Groat (or, more likely, de Groot), a Dutchman, who settled here during the reign of James IV. He had trouble with members of the family who argued about who should sit where at table, so John, to make everyone equal, built an eight-sided house with eight doors and eight windows, with, inside, an eight-sided table. In this way each member of the family (of eight, would you believe) could consider himself 'head' of the family. Another theory is that local magistrates fixed the fee from the mainland to the Orkneys at 4d (a *groat*), and as the ferryman's name was John he became known as John o' Groat. Take your pick.

Meanwhile, in the Tea Room, full dinners were available on the menu. The waitress hovered, clearly expecting someone carrying a backpack to order a mountain of food. I ordered tea and a scone. She *was* surprised. 'Don't you fancy the steak and kidney pie?' she asked with a look suggesting I'd better, or else.

'I'm not really hungry,' I said truthfully.

'Burger and chips?' she asked, with a hint of menace.

I smiled, at the same time preparing to fend off a blow to the head.

'Thanks, but a scone will do fine.'

Surprisingly, without further ado, she brought me the desired fare.

'You'll be bound for Dunnet Head,' she declared (as though it could possibly be anywhere else) and went off with a smile. I knew what she was thinking. I was on a dead-end road and would return via the Tea Room in two or three hours, *then* I'd want my dinner.

Not another walker had I seen today, nor yesterday, nor the day before, nor the day before that. Incredible in a land of tourism. Two miles to go. One mile. Funny, but when you anticipate something it always seems to keep you waiting. So I found myself singing Cliff Richard's 'You Keep Me Hanging On'. It seemed appropriate, if irrelevant. I spotted a path leading across boggy grassland, cutting a corner of the road, and took to it with glee. It was good to walk on soft ground again. It climbed steeply back to the road, the return to nature lasting five minutes. Ahead was a small hill, on the other side of which was Easter Head, the northern extremity of Dunnet Head. There were some grey lochs then, beyond, the Atlantic. Or the Pentland Firth, if you will. I breasted the high ground. Journey's end was yards away.

On my right I spied a platform with one of those telescopes you put a coin in to take in distant views. Resisting the urge to complete my journey just yet, I went over to find a coin someone had inserted in the slot had jammed and the device was inoperable. Well, there's a surprise. Actually, I've long supported a theory that they are made that way.

The production line at Slotmeters Limited. The boss is talking to the foreman.

'I say, Carruthers, that latest batch of coastal telescopes. Have the lenses been checked for accuracy?'

'Aye, guv'nor. No problems.'

'Two bob bits suitably jammed in the slots, I take it?'

'So tight they'll never get 'em out in a million years.'

I went off to explore some derelict buildings, part of the old RAF base. Then it was time to march those final yards to the cliffs by the lighthouse, to the northern tip of mainland Britain. It was something I had looked forward to, wanted to savour alone, as the entire journey had been alone. Then, as though timed deliberately, a motor coach appeared and parked by the lighthouse, and in moments Dunnet Head was infested with old folk. They wandered about, looking at the lighthouse, gazing out to sea, oblivious to my presence. It mattered not that I had this very minute completed a walk the length of the country and wished to be alone. Yet, standing in their midst, I found myself surrounded by a happy throng, a gathering of folk who, in their twilight years, were clearly enjoying themselves. Their presence cheered me, and I handed one of them, a woman who smiled and said hello, my camera and asked her to take my picture. She obliged with a smile. Her companion was looking, and after a while she spoke.

'Didn't I see you walking through Thurso this morning?' she asked. I assured her she must have done.

'Really?' said the one who took my picture, 'you've walked all the way from *Thurso*?' I shrugged. It was nothing.

'No wonder you wanted your photograph taken' said a third, wit a look of admiration. She turned to someone else.

'He's walked from Thurso,' she declared, eager to break the news. She had to tell somebody. Just as you would if you knew the England result everyone was waiting for. Or, perhaps more appropriately, the Scotland result. A few others were casting curious glances my way. It was the turn of an old boy who'd been watching the proceedings.

'Thurso, eh?' he said. 'How far's that, then... twenty miles?'

I told him it was only thirteen. He looked disappointed.

'Actually,' I added, 'I've walked from Lizard.'

I was pleased to tell someone, and waited for a suitable response. But another old soul cast her eyes to the ground.

'Lizards?' she cried, 'I *hate* lizards.'

Others were shuffling their feet.

'I thought I'd read something like that about this place.'

They all turned for the open door of the coach. 'There's big spiders, too,' someone was saying. They were eager to be off to John o'Groats or somewhere. The coach pulled away, the old folk checking for lizards and spiders. I had Dunnet Head to myself at last.

There was Britain's northernmost lighthouse, and Britain's northernmost 'No Entry' sign. Beyond, Britain's northernmost wall, a short stretch of grass ended abruptly at the top of the cliffs of Easter Head. They must be five hundred feet high, more even. I climbed over the wall and ventured to the cliff-tops, as far as I dared. There was an old wooden fence, a bit shaky but good enough to hold and peer over the edge, a foolish thing to do, as the ground overhangs the cliffs, with the possibility of collapse and a fall to certain death. Walking the length of the country wasn't supposed to include plunging into the sea at journey's end, so I returned to the safety of the wall, reflecting on the fact that I was the northernmost person on mainland Britain, and I was now nearer Oslo than London. Just a thought. In fact, I had many thoughts just then. There are occasions in life when one does. So I rested by the wall, and took a few photographs to mark the occasion. They include one of my legs and feet. They'd earned it.

I lingered, reflecting on my journey: of places visited; of people encountered; of the weather's extremes – the scorching sun of Cornwall and the Wye Valley and Scotland's west coast, the rain of northern England and Skye, the storms of Harris. I felt I had achieved. But, as I said at the start, there are others who walk farther, climb higher. The satisfaction is personal, the sense of achievement mine alone. But then I didn't walk the length of Britain for anyone else.

I walked it for me.

***

I turned my gaze to the south, across the grey Caithness wilderness. Dunnet Head is higher than its hinterland and the view is surprisingly extensive. Scotland is a land of mountains, but not here. There was a small, insignificant loch or two, distant houses, Brough or Dunnet village, I was uncertain. I didn't care, anyway. There was nothing left of my journey now. It was time to go.

I took to the road. All was quiet: no cars, no people. I must have walked in a dream, for I can recall nothing of the journey to the Tea Room. The waitress had gone, and I still wasn't hungry. The proprietor gave me a card with puffins on it and wrote a 'well done' message. As I headed for Dunnet village, a woman roared up behind me in a big car and screeched to a halt, window down. She was wearing a low-cut dress and a big smile.

'Would you like a lift to Wick?' she asked.

This suited me. After all, I'd been to Thurso, and either town would do to catch public transport back to civilisation. Strangely, I decided I wanted to be alone. I shook my head. But she wasn't giving up.

'I can show you the harbour at Castletown.'

It's my legs, I reasoned. She wants to have them in her car. Or she wants my autograph. Or maybe she's a reporter: she's recognised me and wants a scoop. I'd be in the *News of the World*. Or maybe she's a latter-day Caithness mermaid. Never mind sitting on rocks getting drenched by the sea, they drive around in cars nowadays. She was trying to lure me to her secret lair, never to be seen again. I shook my head and thanked her for her kindness. As I watched her drive off I wondered if I'd been away from civilisation too long.

At Dunnet village I took my sack off and sat in a bus shelter. When the bus came I enjoyed the thrill of being transported on wheels. Later, as Mr Fidget escorted me to my room, I mentioned the completion of my journey. It was nice to tell someone. My words fell on deaf ears. Even I spoke he was in overdrive.

'I wonder if that chap will be coming from John o'Groats,' he was saying, adding something about the time and a bicycle – all without punctuation, of course. He wasn't being rude: he was just being himself, lost in his world of fuss. It would have mattered not had I said 'I've just walked to Dunnet Head where I strangled fifty senior citizens and had sex with a three-legged haggis.' He wasn't listening, you see. He's one of life's worriers. I wonder how he'd fare as a detective inspector.

Dunnet Head Lighthouse

So over the hills I'll take my way
And mate with the wild and free,
'Til my dust is flung to the winds
In my hill country.

Ammon Wrigley